D1603957

APOCALYPTIC
TRANSFORMATION

APOCALYPTIC TRANSFORMATION

Apocalypse and the Postmodern Imagination

Elizabeth K. Rosen

LEXINGTON BOOKS

a division of
ROWMAN & LITTLEFIELD PUBLISHERS, INC.
Lanham • Boulder • New York • Toronto • Plymouth, UK

PS
374
.A65
R67
2008

LEXINGTON BOOKS

A division of Rowman & Littlefield Publishers, Inc.
A wholly owned subsidiary of The Rowman & Littlefield Publishing Group, Inc.
4501 Forbes Boulevard, Suite 200
Lanham, MD 20706

Estover Road
Plymouth PL6 7PY
United Kingdom

British Library Cataloguing in Publication Information Available

Library of Congress Cataloging-in-Publication Data

Rosen, Elizabeth K., 1967-
  Apocalyptic transformation : apocalypse and the postmodern imagination / Elizabeth K.
Rosen.
    p. cm.
  ISBN-13: 978-0-7391-1790-3 (alk. paper)
  ISBN-10: 0-7391-1790-4 (alk. paper)
  ISBN-13: 978-0-7391-1791-0 (pbk. : alk. paper)
  ISBN-10: 0-7391-1791-2 (pbk. : alk. paper)
  1. American fiction—20th century—History and criticism. 2. Apocalyptic literature—
History and criticism. 3. End of the world in literature. 4. Apocalypse in motion
pictures. 5. Postmodernism. I. Title.
  PS374.A65R67 2008
  813'.50938—dc22
                                                        2007042286

Printed in the United States of America

It is not the function of the poet to relate what has happened, but what may happen.

—Aristotle

The end of a century always produces a feeling of exhaustion. As one gets closer to a date with two zeros in it, literature suddenly gets deluged by a wave of spleen.

—Umberto Eco

CONTENTS

The following permissions were granted for this book:

ACKNOWLEDGMENTS

I have been fortunate to have some superb readers who were generous with their time and expertise. None of us work in a vacuum, and the people mentioned here were of great help to me in writing and finishing this book.

My thanks to Danny Karlin for his intense reading and willingness to share his encyclopedic knowledge with me, as well as his kindness and patient support. I'm also indebted to Pam Thurschwell, whose ongoing encouragement and criticism throughout the writing process I've very much appreciated.

Adam Roberts, Paul Giles, Peter Swaab, Rosemary Ashton, and Helen Hackett all read versions of this text and offered their thoughts on making it better. Kiki Benzon, Steven Belleto, and Matthew Kapell all read individual chapters for me and made valuable suggestions.

I'm indebted, as well, to Elliot Ravetz for his continuing interest, unwavering support, and extremely helpful comments, and to Roger Sabin, who guided me where the standard databases did not dare to tread. DeZ Vylenz, whose documentary on Alan Moore premiered while I was writing, very kindly shared transcripts of his interviews with Moore. Terry Gilliam took time out from a busy promoting schedule to talk to me about his work. David Smith of the New York Public Library was an enormous help to me when I needed to chase down a source or check a quote.

Finally, I am grateful to have come from a home in which books and learning are so highly prized. Had my parents not been the kind of people who value and encourage education, this manuscript no doubt would never have existed. I thank them with love for their support over the long years as I followed this path.

INTRODUCTION

The story of apocalypse has become a part of our social consciousness, part of a mythology about endings that hovers in the cultural background and is just as real and influential as our myths of origins. It is more than a religious story that has been passed down through the ages. Apocalypse is a means by which to understand the world and one's place in it. It is an organizing principle imposed on an overwhelming, seemingly disordered universe. This accounts in part for the continuing fascination with, and attachment to, stories about the End. Anyone who notes the often alarmist delivery of news reports about global warming or conflicts in the Middle East, or goes to the cineplex to see the latest end-of-the-world scenario avoided (or not), or listens to American presidents speak in terms of evil empires or axes of evil can easily be forgiven for believing we are approaching End-times.

Skeptics might wonder, however, as the protagonist of Saul Bellow's novel *Herzog* does, if we don't love apocalypses a bit too much. Umberto Eco tells a story of attending a millennium-year conference during which he was asked by one of the journalists if he thought people feared the approaching year 2000. When he replied that in reality people couldn't care less, "The journalists then sank into the deepest gloom."[1]

No doubt, we do love apocalypses too much. But given that the world sometimes appears to be coming apart at its economic, political, and social seams and that there is "more and more information, and less and less meaning," our fascination with the apocalyptic myth is certainly understandable.[2]

Apocalyptic literature has traditionally been written to comfort people whose lives are, or who perceive their lives to be, overwhelmed by historical or social disruption. Its purpose is to exhort its readers to maintain faith in the midst of trying times and to assure them that they will ultimately be rewarded for their faithfulness and that their enemies will be vanquished. Such narratives endeavor at least in part to make sense of events which cannot otherwise be reconciled with a community's vision of itself and its history.[3] It is "an attempt by a culture that is genuinely puzzled and deeply disturbed to understand itself and its own time."[4] The promise of apocalypse is unequivocal: God has a plan, the disruption is part of it, and in the end all will be made right. Thus is suffering made meaningful and hope restored to those who are traumatized or bewildered by historic events.

Yet the apocalyptic myth offers more than this sense of ultimate order. It is also a vehicle of social criticism, and has always been so. The apocalyptic genre, at least in its religious incarnation, is usually written by and for the discontented, and often for a minority that is profoundly alienated by its powerless position. It appeals to an audience that, as D. H. Lawrence noted, is underprivileged and frustrated by its impotence, and that responds to the tale of an unjust status quo being returned to what it sees as a just one. The apocalypse is God's ultimate judgment of mankind. His intervention is always depicted as punishment for the ills of society, a corrective response for a people who have not only failed unpardonably, but have also demonstrated an inability even to right its own wrongs.

The apocalyptic sensibility has often been attacked as a means of "withdrawing" from history. That is, the reliance on divine intervention to mete out justice and effectively end history has been seen, most notably by Martin Buber, D. H. Lawrence, and Robert Alter, as a justification for human passivity in the face of history; apocalypse seems at least to accept and perhaps to condone the abdication of personal responsibility for our fate. But if, as other critics have argued, the apocalyptic sensibility reflects a despairing community's sense that its history has been radically disrupted, then that community's passivity may be the inevitable consequence of a collective sense of utter helplessness.

Lois Parkinson Zamora has framed her own analysis of apocalyptic storytelling against this precise context, noting how the "apocalyptist describes the broad strokes of history by which human beings are moved" and is "concerned to create comprehensive fictions of historical order."[5] The operative word here is *order*, for the imposition of the apocalyptic model onto one's experience is a feasible, if extreme, way of making sense of dislocating historical events. An apocalyptic narrative "resists the crisis of change by inculcating change into its very vocabulary," assuring its reader that "the apparent disorder of history will finally affirm order."[6]

The apocalyptic impulse is, in effect, a sense-making one, and one of ancient lineage. Moreover, the traditional apocalyptic template has an advantage over more recently favored sense-making paradigms like conspiracy and chaos theory in that it encompasses a moral dimension. Because judgment is a crucial element of the original myth, the traditional apocalyptic story is naturally a vehicle for the analysis and criticism of behavior, whether of the individual, nation, or cosmos. It therefore stands apart from sense-making theories like conspiracy, with its mysterious and confrontational Us vs. Them sensibility, or chaos theory, with its morally neutral and scientific stance.[7] It is an organizing structure that can create a moral and physical order while also holding out the possibility of social criticism that might lead to a reorientation in the midst of a bewildering historical moment.

The traditional narrative that has come to be known as apocalypse was fully formed only with the advent of Christianity. It has narrative antecedents in the Old Testament, and the individual components of the apocalyptic story can be traced even further back to the ancient civilizations of the Vedic Indians, Egyptians, Persians, Mesopotamians, and Greeks.[8] The etymological root of the word *apocalypse* is the Greek *apokalypsis*, meaning "unveiling" or "uncovering," but the word, as it denotes cosmic events, is not used before it appears specifically attached to the Book of Revelation in the New Testament, where it refers to the divine revelation experienced by St. John of Patmos, who is shown the coming struggle between good and evil and God's ultimate judgment upon the world.[9]

The most notable apocalyptic story in the Old Testament is the Book of Daniel, from which it appears John took much of his source material. John drew on Old Testament suggestions of the inheritance of a divine kingdom to construct his New Jerusalem and he solidified general notions of judgment into a specific Last Judgment. But where the Christian apocalypse really diverged from its Jewish predecessor was in its depiction of an actual Savior resurrected from the dead to defeat evil and lead the faithful to their eternal reward, a life of divine inhabitation in the New Jerusalem.

The events which comprise the apocalypse are very specific in John's revelation: the Great Tribulation, during which the Antichrist will appear and reign on earth; the Second Coming of Christ; Armageddon, the battle between the forces of good and evil in which the Antichrist is ultimately overthrown and the world and its sinners destroyed; the Last Judgment, in which God passes judgment upon all souls, living and dead, and confers reward and punishment as He sees fit; and the descent from the sky of New

Jerusalem, the New Heaven on Earth in which the saved will live eternally with God.

The inheritance of New Jerusalem is a crucial part of the traditional apocalyptic story. Indeed, despite the emphasis on the destructive wrath of God, an emphasis which is made clear both through the pointedly detailed descriptions of the devastation and the proportionately larger amount of time devoted to it, New Jerusalem is still the raison d'être of the traditional apocalyptic narrative.

Yet as scholars who have worked in the field since the 1980s have noted, apocalyptic literature has evolved to include End-time stories that either lack this vital feature of the myth or that have changed it to reflect something quite different from its biblical precursor.[10] Indeed, as Josef Broeck notes in his review of this body of scholarly work, the apocalyptic genre seems to have "emancipated itself from its historical and biblical roots" so that "there is no common agreement on the form, content, or function of apocalyptic thinking and writing."[11]

What seems evident is that there is a second branch in the family of apocalyptic literature which has emerged, a fact which became dramatically clear when, on 12 September 2001, the London *Daily Mail* ran a front-page photograph of the collapsing World Trade Center with the headline reading, "APOCALYPSE!" The application of the word *apocalypse* to this image of destruction was indicative of the profound shift from a descriptive term that referred specifically to the hopeful biblical story of ultimate judgment and reward, to an adjective now understood to be a synonym for the catastrophic or devastating.

The altered colloquial meaning of the term *apocalypse* has been accompanied by an alteration in the original narrative model, as well. This altered form of the apocalyptic paradigm retains some of the elements of the traditional story, but it often leaves out the element of New Jerusalem, the divine kingdom that is the reward of the faithful.[12] The result is that a story which once was grounded in hope about the future has become instead a reflection of fears and disillusionment about the present, a bleak shift in emphasis from the belief in an ordered universe with a cogent history to one in which the overriding sense is of a chaotic, indifferent, and possibly meaningless universe. Where the underlying message of the original narrative was optimistic, anticipating God's intervening hand to make things right, the altered version has more in common with the jeremiad, a lamentation over the degeneracy of the world, and when God intervenes in this newer version of the story, it is not to restore order to a disordered world and reward the faithful, but rather to express a literally all-consuming, punishing anger.

This change in apocalyptic storytelling may be the response of a culture that is "caught up by a crisis that challenges the very undergirdings of its makeup," but it is a significant change, nonetheless.[13] While this change may not be surprising—the apocalyptic myth, after all, is "long-lived" and "patient of change and of historiographical sophistications"[14]—it is careless to brush aside the emergence of what clearly appears to be a unique sub-branch of eschatological literature. These grimmer eschatological tales are strictly stories of endings. Such stories, which I am calling "neo-apocalyptic," are focused on cataclysm. They neither offer nor anticipate a New Jerusalem, per se. This form sees the apocalyptic genre's message of hope largely subsumed by its emphasis on destruction, even though the main intent of the traditional story of apocalypse was to provide its audience with hope of a better world. To this extent, then, neo-apocalyptic literature is a literature of pessimism; it functions largely as a cautionary tale, positing potential means of extinction and predicting the gloomy probabilities of such ends. If these tales exhibit judgment, it is of the sort that assumes that no one deserves saving and that everyone should be punished. The traditional optimistic conclusion and intent to inspire faith disappear in neo-apocalyptic literature, replaced by imaginative but definitive End scenarios.

New Jerusalem and the hope it symbolizes is such an integral part of the traditional apocalyptic model that to ignore or discard the concept creates an eschatological narrative that is different in kind, and not just degree, from the traditional one. My own sense is that this evolution has been so radical that it has resulted in a new genus in the family of eschatological tales. This seems particularly so because the intent of these two kinds of stories is so entirely different. The traditional narrative is meant to lend hope and bolster faith, while the newer version holds out only the promise of undifferentiated punishment, a vastly different matter. While all apocalyptic literature is pessimistic in the sense that it assumes humanity cannot rehabilitate itself, the traditional narrative clearly differentiates between those deserving punishment and those who deserve saving. Moreover, it posits a deity who will intervene to save the deserving. The neo-apocalyptic variant assumes that all mankind is beyond renovation, that this degeneracy is so complete that the Ending can only be so, too. There is nothing beyond this Ending, no hope of a New Heaven on Earth, precisely because there is nothing worth saving.

Perhaps this new strain of eschatological literature is what inspired Frank Kermode, whose book *The Sense of an Ending* is still a crucial study in the field, to write in 1985, "For the time being, the apocalyptic, certainly in Western literature, is out of fashion, and the Gospel is not being written. . . . Popular fundamentalist apocalypticism thrives, but the educated . . . have given it up. Deconstructors write no gospels."[15]

But, in fact, traditional apocalyptic literature, though it may have been overshadowed by neo-apocalyptic storytelling, has never stopped being written. The traditional apocalyptic scheme continues to appear in our secular literature despite the prevailing mood of gloom. It is the goal of this study to show exactly how some contemporary creators, the "deconstructors" to whom Kermode is clearly referring, have continued to engage with the apocalyptic myth, though they have engaged with it on their own terms. The artists whose work I consider have resisted the cultural move toward neo-apocalyptic pessimism, and find themselves more attracted to the message of hope inherent in the traditional apocalyptic model, even when their own lack of religious conviction or their postmodern style of storytelling have obliged them to refigure that hope in other terms.

Indeed, though the dominant apocalyptic paradigm of the second half of the twentieth century appears to have been the neo-apocalyptic one, there is evidence that the biblical archetype has continued to influence creative minds. That influence becomes even more apparent when we take into account the kind of reinterpretation of the New Jerusalem motif that David Ketterer identifies when he notes that the creation of a "new world" is as likely to be an imaginary or philosophical entity as a physical one.[16] Particularly toward the end of the twentieth century, there is a reemergence of the traditional apocalyptic scheme in eschatological stories, a trend which may be due to more than just the proximity of the year 2000; Umberto Eco's anecdote notwithstanding, the approach of the century's end no doubt inspired consideration of endings in general, and the traditional fears about millennium are likely to have focused those thoughts into more specific consideration of the paradigmatic narrative of the End, whether consciously or not.

The notion of an increasingly secularized population which many of the late-twentieth century scholars of apocalyptic literature have taken as a given deserves closer examination. Even granting the perception that increasing secularization accompanied the Industrial Revolution and continued to grow more or less steadily, it is certainly not the case at this juncture in history that we are still moving in that direction. In fact, the exact opposite is true.[17] All the data points to the fact that America is not, in fact, becoming more secularized, if by secularized we mean turning away from religious faiths.

Though many Americans are turning away from organized religious institutions, a 2004 Gallup poll found that 90 percent of the Americans it surveyed professed a belief in God. And recent studies indicate that contrary to an official secularism, the number of Europeans who profess religious belief is also growing. While membership in religious institutions, particularly Christian ones, appears to have been declining over the past several decades in Europe, there has been a simultaneous increase of religious feeling among young people.[18] Moreover, participation in both fundamental and evangelical Christianity appears to be increasing in America, a trend perhaps reflected by the fact that at least three recent presidents of the United States have characterized themselves as evangelical or "born-again" Christians: Jimmy Carter, Ronald Reagan, and George W. Bush.[19] Certainly, interest in End-time theology is not on the wane if the worldwide sales of the Tim LaHaye and Jerry B. Jenkins's *Left Behind* series, a secularized retelling of the events of the Book of Revelation, are an accurate indicator. The series has sold more than sixty million copies, the novels have consistently debuted at number one on many bestseller lists, and one of those novels was the best-selling hardback book of 2001.[20] According to a 2002 *Time*/CNN poll:

> more than one-third of Americans say they are paying more attention now to how the news might relate to the end of the world, and have talked about what the Bible has to say on the subject. Fully 59 percent say they believe the events in *Revelation* are going to come true, and nearly one-quarter think the Bible predicted the Sept. 11 attack.[21]

Such responses to 9/11 appear to be part of a larger pattern of renewed interest in eschatological narrative, and the current direction of that eschatological response—in particular toward renewal—demonstrates the continuing appeal, as well as a psychic need for the idea of a New Jerusalem, in which the End is not merely a neo-apocalyptic annihilation, but is a prelude to something better.

Renewed religiosity coupled with recent anxiety about the approaching end of the second Christian millennium may in part account for an intensified interest in the eschatological vision in general, but what accounts for the renewed interest in the traditional apocalyptic paradigm specifically? Here I am going to posit a convergence of historical events with eschatological implications, a growing climate of fear regarding them, and an equally powerful sense that the paradigms by which we have tried to understand and interpret our world have come to seem inadequate, and perhaps unusable. This nexus of social mood and historical condition creates a climate of anxious uncertainty that the traditional apocalyptic model is well structured to address.

Frank Kermode sensibly fixes on the idea of crisis when he writes that the apocalyptic myth continues "to lie under our ways of making sense of the world" even as our adaptations of the myth evolve. "Our interest in [ends] reflects our deep need for intelligible Ends."[22] Our current sense of crisis seems both pervasive and unremitting. In *After the End*, James Berger argues that this sense of permanent crisis coexists with the notion that the "conclusive catastrophe has already occurred," that "apocalyptic writing itself is a reminder, a symptom, an aftermath of some disorienting catastrophe."[23] But it seems more accurate to say that our mode of fear is constantly evolving both to defer and reimagine what this conclusive catastrophe might be. While the sense of crisis may be permanent, the nature of the crisis we perceive is subject to change; and often we perceive multiple crises, rather than a single crisis. What remains constant, however, is our sense of a disordered world.

It is to this disquieting sense of disorder that the apocalyptic myth speaks, reasserting teleological design and cosmic meaning. One need not be part of a persecuted community for the sense-making element of apocalypse to have an appeal; it is enough merely to be part of a community that believes its continuity has been disrupted. In the post–Cold War age, we have experienced historical and cultural disruptions along with the collapse of many of the structures that previously provided a sense of stability.

No doubt the nuclear arms race has contributed to this sense of permanent crisis. The atomic bomb is a tangible reminder that the End (or one Ending) is only a missile flight away and that it cannot be ignored. It relocates considerations of the End from the realm of the theoretical and places them squarely in the realm of the possible. The Cold War existed simultaneously as a world-ending threat and a way to understand the world. While the binary superpower model of world politics may have elevated our sense of apocalyptic danger, it nonetheless anchored us in an interpretative stance where everyone and everything had its place. With the collapse of the Berlin Wall and the Soviet Empire, we are left with the same apocalyptic threat, perhaps even greater now, but are deprived of a clear and credible hermeneutic strategy by which to identify and make sense of that danger.

Indeed, as the potential apocalyptic dangers seem to increase, the interpretative strategies we have relied on for comfort and stability have continued to shift uneasily under our feet and sometimes disintegrate altogether. Kermode mentions the paradigms of Empire and decadence as examples, but one could think of many others. The Newtonian vision of the universe has been radically altered by discoveries in quantum physics. The teleological idea that evolution is progressive was challenged by Darwin. The capitalist model has been challenged by globalization, postcolonial studies, and terrorism. The accelerating proliferation of information that has been generated by an omnipresent electronic media and particularly the Internet has made it correspondingly more difficult to create interpretive strategies to help us understand the universe and our place in it.

At the same time that our interpretative structures have grown more unsteady, several historic events have caused our apocalyptic anxiety to grow more acute during the second half of the twentieth century, thereby causing the kind of psychological and physical disruption which inspire apocalyptic storytelling. The explosion of the nuclear bomb at mid-century was the first of these, but since then, two other global phenomena in particular have lent credence to apocalyptic fears. The threat of global pandemic has become a reality, first with the HIV/AIDS epidemic that has so far killed an estimated twenty-two million people, infected another 42 million, and will, it is estimated, see another 50 to 75 million people infected by the year 2010.[24] On the heels of the HIV epidemic we now have the avian influenza which threatens to become a pandemic if the virus mutates to spread from person-to-person.[25] The second event of apocalyptic import is the disastrous climate change that is occurring because of global warming and worldwide ecological destruction that is already underway.[26]

The threats of viral pandemic and the destruction of the ecosystem are the two conditions that are not only as potentially dangerous as the nuclear bomb, but also have analogous biblical—that is, apocalyptic—motifs in plague and world destruction. The all-encompassing nature of these crises threaten human existence on a global level. Their fearful nature and a steadily expanding awareness of their enormity contribute to a growing sense of uncertainty about the survival of our planet and the viability of our future on it.

As we have seen, the traditional apocalyptic story offers a means of making sense of radical discontinuity by maintaining that crises are part of a deliberate and purposeful underlying design. Lois Parkinson Zamora contends, "That the appeal of [Christ's] promise continues . . . 2,000 years after it was made and despite innumerable falsified predictions of the end, suggests the deep psychological needs to which it responds."[27] If we want to understand why the creative imagination seems to have gravitated toward the traditional paradigm at the end of the twentieth century, we might argue that as the psychological need for this sense-making narrative has become somehow more acute, the corresponding desire for what Richard Cizik calls "moral certitudes in a world without any certainties" has grown.[28]

Moreover, such social and psychological disruption almost certainly stimulates a critical response on the part of artists. It is true that the adoption of the traditional apocalyptic paradigm as a critical stance against the current social order is paradoxical since apocalyptic rhetoric assumes no rehabilitation is possible and "[emphasizes] that no social reform can cure the world's diseases." Apocalypse assumes that "[e]very structure of the old world is infected and only an absolute, purifying cataclysm can make possible an utterly new, perfected world."[29] Yet the apocalyptic narrative allows a recitation of everything that we perceive as dangerously wrong with humankind, all those things that support the indictment that the world is beyond rehabilitation. Apocalypse, as a prophetic revelation, does not propose to change these "evils," merely to catalog them. But the very process of cataloguing is an inherent social criticism, and the apocalyptist's "dissenting perspective" makes both possible and likely his criticism "of present political, social, spiritual practices."[30] But perhaps what is most important is not that authors use the apocalyptic paradigm, but that they so deftly "manipulate that apparent apocalypticism to make vital observations about the world as it now exists."[31] One conclusion we might draw from this observation about contemporary apocalyptic literature and film is that its aim may not be merely to rework the paradigm, but rather to use it as the most effective vehicle for their social critique.

There is a certain group of writers and filmmakers, however, whose social criticism extends to the apocalyptic myth itself. Many believe that postmodernism in the arts often reflects exactly the uncertainty caused by historical and cultural disruptions such as the ones described. Postmodernism challenges traditional sense-making structures, which it calls grand or metanarratives, refusing to impose one point of view or privilege one kind of "culture" over another, and playfully celebrating the kind of fragmentation and lack of coherency in doctrines which has been the source of anxiety or gloom for some. It is "hostile to any overarching philosophical or political doctrine, and strongly opposed to those 'dominant ideologies' that help to maintain the status quo."[32]

Yet postmodernists have remained interested in the apocalyptic myth, even as they reject the myth's absolutism or challenge the received systems of morality that underlie it. Postmodernists often seem to recognize the need for the conclusiveness provided by the apocalyptic story, even as they seek to challenge, explode, or undermine the belief system or assumptions underlying this particular grand narrative.

Some might argue that the apocalyptic myth is "irony-proof," that the reason it is such a powerful and long-lasting myth is because it can resist the sometimes smug, squirrelly, or querulous tone of postmodernism. Yet, apocalypse is hardly irony-proof. It is a narrative riddled with ironies and paradoxes, a story that "mocks the notion of conclusive ends and endings even as it proposes just that—the conclusive narration of history's end."[33] As James Berger notes:

> The end is never the end. The apocalyptic text announces and describes the end of the world, but then the text does not end, nor does the world represented in the text, and neither does the world itself. . . . something remains *after the end.*[34]

What other word is there but "ironic" for a myth that is built on an earnestly predicted End that doesn't arrive, only to repeat itself with equal earnestness and the same unrealized expectations? Moreover, if postmodernism's roots are political and its interests are truth(s) and power, then the apocalyptic genre is a natural one for postmodernists to take up because "apocalyptic writers are a quintessential technology of power/knowledge."[35]

For those who are skeptical about whether postmodernists can successfully appropriate the apocalyptic myth, I point to the writers and filmmakers in this study, who clearly *have* appropriated the myth and done so in a distinctly postmodern way. Their reasons for adapting the apocalyptic myth are, ironically enough, traditional ones. That is, they, too, use the apocalyptic myth as an instrument of criticism. But their postmodern style has profound implications for the apocalyptic paradigm itself, as I hope to demonstrate.

Before discussing some of the effects of postmodern adaptations of apocalypse, it is necessary to differentiate between apocalypse as a myth and apocalypse as a narrative. For apocalypse is, of course, not just a kind of prophecy, but also a kind of plot. Indeed, one might argue that the "biblical apocalyptist proposes nothing less than God's own plot for history" and therefore apocalypse might "be proposed as the very model of narrative plot."[36]

And, of course, apocalypse itself does have a plot, one that the Society of Biblical Literature Genres Project undertook to define in 1979. The goal was to delineate the apocalyptic genre as precisely as possible, and the Society produced the following definition: "a genre of revelatory literature with a narrative framework, in which a revelation is mediated by an otherworldly being to a human recipient, disclosing a transcendent reality which is both temporal, insofar as it envisages eschatological salvation, and spatial insofar as it involves another supernatural world."[37]

What is most surprising about this definition is that the elements of "plot" which are traditionally considered to comprise apocalyptic narrative are not mentioned in this definition at all. Indeed, this definition is arguably both too loose and too restrictive; it is too restrictive in that it suggests that without the revelatory element a work cannot be considered apocalyptic, and it is too loose because it does not take into account some of the vital components of the traditional story of apocalypse.[38] There is no mention of judgment, for instance, nor of the destructive aspect which is the result of the judgment. The use of "otherworldly being" suggests a hesitance even about claiming that apocalyptic literature is a narrative whose crux is God, a problematic stance in a definition that is looking specifically at biblical, rather than secular, apocalyptic stories. And yet even secular adaptations of the apocalyptic paradigm include motifs of destruction (if they are neo-apocalyptic) and renewal (if they are more traditional).

Perhaps the cautiousness here is an acknowledgment of the extraordinary flexibility and resiliency of the apocalyptic story. The traditional story of apocalypse is fundamentally one in which God is the central actor and judgment the main action. The result of the judgment is the destruction of the old world on the one hand, and creation of a revitalized new world on the other. This general plot is discernible whether we examine the Christian apocalypse of John or more ancient, cyclical versions of cosmic destruction and renewal.[39]

Because the apocalyptic genre's roots are religious, secular authors face certain challenges in adapting it in their narratives. If apocalypse is, at heart, a narrative about a higher power correcting the moral imbalances of the world, how does one translate this tale into secular terms? How does one translate the New Heaven on Earth? And what is the result when the story of apocalypse is removed from its theological setting? Despite these significant challenges, secular adaptations of the traditional paradigm manage not only to retain the basic three themes of judgment, catastrophe, and renewal, but also the more specific motifs of deity and New Jerusalem.[40]

For example, the Judeo-Christian deity of the paradigm might be replaced with an alternative deity figure. Godlike qualities may be relocated in a human figure, one who possesses the power to give or take life, or who seems to be omnipotent or omniscient in some other way. In other cases, the alternative deity figure can take the form of a specific apotheosized object, idea, or even ideology.

The apocalyptic "world" which is destroyed can also be flexibly interpreted in these secular versions. Whereas science fiction writers may create actual worlds in their apocalyptic tales, mainstream writers often replace the real world with a figurative one. They may interpret or restrict a "world" to be a specific community (Nathanael West's *The Day of the Locust*), an individual (Ralph Ellison's *Invisible Man*), or even an individual mind. This last reconception is especially popular among contemporary filmmakers. Films such as *Vanilla Sky* (2001) and *Donnie Darko* (2001) revolve around the tension between the perceived world of the narrator and the "real" world of the film, and the destruction of one and creation of the other.

Of all the original apocalyptic concepts, New Jerusalem is perhaps the most difficult to translate into secular terms, particularly since it is often confused with ideas of utopia. But utopia is a "human construct," a vision of a political, moral, and inclusive community created by humans.[41] New Jerusalem stands outside of ideas of politics and human community; it is a reward from God, an elitist and divisive gift that forever separates the damned from the faithful, and it cannot be attained or created in any other way.[42] In the biblical story, New Jerusalem is an actual place that is inherited by the faithful, and creating a secular equivalent has posed an uncomfortable challenge for artists. Many have found a solution in the fact that while, in Revelation, John is told that New Jerusalem will be a real place, what he experiences is a *vision* of this idealized and perfected place, and not the place itself. In postmodern apocalyptic narratives, New Jerusalem is less a place than a new way of seeing: a new vision. Characters do not inherit a new world. Often, they inherit a new way of understanding the old world. And this new way of understanding allows them to see the old world *anew*.

In postmodern adaptations, there are three areas of the original apocalyptic paradigm that are tangibly affected when translated into secular terms, and, as one might suspect, all three are related to the absolutist nature of the traditional story.[43] The first of these is how deity is portrayed in these recent reworkings. One finds a "humanization" of the deity. Nietzsche's dictum that God is dead is perhaps not taken as the rule in postmodern versions, but He may no longer be the perfect entity of the biblical version. These secular deities are often imperfect characters, neither absolutely omniscient and omnipotent, nor absolutely benevolent. The absolutist Judeo-Christian depiction of God ceases to be a factor; plurality and ambiguity are stronger influences here.

As a result, writers often create more than one deity for their stories. Sometimes they split the "traits" of God between their characters, emphasizing the Judeo-Christian God's wrathful side in one character and His forgiving side in another. Sometimes authors conflate the separate Book of Revelation roles of Savior and Antichrist into one deity figure who is subject to the very moral ambivalence that traditional apocalypse is held to shun. Where the concept of apocalyptic deity is represented in a person (rather than an abstraction), there is often an accompanying tendency to question what it means to *be* a god.

A second area affected by translation is the conception of time. The apocalyptic conception of time is inherently a complicated one, for the story of apocalypse is simultaneously about the ending of everything and yet suggests a time afterward. Moreover, on the more local level of narrative in Revelation, St. John occupies two times simultaneously since he is both in the present being shown the future and in the future experiencing it. There is a tension therefore between time as a principle (a continuum of successive individual moments) and time as a narrative concept (a method of juxtaposing different moments in a story). In Christian apocalypse, the overall structure of time is linear, but St. John's viewing of it is not: through his vision he occupies more than one place on the continuum of that line simultaneously. While malleability of visionary time is a distinguishing trait of traditional apocalyptic narrative, it is distinct from the issue of the structure of time overall. Despite these complexities, traditional apocalypse is based on a linear notion of time and is a story about the end of history.

What we find in the postmodern versions of apocalypse, however, is that the story about the End of Time becomes instead a story about the end of one time. This marks a return to a view of time which is cyclical rather than linear, and which is more akin to that of the end-of-cosmos stories found in ancient cultures. It marks a movement away from the Judeo-Christian notion of linear time with a beginning, middle, and end. In this shift one can see again how rigid delineations are abandoned in favor of a more flexible interpretation: endings become beginnings and vice versa. Moreover, *absolute* beginnings and endings disappear. Mircea Eliade notes that most eschatologies hold a common belief that only absolute destruction of the old world can result in absolute renewal.[44] What is played out more often in postmodern versions is a partial destruction, a surgical strike of sorts, with the result that there occurs a blurring of beginnings and endings, a logical consequence of depicting New Jerusalem as a radically reoriented understanding of the world, rather than as a different world. Contemporary writers who revise the traditional apocalyptic story to reflect a cyclical rather than linear time structure may be responding to the postmodern sense of skepticism about the singularity of events, rejecting the rigid tyranny of time which is part of the original apocalyptic narrative.

The third feature affected by translation is the concept of judgment. Because of postmodernism's refusal to privilege one culture or point of view over another, judgment often becomes an amorphous and ambiguous concept in postmodern apocalypse. In part this is a result of imperfect deities. These reconceived deities are often soul-searching, Hamlet-like characters. Unlike the God of the Bible, their moral bearings are sometimes unsteady. They are fully aware of, sometimes even paralyzed by, the moral complexities of the modern world, and they are frequently unsure what is "right" and what is "wrong." Part of what is at stake in postmodern apocalypse is the question of whether objective judgment is possible.

In the following study, I have chosen not to limit my examination to a single genre of storytelling, but instead to look at a variety of media— literature, film, and the graphic novel. In part, this is because my interest is in culture-wide apocalyptic storytelling, and in part it is because the story of apocalypse has, almost from its inception, been represented in multiple mediums, having been as often treated in visual forms as in literature. Revelation is one of the most illustrated of all the biblical books and has inspired countless images and works of art. If we want to see how the apocalyptic myth is being used by contemporary creators, we cannot ignore film and graphic novels, two genres which have become important vehicles of storytelling. But I wish to emphasize at the outset that this study is not primarily intended as an examination of genre. Though different media do represent the apocalyptic paradigm differently from each other, my main focus is on exploring how these artists make use of the story of apocalypse within their chosen genre.

Some of the authors I have included here, Kurt Vonnegut and Robert Coover in particular, have been discussed in earlier scholarly studies on apocalyptic writing. However, neither they, nor any of the other artists I discuss, have been examined specifically as postmodern writers of apocalyptic narrative. Indeed, there has been little or no analysis of postmodern apocalypse at all,[45] and scholars such as Northrop Frye and Frank Kermode, whose work on apocalyptic narrative is seminal, are concerned primarily with modernist (not postmodernist) apocalyptic narrative. Indeed, Kermode has written that "[what] we think of as truly Modern or Modernist is always relatively apocalyptic."[46]

The seven authors and filmmakers examined here were chosen not only for their reputations as postmodernists, but also because each has demonstrated more than a passing concern with the idea of apocalypse and so offers a body of apocalyptic work to consider. The texts that I have chosen are in the traditional apocalyptic, rather than neo-apocalyptic, mode. Kurt Vonnegut's body of work, for example, also includes neo-apocalyptic texts, but it is the intent of this study to examine only texts which are working with the traditional apocalyptic form, and then to examine how these works transform a religious story into a secular one, and to think about what each artist gains from choosing to work with the classic rather than new paradigm.

The word *choosing* need not imply conscious design. While the existence of more than one apocalyptic text in these authors' oeuvres argues for the idea that they may indeed be making a conscious choice, it is not necessarily the case that they are. Apocalypse is an idea that is now deeply embedded in our collective consciousness, and in the post-Hiroshima world, where the eschatological tenor of events has throbbed steadily in the background, it may be present even when we are not conscious of it. Authors who write apocalyptic texts may not be under a direct influence so much as reflecting a subterranean current of our communal lives.

These artists were also chosen for analysis because, with the exception of Coover, almost all of the work represented here was created within the last twenty-five years of the twentieth century, and thus it may tell us something more general about the artistic engagement with the apocalyptic myth as the century drew to a close. Because in some cases during this time period, we find authors like Kurt Vonnegut, who previously produced works more reflective of the neo-apocalyptic paradigm, suddenly creating texts which return to the traditional paradigm, it seems worthwhile to examine various apocalyptic narratives of the same period, particularly in the light of their closeness to the year 2000, to question whether and how the use of the paradigm might be reflecting other concerns of the period. And if, as Debra Bergoffen believes, apocalypse is "a symbol of time which articulates a people's experience of their being-in-the-world," this grouping of apocalyptic texts may be able to tell us something about the experience of "being-in-the-world" at the end of the twentieth century.[47] Simply being aware that all of these works possess narrative traits that we recognize as "postmodern"—indeterminacy, irony, unstable identity, the mixing of high and low culture, pluralism and multiplicity, skepticism of authority, and skepticism about grand narratives—may reveal how these distinctive artists are shaped by, understand, and seek to reflect aspects of the postmodern sensibility through the apocalyptic myth.

I have organized this study not by medium (film, novel, and graphic novel), but rather along a continuum of apocalyptic approaches. That is, while Alan Moore and the Wachowski Brothers both work in visual media, their approaches to the material and mythic structure reflect different interests. The movement, therefore, is from texts that deliberately flaunt their use of the paradigm to those which approach apocalypse more metaphysically. The line of division is by authors who use the apocalyptic paradigm to explore other themes and authors whose theme is the exploration of the apocalyptic paradigm.

Chapter 1 examines texts by Alan Moore, whose work in the comic book genre has made him perhaps the best-known writer in that field. The production of a graphic novel is usually a collaborative effort between a writer and artist, so it is reasonable to ask whether one can properly consider a single person as the author of a graphic work.

Because Moore tends to conceive his stories in visual terms and because he provides copious instruction to his artists as part of his scripts, I am satisfied to refer to these works as "his," though this in no way is meant to discount the extraordinary role which artists such as Dave Gibbons, Stephen Bissette, John Totleben, J. H. Williams III, and others have all played in realizing and contributing to Moore's stories.[48]

While I begin with Moore on the argument that his texts are the most obviously apocalyptic of those examined here, there is nonetheless a more subtle use of the paradigm at work in his texts: for Moore uses the apocalyptic myth to criticize not only the ills of society, but also to comment on elements of the myth itself. His *Swamp Thing* is a veritable collection of apocalyptic stories, stories that in part explore the numerous ways in which the paradigm has been adopted. In them, there are personal apocalypses and communal ones, fictional apocalypses and "real" ones. Even the Swamp Thing creature is conceived of as a symbolic representation of apocalyptic ideas: he is a walking personification of the kind of "vegetation myth" which Carl B. Yoke identifies as belonging to the category of re-creation or end-of-the-world myths.[49] While Moore uses the apocalyptic myth to criticize society on a local level, as he does in issues which deal with slavery, misogyny, and gun violence, he also examines some of the thornier issues of the paradigm itself: the nature of New Jerusalem and theodicy. In *Watchmen*, Moore creates a world in which the people have for so long lived with a looming sense of apocalyptic dread that they have become desensitized and complacent, and so are unable to detect the real thing when it appears. In doing so, Moore invites a consideration of the real apocalypticism with which we live by positing a "What if" scenario which takes advantage of and extrapolates from those fears. Both *Watchmen* and Moore's more recent eschatological series *Promethea* explore the idea of apocalyptic deity. *Watchmen* examines various depictions of deity, occupying itself with questions about human conceptions of the deity and God's perception of us. In *Promethea*, Moore's goal is larger: to challenge our entire conception of what apocalypse actually is. While at the heart of this story there is an apocalyptic goddess, Moore's aim is a return to thinking about apocalypse specifically as "revelation," rather than as cataclysm or divine punishment.

Unlike Moore, Kurt Vonnegut does not want to humanize the deity at all. On the contrary, human beings are practically incidental in his apocalyptic novel *Galápagos* in which natural selection is made the deity figure. In *Galápagos*, the author makes literal the idea that science has become a religion. In chapter 2, I'll examine how, by elevating evolution to the position of apocalyptic deity, Vonnegut succeeds not only in finding a way to reconcile two sense-making paradigms—evolutionary science and religion—which have usually stood in opposition to one another, but also finds a means to criticize two of the grand narratives of our time: apocalypse and Darwinism. In uniting evolutionary and apocalyptic time the author is also able to "[provide] a 'logical' solution to a theological dilemma": namely, of the existence of suffering, thereby "[enabling] the believer to redefine any *apparent* evil or calamity as a positive good by situating it within the temporal frame of mythic narrative," something which the scholar Stephen D. O'Leary argues is the point of the apocalyptic paradigm.[50] Catholic historian Jean Delumeau has commented that "for as long as we are living in time, we are not able to understand the reason for the colossal enigma of . . . suffering," but Vonnegut suggests that if we only lived for a long enough time we might understand, and that what we would discover is that it was nothing personal; it was just another bump along the continuum of human evolution.[51]

Chapter 3 is concerned with the apocalyptic work of the filmmaker Terry Gilliam. Gilliam has several times appropriated the apocalyptic narrative as the basis for his films. In some instances, he explores the redemptive and positive apocalyptic vision, as in *The Fisher King*, while in others, such as *Brazil* and *12 Monkeys*, his focus has been on the dystopian and destructive elements of the myth. But in each of these films, Gilliam moves the site of apocalypse to an internal landscape: that is, into the minds of his characters. Such films can be seen as part of the apocalyptic tradition described by M. H. Abrams when he argued that the Romantics, after their disillusionment with the French Revolution, rechanneled their actual hopes for an apocalyptic renovation of humankind into a more metaphoric desire for an "apocalypse of imagination."

Gilliam's films also focus on specific elements of the traditional apocalyptic story. *Brazil* explores the New Jerusalem and judgment elements of the myth, while *12 Monkeys* examines the figure of the apocalyptic prophet with the same exactitude that Alan Moore uses to explore apocalyptic deity in *Watchmen*. In all of Gilliam's apocalyptic works, however, apocalypse is transformed from a communal and external event to an internal and individual one. Whereas the Wachowski Brothers will link that interiority to technology in their work, for Terry Gilliam the connection is a far more organic one in which the apocalyptic myth intersects with the mind itself. In *The Matrix* trilogy, the apocalyptic myth is organized around the conceit of virtual reality, but in Gilliam's apocalyptic work these apocalypses of the mind are organized around the conceit of actual reality, and specifically around the trope of insanity, one of Gilliam's favorite themes.

Chapter 4 identifies evolution as an important theme in the Wachowski Brothers' *Matrix* movies, but the trope is used in a completely different way than in Vonnegut's novel. What at first appears to be a rather straightforward reworking of the story of Christ's resurrection becomes far more complicated as the trilogy progresses. In fact, one way to read the trilogy is as a story in which apocalypse itself evolves. *The Matrix* is thematically concerned with epistemology, a branch of philosophy that studies the nature and theory of knowledge, but rather than use the apocalyptic paradigm to address their theme, the Wachowskis use their theme to speak to the apocalyptic myth. Hence, each of their films "sees" apocalypse through a different point of view. Like Gilliam's films before them, *The Matrix* films intersect with the Romantic "apocalypse of the mind," but in a quite literal way: through the "jacking in" of minds to the larger matrix, as well as with its overall concern about perception.

Chapter 5 focuses on the work of Robert Coover, whose apocalyptic novels precede the other texts in this study by roughly twenty years. But Coover is the first of the postmodern authors here for whom the plot of apocalypse is less important than the metaphysics of it. Coover's interest in the apocalyptic myth manifested itself as early as his first novel, *The Origin of the Brunists*, a tale about a millennial cult in a small town. Coover is known primarily for his work in metafiction, and so his use of the apocalyptic paradigm is often simultaneously an exploration of storytelling and language. Since Coover has stated that one of his abiding intentions as a writer is to examine the myths and structures by which we organize our lives, the "apocalypse" he offers in his work is often one of language and narrative method, and the "New Jerusalem" he envisions is the freedom left behind when such forms are exploded.

Chapter 6 discusses the fiction of Don DeLillo, an author who one critic has said has "the white-hot fury of a latter-day prophet, full of discontent and desperation" and who is "predisposed to seeing a culture in permanent crisis."[52] DeLillo has written a number of novels that investigate different aspects of apocalypticism, but it is in *Underworld* that he addresses the subject most directly through the lens of nuclear fear. Like Vonnegut, who posits a new religion based on science, DeLillo also builds his novel around a religious sensibility, only the religion that he uses is nuclearism, the religion of nuclear weapons. Recognizing that the atomic bomb "has completed the process of secularization that apocalyptic thinking has undergone since medieval time,"

DeLillo locates the site of nuclearism, not at Hiroshima, but at the moment when nuclear confrontation seemed inevitable: the Cuban Missile Crisis.[53]

Of all the authors examined in this study, DeLillo is the least interested in the specific plot of apocalypse or its translation into a secular literature. Instead, his interest is in how the idea of apocalypse affects us. The question of the unthinkable end is addressed by DeLillo in his novels *End Zone* and, less specifically, in *White Noise* where the topic is largely reframed as being that of the "indescribable." In DeLillo's apocalyptic novels, he wonders, as one linguistic specialist did in 1965, whether with the atomic bomb it is "possible that in spite of our vast and ever-growing vocabulary we have finally created an object that transcends all possible description."[54] Aware that the bomb was and is "a power that defied the military and political vocabulary that first tried to encompass it," the paradox of the existence of the bomb and our simultaneous inability to adequately discuss it leads to some of the funniest scenes in these two earlier works."[55] But in *Underworld* and *Cosmopolis*, DeLillo extends his exploration of language to the apocalyptic sensibility overall. Recognizing in the bomb a force which "demands not only an entirely new vocabulary, but a new way of thinking," DeLillo examines this new way of thinking, considering matters as varied as our perverse desire for punishment, the sense-making potential of the paradigm, and the effect of failed apocalyptic prediction.[56]

Postmodernism has now been around long enough for us to examine how some of its leading practitioners have addressed the apocalyptic myth. The conclusion will address the question of why postmodernists continue to show interest in the traditional story of apocalypse and why postmodern apocalypse matters.

NOTES

1. David, *Conversations about the End of Time*, 174.
2. Baudrillard, *Simulacra and Simulation*, 79.
3. There is a wide consensus among scholars that the apocalyptic genre is one born of sociopolitical crisis. Leonard L. Thompson and John J. Collins both offer alternative views, however. Collins rejects this theory outright, and Thompson, claiming the consensus view is reductive, suggests that "perceived crisis" more accurately describes the motivation for writing apocalyptic stories. Collins bases his rejection on an examination of the social and political contexts surrounding the creation of certain well-known apocalyptic literature. Thompson's theory hinges on a semantic nicety. To my mind it matters little to the person or community which believes it is

in crisis whether the world at large would judge it to be; perception is all in this matter, and it would be accurate, I believe, to claim that the apocalyptic literature created by such a community is still motivated by crisis.

4. Dewey, *In a Dark Time*, 10.

5. Zamora, *Writing the Apocalypse*, 3, 4.

6. Dewey, *In a Dark Time*, 11.

7. See Michael Barkun, "Politics and Apocalypticism," for more on conspiracy and its relationship to political apocalypticism.

8. See Cohn, *Cosmos, Chaos and the World to Come*.

9. Collins, *The Apocalyptic Imagination: An Introduction to the Jewish Matrix of Christianity*, 3

10. For scholars who argue that such stories without New Jerusalem should still be categorized as apocalyptic, see Zbigniew Lewicki, *The Bang and the Whimper: Apocalypse and Entropy in American Literature*; Douglas Robinson, *Apocalypses: The Image of the End of the World in American Literature*; John R. May, *Toward a New Earth: Apocalypse in the American Novel*; James Berger, *After the End: Representations of Post-Apocalypse*. For scholars who argue for a reinterpretation of the New Jerusalem element, see Joel W. Martin and Conrad E. Ostwalt, Jr., *Screening the Sacred: Religion, Myth, and Ideology in Popular American Film*; David Ketterer, *New Worlds for Old: The Apocalyptic Imagination, Science Fiction, and American Literature*; and Marlene Goldman, *Rewriting Apocalypse in Canadian Fiction*.

11. Broeck, "The Apocalyptic Imagination in America; Recent Criticism," 94.

12. Different scholars account for this omission in different ways, though most argue it has to do with increasing secularization. Pointing to the many social and economic changes happening in the nineteenth century, including secularization of society, Zbigniew Lewicki ties the loss of New Jerusalem to the increasing dominance of entropy as the representative trope of universal endings. John R. May attributes the newer, pessimistic strain of apocalyptic narrative to a loss of faith that has led to translating the traditional apocalyptic paradigm into a "secular or worldly analogue" (*Toward a New Earth*, 215). Acknowledging the vagueness of the term *apocalyptic* and using the root *eschaton* ("the furthermost boundary") as his prompt, Douglas Robinson has proposed reading apocalyptic narratives not as visions of the end so much as of transition, and thus regards as apocalyptic a variety of eschatological tales, some without New Jerusalem, the figure of God, or even an End. David Ketterer does not discount New Jerusalem as an identifying feature of the genre, but interprets it far more flexibly than the original paradigm does. Joseph Dewey, W. Warren Wagar, and Frances Carey have all connected the ascendance of the pessimistic strain of apocalyptic literature specifically to the twentieth century and its events. Carey, who edited the impressive catalogue that accompanied the British Museum's 1999 exhibition on apocalypse, argues for a connection between the changed tone of apocalyptic work and the pessimism and alienation that are part of Modernism. Dewey and Wagar both trace the noticeable change in apocalyptic narrative to the first nuclear explosion.

13. Dewey, *In a Dark Time*, 10.

14. Kermode, *The Sense of an Ending*, 29, 8–9.

15. Kermode, "Apocalypse and the Modern," 102–3.

16. Ketterer, *New Worlds for Old*, 13.

17. Swatos, William H., Jr., and Kevin J. Christiano, "Secularization Theory: The Course of a Concept," in *The Secularization Debate*, 8.

18. See Chu, "Oh Father, Where Art Thou?" 25; Douthat, "Crises of Faith"; and Dionne, PBS: "Frontline: The Jesus Factor—Interview with E. J. Dionne, Jr."

19. Cizik, "PBS: "Frontline: The Jesus Factor—Interview with Richard Cizik."

20. McAlister, "Prophecy, Politics, and the Popular: The Left Behind Series and Christian Fundamentalism's New World Order," 773.

21. Gibbs, "Apocalypse Now," 42.

22. Kermode, *The Sense of an Ending*, 28, 8.

23. Berger, *After the End*, xiii, 7.

24. Until There's a Cure (Until), http://www.until.org/statistics.shtml. See also UNAIDS, http://www.unaids.org/en/AboutUNAIDS/default.asp

25. Center for Disease Control and Prevention, http://www.cdc.gov/flu/avian/outbreaks/current.htm

26. See Global Warming International Center, http://www.globalwarming.net/index.php?option=com_frontpage&Itemid=1

27. Zamora, *Writing the Apocalypse*, 11.

28. Cizik is the vice president for governmental affairs for the National Association of Evangelicals. Cizik, PBS "Frontline: The Jesus Factor." Cf. Wagar, *Terminal Visions*, 66–67, who attributes contemporary eschatological interest to three kinds of modern anxiety: private/individual fear of death, isolation, and separation; dread of natural forces; and anxiety over man's own destructive ability.

29. Berger, *After the End*, 7.

30. Zamora, *Writing the Apocalypse*, 3–4.

31. Steinberg, "Bernard Malamud and Russell Hoban: Manipulating the Apocalypse," 166.

32. Butler, *Postmodernism: A Very Short Introduction*, 29.

33. Zamora, *Writing the Apocalypse*, 17.

34. Berger, *After the End*, 5–6. Emphasis Berger.

35. Quinby, *Anti-Apocalypse*, xiii.

36. Zamora, *Writing the Apocalypse*, 13–14.

37. Collins, *The Apocalyptic Imagination: An Introduction to the Jewish Matrix of Christianity*, 4.

38. See Collins for more on this problematic definition.

39. See Eliade, *The Myth of The Eternal Return*, for a discussion of these more ancient apocalyptic myths.

40. Other elements of the traditional paradigm, such as the figure of the apocalyptist, the battle of Armageddon, or the figure of the Antichrist, are easily incorporated into secular adaptations because contemporary society has already become

accustomed to using the rhetoric of apocalypse to describe real events. The word *Armageddon*, for instance, has often been used to describe armed conflicts of particularly large or violent kinds, while the number of tyrants, political figures, and malefactors who have been called or thought of as the Antichrist is too numerous to mention. See Robert Fuller for a more complete discussion of how the figure of the Antichrist has been co-opted for political and religious ends, particularly in America.

41. Carey, John, *The Faber Book of Utopias*, xi.

42. Zamora distinguishes between New Jerusalem and the "return to Eden" motif, saying that the former completes history whereas the latter is based on "undoing of historical experience." "If *innocence* inhabits Eden," she writes, "it is *virtue* which gains New Jerusalem" (*Writing the Apocalypse*, 18. Emphasis Zamora.)

43. One notes that while artists' handling of the thematic elements of apocalypse may vary widely, the handling of the translation of apocalyptic form is, by necessity, a commonality between them. Apocalypse is not just the story of a vision; it is told in a vision. It has a visionary format. Authors who work with the apocalyptic paradigm may choose not to deal with this element in their narratives, but by virtue of the fact that there is a formal translation from a visionary form to speculative and imaginative texts such as novels or films, they, in fact, maintain a sense of this visionary format. One way to think about the secular adaptation of apocalypse would be to locate its formal translation from visionary to creative texts such as the ones discussed here.

44. Eliade, *Myth and Reality*, 51–52.

45. Richard Dellamora's *Postmodern Apocalypse: Theory and Cultural Practice at the End* is the one exception, though its focus is more theoretical than the thematic one I am concerned with here.

46. Kermode, "Apocalypse and the Modern," 101.

47. Bergoffen, "The Apocalyptic Meaning of History," 11.

48. Levels of collaboration vary remarkably between different people in the field. Some writers provide only the dialogue and description of action and leave all the illustration to their artist, while others discuss panel illustration beforehand. Within the industry, however, Moore is known for the unusually large amount of detail he provides to his illustrators as to how many panels a page should have, the layout, the detail within them, and so forth. Moore's colleague, artist Todd Klein, writes that, "Alan's scripts have been notorious for their great length and detail, but what makes up that detail? Plenty of description, sure, but beyond that, Alan brings everyone reading his scripts into his personal world and vision of the story, not only describing every detail he can think of, but reaching out to you, asking you to join him in collaboration" (Khoury, *The Extraordinary Works of Alan Moore*, 190).

49. Yoke, "Phoenix from the Ashes Rising: An Introduction," 3.

50. O'Leary, *Arguing the Apocalypse: A Theory of Millennial Rhetoric*, 42. Emphasis O'Leary.

51. David, *Conversations about the End of Time*, 53.

52. Dewey, *Beyond Grief and Nothing*, 6.
53. Ketterer, *New Worlds for Old*, 94.
54. Boyer, *By the Bomb's Early Light*, 250.
55. Dewey, *In a Dark Time*, 5.
56. Dewey, *In a Dark Time*, 4.

1

SENTIENT VEGETABLE CLAIMS END IS NEAR!

The Graphic Novels of Alan Moore

The Book of Revelation is perhaps the most visually oriented of all the biblical books. It is also one of the most illustrated, a fact made plain by the 1999 British Museum exhibition "The Apocalypse and the Shape of Things to Come," which drew together apocalyptic art from medieval manuscripts to contemporary artists such as Jake and Dinos Chapman and filmmaker Ingmar Bergman. Much of Revelation's power derives from its detailed and compelling descriptions of the Four Horsemen, the Whore of Babylon, the throne of Christ, New Jerusalem, and the many plagues visited upon mankind, and Revelation continues to be reinterpreted by visual artists, an attestation to its powers of inspiration and the flexibility of its symbols.

It comes as no surprise that various incarnations of the apocalyptic myth have been a part of the comic and graphic novel medium almost from the beginning. Stories of potential ends of the world are, after all, a clichéd plot in the most familiar genre of comics, the superhero story. Yet some of the most interesting and clever postmodern adaptations of the apocalyptic myth have also occurred in this creative medium, and Alan Moore is responsible for a number of them.

Moore, who turned fifty in 2003, has been lauded in his own field for his extraordinarily fecund imagination and outstanding writing.[1] He is regarded as an innovator, as well as a clever and imaginative storyteller, and yet his name remains largely unrecognized in the literary world. This, however, is starting to change.[2] Writers such as Michael Moorcock and Dylan Horrocks note that Moore "has remained uncomfortably original, temperamentally unable to rest on his laurels or exploit his early dynamic," and praise his "ability to take a trashy formula or forgettable character and shape them into something fresh, profound and beautiful—while at the same time managing to impart a genuinely respectful sense of what was precious about the original."[3] Moore's skill at discerning the possibilities for characters and even genres has meant that some of his work has been groundbreaking, while at the same time the breadth of this autodidact's own reading has allowed him to make connections in his stories more often thought of as "literary" than "comic-like."

It is clear from reading interviews with Moore that he has given a great deal of thought to the myth of apocalypse. He has said that writers will always look to extreme situations for creative tension because it gives them an opportunity to "examine the human world and human beings" under those radical conditions:

> there are really only two extreme points that you can project the world to. One of them is Utopia, the other is Apocalypse. I mean, in actual real life, we'll probably muddle on somewhere between the two, probably for thousands of years yet. But I don't have thousands of years to wait and I'm a writer of fiction. . . .[4]

He seems also to have considered the malleability of the concept of apocalypse and how certain elements of it might be reinterpreted. In the documentary *The Mindscape of Alan Moore* (2003), he notes how "apocalypse," though strictly meaning "revelation," has now come to mean the end of the world, but that this is a flexible concept:

> As to what the end of the world means, I would say that probably depends on what we mean by world. I don't think this means the planet, or even the life forms upon the planet. I think the world is just a construction of ideas, and not just the physical structure, but the mental structure, the ideologies that we've erected. That is what I would call the world. Political structures, philosophical structures, ideological frameworks, economies. These are actually imaginary things, and yet that is the framework that we've built our entire world upon.

Moore is thus poised to reinterpret the apocalyptic myth in distinctly postmodern ways, experimenting with the notions of the apocalyptic "world," challenging strictly dualistic notions of morality, and incorporating the multiplicity and indeterminacy that postmodernism endorses. This chapter examines how Moore's adaptation of the traditional paradigm in three works, *Swamp Thing*, *Watchmen*, and *Promethea*, has provided him with a vehicle to address themes of concern to him and to examine the myth of apocalypse itself.

Moore's apocalyptic "framework" is formal, as well as thematic, so a short discussion of the graphic novel medium is necessary. Comics are a unique hybrid of text and image, and because of this, they are able to manipulate the time and space within a narrative in special ways. Indeed, some might argue that the manipulation of time and place is a defining trait of the comic medium. Will Eisner, a founding father of the medium, defined comics as "sequential art" specifically to stress the vital role time plays in the comic form.[5] Yet Eisner did not mean a sequential or chronological narrative when he used this term. He meant a sequence of images linked by juxtaposition, rather than chronological order.

A pivotal tool for understanding this sequentiality is what is known as "closure." Closure accounts for the intense relationship between text and image that is found in sequential art. When two images, or panels as they are called, are laid next to one another, the space between them is called the "gutter" and it is here, Scott McCloud argues in his book *Understanding Comics*, that both time and place are uniquely manipulated through closure.[6] Panels or frames:

> have no *fixed* or *absolute meaning*, like the icons of *language*. . . . Nor is their meaning as *fluid* and *malleable* as the sorts of icons we call *pictures*. The panel acts as a *general indicator* that time or space is being divided. The *durations* of that time and the *dimensions* of that space are defined more by the *contents* of the panel than by the panel itself. . . . In learning to read comics we all learned to perceive time *spatially*, for in the world of comics, *time and space* are *one and the same*.[7]

Closure happens when the reader fills in the missing bits that occur *between* panels. In the "blank" space of the gutter, a reader does not merely fill in the action linking a movement that is started in the first panel and completed in the second, as they do between frames of film. It is far more complicated than that. How a reader fills in the gutter is dependent upon the content of the two panels. Depending on what a panel shows, readers may "fill in" the gutter with missing action, plot, changes in locale, and so on.[8] McCloud illustrates this with an example of a panel showing a character holding an upraised axe over a second person and saying, "Now you die!" followed by a second panel showing the night sky and the word "EEYAA!" Explains McCloud:

> I may have drawn an *axe* being *raised* in this example, but I'm not the one who let it *drop* or decided how *hard* the blow, or *who* screamed, or *why*. *That*, dear reader, was *your special crime*, each of you committing it in your own *style*. All of you *participated* in the murder. All of you *held the axe* and

chose your spot. . . . the reader's *deliberate, voluntary closure* is comics' primary means of simulating *time and motion.*[9]

By its very nature, the narrative style of the comic book has a strong affinity with that of the Book of Revelation in terms of its manipulation of time and place. Revelation exhibits something very similar to this "closure" of time: St. John can witness the entirety of an event in a single vision, though the event itself may take place over a space of days or months, as it does, for example, in Rev. 11:7–12 where John simultaneously observes the two prophesying witnesses die, lie dead in the streets of the great city for three and a half days, and then resurrected and taken up to heaven.[10] The sudden movement from locale to locale in comics is also a feature of Revelation, as in Rev. 4:1–2 where John is simultaneously on Patmos receiving his vision and taken up to heaven where he observes the future, or in Rev. 13:1 where John is suddenly moved from heaven to stand "upon the sand of the sea."

DC Comics' *Swamp Thing* was Alan Moore's American debut and eschatological fears run thick through it.[11] Of all his work, this is the one where the author's fascination with apocalypse is most apparent. But as Moore worked on the *Swamp Thing* and *Watchmen* series concurrently, it is perhaps no coincidence that both comics have apocalyptic themes. *Watchmen* confronts the complex issue of apocalyptic deity, while *Swamp Thing* is Moore's meditation on New Jerusalem. In the original apocalyptic paradigm, New Jerusalem is a literal place inherited by the faithful. In Moore's postmodern interpretation it becomes a new perspective rather than a new place, a twist that becomes explicit in Moore's more recent apocalyptic work, *Promethea*.

Swamp Thing had not always had apocalyptic tendencies; it had started off as quite a different kind of tale. The character was originally the creation of Len Wein and Berni Wrightson, who introduced him in the DC horror comic *HOUSE OF SECRETS* (1972), but the series became defunct after twenty-five issues, not long after the original creators left.[12] In 1983, Moore began writing the series with Stephen Bissette and John Totleben as his primary illustrators.[13] During the course of Moore's three-year tenure as writer, the character of the swamp creature was essentially remade.

In the original Wrightson/Wein story, scientist Alex Olsen—whose name was later changed to Alec Holland—had been working on a "biorestorative" formula when an act of sabotage dumped both him and his formula into the Louisiana swamp where his lab was located. He emerged as the Swamp Thing, a plantlike humanoid of lumbering strength and human intelligence. The motivation of the original Swamp Thing was his desperate drive to find a means of restoring himself to his human form, but the limitations of this original idea seemed obvious to Moore: "It was obvious to even the slowest reader that Alec Holland—the Swamp Thing—was never going to find some way to turn himself back to Alec Holland because the moment he did, that would be the end of the series."[14] Taking pains not to destroy the character's previous continuity, Moore set about reinterpreting Swamp Thing's history so that he could essentially start the tale fresh.[15]

His first issue establishes the fact that Swamp Thing can never find a way to return to his human form because he is no longer human. He is not Alec Holland in plant form. He is a plant who only believes he is Alec Holland. He is, in Moore's new mythology, a plant elemental, a living embodiment of "the green," the plant life of the world. Connected to the earth and its vegetation, Swamp Thing feels its pain and can manipulate its strength. He *is* this plant world.

With this change, Moore created a character for who the subtextual possibilities were remarkably rich. This more complex character lent itself to certain themes in particular. In *Swamp Thing*, there was a natural overlap between the eschatological themes that fascinated him and Moore's concerns about environmental destruction. Indeed, for this one work, Moore created four apocalypses, each of which interprets the idea of the apocalyptic "world" differently. These different versions of apocalypse, all interrelated and arranged in concentric circles, encompass ever-larger universes.

Moore makes it clear from his first issue that his *Swamp Thing* series is going to be a story of potential and literal apocalypses. The initial four issues, which comprise the first story arc, are the story of apocalypse written in miniature. In it, Moore reintroduces an old DC villain named Jason Woodrue, a.k.a. the Floronic Man, who is also a plant/human creature. In Moore's hands, Woodrue becomes a kind of anti–Swamp Thing, the green world personified and gone mad. Woodrue rants indignantly about the injuries done to the plant world by humans. His threatened revenge is just part of the first issue's dual apocalyptic strains, for Moore clearly outlines the first of his many potential apocalypses in the Floronic Man's condemnations: that of an environmental apocalypse. This apocalypse, as *Swamp Thing* suggests repeatedly throughout the series, is not so much potential as imminent.

This theme is not always as prominent as it is in the first story arc, but because Swamp Thing himself is tied so closely to the environment, the reader never loses sight of it. Moore maintains this subtext visually by inserting the odd bit of garbage in panels meant to be showing lush vegetative panoramas. For example, the splash page for issue #25, "The Sleep of Reason," shows Swamp Thing underwater in his swamp.[16] In addition to the distinctly sick-looking shade of green in which this illustration is rendered, there is a discarded hubcap sitting in the silt. Also pictured are a crayfish and a catfish, both creatures which usually dwell in murky water. This strategy is also used in "Growth Patterns" (#37), in which Swamp Thing grows himself a new body.[17] The spot in the swamp where he begins to sprout anew is in the shadow of a discarded tin can. Throughout the issue, he is always pictured juxtaposed against this piece of trash. Even when his girlfriend, Abby, discovers and begins to care for him, it does not occur to her to remove this piece of garbage from the Edenic landscape.

A more striking example revolves around the illegal dumping of radioactive waste. In "The Nuke-Face Paper, Part I" (#35), artists Bissette and Totleben illustrate a remarkable three-page sequence of the burnt-out, polluted, and ironically named town Blossomville where the environmental consequences of ill-managed energy policies are made dreadfully apparent. The skies are lit orange and red as if reflecting flames, and red smoke drifts across the panels. Swamp Thing walks through scenery suggestive of a post–nuclear war landscape. In the background is the distinct shape of the Three Mile Island nuclear facility that Blossomville is clearly meant to call to mind. The ties to Hiroshima and Nagasaki are implied both in the art and Swamp Thing's narration that talks about curdled soil and stillborn birds. "Something bright and awful kissed the world . . . and left . . . its smeared . . . blue . . . lipstick-print," Swamp Thing muses as he surveys twisted metal hunks, bubbling green puddles, eerie vapors, and malformed fungi.[18] The rhetorical cadences of Moore's effusive prose, used here to describe the most terrible of landscapes, serves to intensify the reader's horror, and the sequence ends with the creature on his knees among the smoldering detritus with his hand covering his mouth in what at first appears to be nausea, but a close-up of the creature shows that he is not ill, but weeping for the decimated land.

Such scenes contextualize the Floronic Man's histrionic excuses for wiping humankind off the planet, a point of view the reader might find compelling, given Moore's reiteration of exactly this point throughout the series. This specter of environmental apocalypse is constantly in the background of Moore's tenure on the series, and for good reason: it is the only one of the four apocalypses he depicts which has the potential for actually occurring, the only one which affects the reader literally. The other apocalypses only affect the comic book characters in their comic book universe.

To emphasize the reality of the threat and make clear that this is not merely the work of the author's nightmarish imagination, panels in this particular two-part issue are littered with newspaper pages on which actual stories about toxic fumes, nuclear accidents, sunken uranium shipments, deadly acid spills, and the ongoing political tussle over waste disposal are all clearly readable. These news articles bear witness to ongoing environmental damage, and act as a bridge between the fictional world of Swamp Thing and our own world from which the newspaper stories are taken. The overlay of real environmental news over fiction is an example of extremely complex closure, and here is used to reiterate the reality of the danger.

The first story arc also anticipates Moore's work on apocalyptic deity in *Watchmen*. Though Moore ultimately makes Swamp Thing the primary deity figure of the series,[19] in this first story arc, Moore splits his apocalyptic deity in two, with the Floronic Man acting out the role of the wrathful Judge of the seven seals, and Swamp Thing acting out the role of the gentle, forgiving God. This multiplicity of gods is a strategy he will repeat in *Watchmen* and *Promethea*. Moore refuses to privilege a particular notion of god; his own deity figures incorporate allusions to gods from a host of pantheons: Greek, Judeo-Christian, Buddhist, Norse, and Pagan.

Woodrue doesn't start out as a deity figure, but becomes one when he attempts to elevate his own consciousness by tapping into the unconscious Swamp Thing's. It is an experiment that not only gives him the knowledge he wants about the plant world, but also changes him entirely, turning him into an evil doppelgänger of the plant creature, "Swamp Thing's darker self."[20] Like all fairy tale transformations, this is a painful one, as the blurred images and jagged lines of the two-page illustration seem to imply. The pages are dominated by an image of Woodrue's eyes, and at least three other panels include the image of eyes, clear reference to the fact that, with his elevation, Woodrue now sees the enormity of the natural world and, through it, Swamp Thing's power. Depicted with a leafy crown and loincloth and striking a statuesque pose, the images of the Floronic Man at the moment of his transformation call to mind classical representations of Spring or nature gods or demigods such as Oberon or Pan. The celebratory rain of blossoms confirms his ascension.

This apotheosis drives Woodrue mad, transforming him into the wrathful apocalyptic deity, as becomes clear from both by his language, laden with Book of Revelation references, and the way he is drawn. Once deified, he is pictured as a more threatening, demonic presence, with his eyebrows and eyelashes drawn as spiky horns, his fingers clawed, and his eyes either white or red holes.

The demonic implication of these drawings is not accidental, for Moore not only plays with a multiplicity of deity figures in his apocalyptic works, he also conflates the God/Devil binary structure of the traditional apocalyptic paradigm in order to represent a far more shaded morality than Revelation allows. Such a shading is possible because, as writer Ramsey Campbell notes in his foreword to the collection, Woodrue's anger is justifiable; he is as sympathetic as horrifying precisely because he expresses genuine concerns about environmental destruction. Indeed, in these early stages, the apotheosized Floronic Man seems to embrace nearly all the divine roles in the Book of Revelation, a conflation of false prophet, avenging angel, Satan, and God. Referred to alternately as a "green messiah," an "annihilating angel," a divine messenger, and even—in an explicit reference to Lucifer—a character who has fallen from grace, he tells his victims:

> I am one with the wilderness . . . Its will works through me. For I asked of it, saying, "What would you have me do?" And it said "Purify." And it said "destroy." [. . .] "Cut them down, like blighted wood. Let us have another green world!"[21]

At the same time that Woodrue is being developed as the Antichrist, Swamp Thing is developed as a deity. As the rightful representative of the natural world, Swamp Thing is deliberately tied to the savior role. His larger view of the world as a complete organism means salvation and forgiveness for mankind; he gently reminds Woodrue that the humans he wants to destroy are necessary for the survival of the plant world which needs the carbon dioxide they produce. In this instance, Swamp Thing's view is patently divine and all-seeing. Later in the series, Abby will also eat the fruit which grows on her plant boyfriend, and while Moore is definitely having fun with the sexual connotations here, there is no question that the reader is supposed to make the connection between this act and Christ's command to "eat of my body," a link which Moore makes explicit by having Abby ask Swamp Thing for exactly that, some form of communion between them.[22]

The artwork unequivocally makes this connection. The final panel of the first story arc contains explicit crucifixion imagery with the Swamp Thing in the place of Christ. With arms outstretched, head thrown back, and one leg bent at the knee, Swamp Thing is clearly meant to imitate the classic pose of Christ on the cross.[23] The crucifixion image is set against a blood red orb, a clever visual link between the ecological concerns of the text and its apocalyptic framework since the moon or sun only look brilliantly red like this when air pollution causes a particular refraction of light. Simultaneously, there is an apocalyptic overtone to the color in this image, a subtext suggesting the potential apocalyptic consequences of our environmental destruction.

Emphasizing the reality of the threat, Swamp Thing's fingers extend beyond the borders of this final panel, as if to say to the reader that what he represents here extends beyond the pages of the comic book and into the real world. While Moore will rarely be this explicit again, neither will he let the reader forget the potentially apocalyptic consequences of our environmental "sins." Throughout the remainder of his writing tenure, he will continue to hint at this potentially real apocalypse even as he is adapting the apocalyptic myth in other ways.

There are three other apocalypses in the *Swamp Thing* series, and the first of these is also laid out in the first story arc. Unlike the others, it reimagines apocalypse as an interior process, and allows Moore to begin to play with the concept of an apocalyptic "world." In this case, the "world" destroyed is Alec Holland's identity. The New Jerusalem that replaces it is more than just his new identity as a plant elemental called Swamp Thing. It also encompasses a new understanding about the nature of the universe, and as with many other postmodern versions of apocalypse, New Jerusalem is reconceived as a new worldview rather than a literal new world.

The identity apocalypse begins with Woodrue's discovery that Swamp Thing cannot return to his human form. When Swamp Thing reads Woodrue's report and realizes that his former human self is unattainable, the effect of this news is devastating. He lies down in the swamp and becomes rooted there. That Woodrue is the agent of apocalypse in the identity story is appropriate given that he has become a figure of destruction and an agent of purification. Keeping watch over the rooted creature, Woodrue recognizes that Swamp Thing is not dead, but undergoing a psychological transformation of some kind in which he will have to give up his idea of himself as human. The question Woodrue poses about what will replace Swamp Thing's humanity is a central preoccupation of the entire series. It will take Swamp Thing a long time to understand exactly what he has become, but long before then, the reader will understand that he is nature personified, that he has essentially become a deity figure.[24]

In the meantime, the apocalypse of his former self is total, and is illustrated in a series of four dreams the creature has while rooted. These dreams incorporate Alec Holland's past, his self-loathing of the "monster" he has become, the paranormal adventures of Swamp Thing's previous incarnation, and a debate about identity and humanity. Each of these dreams moves Swamp Thing just a bit closer to relinquishing his conception of himself as human.

The first of these dream sequences finds Swamp Thing reliving Alec Holland's wedding reception. His wife Linda, who died in the same sabotage, tells her husband that she doesn't feel well and begins to sink into the ground. Alec's urgent exclamation that Linda is buried and must be dug up is the first reference to burial, and the word is highlighted because burial is going to be vital to Swamp Thing's resolution of his identity crisis. Additionally in this dream, Alec is dressed in a "mud-suit." This mud suit looks exactly like the Swamp Thing, and the mud functions in this case not only to tie Swamp Thing to the earth, but also almost certainly as a sign of disgrace and disgust for that new identity. When a guest points out that Alec cannot breathe inside this suit, and they begin to dig him out of it, they discover only an empty shell. The dream sequence ends with a panel that straddles Swamp Thing's dream and real worlds, with the illustration being of the comatose creature in his real world, but the narration being the final words of the dream: "Alec isn't in there." These words function on a dual level, indicating both what the dream guests have found inside the mud-suit, as well as Swamp Thing's real and current identity dilemma.[25]

Both Alec and Linda Holland appear in the second dream, as well. Carrying the unconscious Linda, Swamp Thing discovers a group of Planerian worms holding a barbeque with the corpse of Alec Holland as the main dish.[26] What becomes apparent in this dream is that Swamp Thing equates his former identity with his humanity. Having eaten the corpse of Alec Holland down to the bones, the worms tell Swamp Thing that they have left him the best part, the humanity, and they advise him not to lose it. The dream ends with Swamp Thing mournfully cradling the skeleton of his former self as he abandons his wife, telling her that he can only carry one of them.[27]

From here on in, the struggle is one to decide whether one must be human to have humanity. If so, then Swamp Thing is the monster he regards himself in the third dream sequence where a pack of monstrous figures set upon him. Holding the skeleton in his arms like a baby, Swamp Thing pleads with them not to take it because his humanity is all he has left. When the horde plucks at the bones, Swamp Thing breaks into a frenzy of violence, and tears the assailants to shreds. It's no coincidence that one of the monsters torn to bits, and, indeed, the one on which the final panel of this dream sequence focuses, is Frankenstein's monster. The allusion calls attention to the pathetic bind of Shelley's creature who, though monstrous-looking, does have humanity. Interestingly, in the first panel depicting Frankenstein's monster, its eyes are normal, but in the final panels, the eyes look more like scratched coins. The coin reference alludes to the ancient burial rites of placing coins on the eyes of the deceased in order to pay Charon, the Stygian ferryman, and so the destruction of the monster with coins on its eyes perhaps indicates the death of Swamp Thing's view of himself as a mere monster.[28]

The last of these dreams occurs immediately before the Floronic Man's apotheosis, and therefore acts as its parallel: both Swamp Thing and Woodrue are now coming into some knowledge which will utterly transform them. In this final dream, Swamp Thing runs through the swamp holding a debate with what is left of his skeleton held tightly in his huge, clenched fist. He demands to know why he cannot stop and rest. The answer is a pun on "human race" with his skull pointing out that Swamp Thing cannot put him down:

> Because I'm your humanity. I'm important. I'm what keeps you going. You could let go of Linda, but you can't let go of me. Oh, I know I'm a little beaten up and battered, but I'm still worth all the effort, aren't I? After all, without me there'd be no point in running, would there?[29]

The illustration makes clear that this is the turning point for the creature. The dialogue is followed by two panels, one of the Swamp Thing silently slowing, and the second of him stopped entirely, staring at the skull in his fist. Both panels show the action from behind, as if we, the readers, have been watching Swamp Thing run away from *us*. The flight away from his human readers further reinforces his own identity dilemma.

The second panel shows him entirely stopped, contemplating the skull of his former self, the first of two times that Hamlet is evoked in the identity apocalypse. The additional fact that all sense of movement around him has also been removed gives this panel a sense of stillness that reflects not only the sudden cessation of physical movement, but also of the parallel mental process coming to a halt. The single word that Swamp Thing speaks in this panel—"No"—reinforces this quieting. The plant elemental then sits on a tree stump and even his badgering skull's warning that he will be disqualified from the human race if he stops running cannot make him take up his flight again.

The perspective of the action begins to swing around to the front of the creature now; the first view of him seated is a profile in which his resigned slump is still very much apparent, but his downcast face is now also partially seen, as is his gradually loosening grip on the skull. Ensuing panels continue to swing the perspective to the front of the character. By the time there is a panel focused on Swamp Thing's face, he has lain down and taken root on the tree; the expression on his face is blank and staring and he has completely released the skull which symbolizes his former identity. The final image of Swamp Thing in this issue is of him mossy and overgrown, rooted to his tree stump in the swamp.

Strangely, in the process of accepting the loss of his human identity, Swamp Thing does, in fact, begin to resemble a Judeo-Christian deity. Through his plant consciousness, comprised of all the plant life of the planet, Swamp Thing has a level of extreme awareness that nears omniscience. As later issues will show, his control of the plant world makes him nearly omnipotent. A plant consciousness that makes him simultaneously aware of and feel disturbances in the plant world all over the earth, combined with an ability to shed his body and regrow instantaneously anywhere on the planet where there is plant life to shelter his consciousness, means he approaches omnipresence.

Though Swamp Thing will shake himself free of his catatonic state in the following issue in order to defeat the Floronic Man, his identity apocalypse is not finally resolved until several issues later in "The Burial" (#28). However, the process is clearly begun. After defeating the Floronic Man, Swamp Thing informs Abby that Alec Holland is dead. When she asks who *he* is then, he replies, "I? I am . . . the Swamp Thing."[30]

This panel is taken up with the lush, beautiful bulk of the Swamp Thing's torso and most of his head. Behind him is the night sky with one star shining especially brightly over his left shoulder, while over his right, the word bubble containing "I?" is placed against the backdrop of the night sky. The effect is to float this question in a celestial backdrop and make the question a profound, almost divine inquiry. The other dialogue bubble is set against the muscular bulk of the Swamp Thing's body, so that when he declares himself, this identification is backed by a visual reinforcement. His pose is indicative, as well. With one hand to his chest and head slightly bowed, the impression is of a gentleman introducing himself. In this image, Swamp Thing's face is made particularly human, with a softening of the usual alien red eyes, and a flattening of the reptilian crest of his nose. Posed like a gentleman, his demeanor thus undermines the notion that he is merely a "monster."

Once again, the panel cannot hold all of the Swamp Thing. Only part of his body and head are visible. In the context of the accompanying narrative, the implication is that he is bigger than the story he is in, too large to be properly displayed. The effect of the Swamp Thing's body extending beyond the panel borders in this case is different from the one discussed previously. In that case, his body came through the borders, calling the reader's attention to both the panel's artificial nature and how Swamp Thing reaches out from the comic into the real world beyond. This is apt for an image having to do with a potential "real" apocalypse. But in this second case, the panel borders hem him in, making him seem impressive and superhuman. We are now safely within the confines of a fictional story, and as the apocalypse here is a personal but fictional one, Swamp Thing's body must not come out of the comic, but must remain within its limits. Nonetheless, the implication is that the comic is no longer big enough to hold what he has become. It gives readers the sense that they are looking at a character grown divine and godlike.

It seems unnecessary, even redundant, to give Swamp Thing's former human self a formal burial, but this is exactly what happens in "The Burial," the issue in which the identity apocalypse is resolved. Writer Neil Gaiman notes, however, that this issue has a larger significance in the comic book world:

> Alec Holland is buried and put to rest in this issue; but that's not all that's buried. It's the end of an era—a celebration of and memorial to the original Len Wein and Berni Wrightson stories, and is the story that gave THE SAGA OF THE SWAMP THING the freedom to move on. The shaggy swamp creature, turning brown with approach of autumn, stares at the smooth and root-laced Wrightson Swamp Thing, fresh out of the swamp, and we see how far we have come.[31]

The issue's mournful tone and its somber use of a mostly dark register of color appropriately mark it out as the tale of endings. The opening image of Swamp Thing digging a grave in the rain and the handfuls of mud he scoops out recall the mud-suit of the first dream and links the issue to the earlier sequence, and thus to Swamp Thing's struggle with his new identity. In the issue, the ghost of the original Swamp Thing rises from the swamp to confront the new one. Each creature reaches for his double, but their hands pass through one another's. Moore's Swamp Thing agitatedly protests that there is so much he must tell his ancestor about his future, but the Wrightson incarnation solemnly raises an index finger to its mouth to indicate silence and then points toward the swamp before fading away again. Following the ghost's gesture, Moore's Swamp Thing is able to find and retrieve the bones of Alec Holland, and thus give him a proper burial in the grave he himself has dug. Moore lovingly pays homage to his creature's past by having Swamp Thing rip off a piece of his own body, a two-pronged root, to mark the grave where his own history and past are now buried.

This, then, is the culmination of a dual apocalypse: one for the fictional character *in* the story, and one for the fictional character in the *real* world. The identity apocalypse encompasses both the individual Swamp Thing, as well as the individual authors/artists of it. As Swamp Thing begins to understand and accept his new self, this more complex identity begins to resemble, for him, a New Heaven on Earth.

From this point forward, the apocalypses are going to be relatively straight-forward ones, at least in the comic book world. Where Moore has largely been focused on environmental themes until now, the next two versions of apocalypse are going to address apocalyptic morality. Not surprisingly, given his postmodern affinities, Moore is going to complicate the simplistic view of good and evil that is so pivotal to the traditional apocalyptic myth.

Moore signals his use of the paradigmatic text both by repeatedly allud-ing to the Book of Revelation and with an actual return of the Devil, a char-acter named Jason Blood, also known as the rhyming demon Etrigan. But the depiction of Etrigan is a good example of how Moore's postmodern style affects his apocalyptic adaptation. Etrigan is going to turn out to be *a* devil, rather than *the* devil. Moreover, he ultimately fights on the side of good, ex-plaining that evil is no simple matter, and that he prefers to choose the devil he knows rather than one he does not.[32] Etrigan's logic is not going to be-come totally clear until the denouement of this apocalypse, but he is not the only character used to suggest that morality defies simplistic calculations. Many of the superheroes who appear in *Swamp Thing* during Moore's tenure are morally ambiguous.

It is clear, however, that Moore is playing with the apocalyptic myth. In "Revelations," the issue in which Etrigan returns, the devil's reappearance is heralded by "signs" and omens: the sky has turned an ominous shade of red; there is rioting in the streets with people literally losing their minds; and the narration tells us that "Time *buckled*, collapsing *in* upon itself, *fu-ture* and *past* embedding in the *present*," a neat description of Revelatory time and space.[33] The references to Revelation keep coming, with different characters mentioning the prophecy of Armageddon, the millennium, the day of judgment and resurrection, and the expected return to Earth of some terrifying evil.[34]

The apocalypse that Moore is foreshadowing with such references is two-fold, and some comic book history is necessary to understand it. The fictional comic book universe is particularly complicated by its serial nature, its long history, and the migratory tendencies of those who write and illustrate the individual books. Characters who had been at the height of their popularity in the Golden Age of comics but had lost favor or become outdated were of-ten reinterpreted later on in the Silver Age, or again in the present day.[35] Si-multaneously there might be in production multiple comics involving the same character, but at different ages of his life, or living in different locales, or indeed even in alternative universes. These multiple realities and parallel universes are known in the comic book world as the "multiverse."

By the 1980s, this creative freedom was causing difficulties because it in-terfered with the continuity of the characters' histories. How to explain that

Batman is perpetually in his mid-twenties in his ongoing serial, but in his battered forties in stand-alone graphic novels? How to explain casts of characters, some of whom might have been minor or completely different from the ones bearing their same names, but who had been brought "back to life" by more recent creators?

> Years of accumulated history were beginning to slow down DC's mightiest champions, and the "parallel worlds" theory that allowed superheroes from the 1940s and the 1980s to co-exist was starting to interfere with the ideas of a new generation of comic writers, who wanted the freedom to re-interpret their childhood heroes. . . . The issue of parallel worlds and universes was becoming problematic by the 1980s.[36]

By mid-decade, a decision was made to conflate these parallel universes and essentially clean house. The result was the groundbreaking, controversial plan which became the twelve-part *Crisis on Infinite Earths*. In it, characters from parallel DC universes mingled freely, all of them working to stop the crisis of the title. Many characters, some of them major, were killed off. Chronologies and character histories were made definitive.[37] The endeavor took extraordinarily detailed plotting and planning, and every writer who was then in control of a serial was warned, indeed directed, to incorporate the plot into his or her individual series.

This apocalypse of the multiverse is the backdrop for the latter half of Moore's *Swamp Thing* tenure. The first *Crisis* reference is made in the "Revelations" issue when Swamp Thing is whisked off to an organizational meeting of all the serial heroes. Within the panels that show this visit, the reader glimpses Batman, Superman, Plasticman, Alex Luthor, and a host of other recognizable characters from the DC world. During this meeting, Swamp Thing's "handler," John Constantine, acknowledges and explains the crisis to the ignorant creature and any reader who does not already know about it:

> The *world*? The *world* isn't ending. It's the *multiverse* that's *ending*. . . . A whole series of parallel *universes*, parallel *earths* . . . Something's eating its way *through* them, like a *maggot* munching through a stack of *maps*. In order to survive, the *remaining* worlds are being sort of folded together, making them stronger. It'll work. . . .The *material* world will be saved, but there's more to *life* than the *material world*.[38]

This final statement is the first hint that the author is up to something unusual. Moore has the reputation of a maverick. In addition to his long-standing resentment against the comic book companies' financial and licensing rights to creative properties, he simply does not like being told what to do.[39] The warning that the material world and the spiritual world are two separate things is

Moore's defiant response to his corporate financers. With his hand forced, he incorporates the *Crisis* storyline into *Swamp Thing*, but in the end, he makes it completely his own story by turning the comic book multiverse apocalypse into a smaller element in the *Swamp Thing* apocalypse.

In retrospect, a reader realizes that this strategy has been foreshadowed earlier when Constantine has joked that it's not the end of the world that there's an apocalypse happening outside.[40] The use of *an*, rather than *the* to refer to the apocalypse, and Constantine's punning assurance that this apocalypse is not the end of the world confirms that Moore is readapting the apocalyptic paradigm according to postmodern tenets: Which apocalypse? And is it really the End? The multiplicity of apocalypses that Constantine suggests here is literally embodied in the numerous apocalypses which Moore depicts in the series.

Once Moore has fulfilled his duty by mentioning *Crisis*, he leaves it behind and does not refer to it again. Almost immediately, he begins to steer towards the Ending he has envisaged as the subject matter of *Swamp Thing*. Constantine's explanation has made it clear that fixing the crisis will necessarily entail apocalyptic destruction, so the question which begins to preoccupy the plant elemental—what *will* New Jerusalem look like?—is going to be Moore's objective now. First, however, he must differentiate the *Swamp Thing* apocalypse. According to Constantine, the physical collapse of the multiverse will have dire psychic ramifications in the *Swamp Thing* world, allowing a group called the Brujería to bring back some unspeakable entity that will destroy heaven itself.

With one fell swoop, Moore both incorporates and trivializes the *Crisis* plotline. What's the folding of the multiverse, after all, when heaven is in danger of being destroyed? The Brujería want a new universe, and lest the reader miss the allusion, Moore makes the apocalyptic parallel explicit:

> This is the *ultimate* dark, *ultimate* light. The *forces* and *stakes* here are *fundamental* and *absolute* . . . and *whichever* side meets its *final destruction* this day, *everything* will be *changed*.[41]

Moore has set himself quite a task now: what exactly *is* this apocalypse going to entail? He handles the return of the evil entity with the same multiplicity he has used elsewhere. Each character understands this thing to be something different, whether it is Satan, Cthulhu, an energy field, "the primordial shadow," or the "complete absence of divine light."[42] The visual representation of this ultimate evil is a rolling black wall, the epitome of postmodern image-making since each reader can also project his own fears and interpretations onto this blank space.

One after another, the gathered heroes attack the mysterious evil entity, but each time, the entity engulfs its attacker, holding him prisoner inside itself and demanding an answer to a sphinxlike question about its basic nature. Because each of the first three heroes—Etrigan, Dr. Fate, and the Spectre—are bound by a traditional view of good and evil, their answers are also bound by that rigid duality.[43] They can only see the entity through this Manichean lens and call it "evil." Moore's postmodern response to that traditional Revelation morality is to have the entity spit each out in contempt.

As a postmodern deity, Swamp Thing's perspective will not be so rigid. He is uniquely prepared for this postmodern Armageddon because throughout the series he has been pondering the very complex and shaded questions that the entity now poses about the nature of evil and its purpose. Swamp Thing responds to the riddle according to what he has learned in his new role as a nature deity. He draws an analogy from nature, in which death and decay feed new life and both are part of an ongoing circle of existence. He answers thoughtfully, "Perhaps evil . . . is the humus . . . formed by virtue's decay . . . and perhaps it is from . . . that dark, sinister loam . . . that virtue grows strongest?"[44]

This, then, is Moore's New Jerusalem: not a place, but a new understanding, one which encompasses both evil and good, seeing them as part of the same thing. Paradoxically, this solution is not new at all. The notion that evil and good are two parts of a whole has very old roots, particularly in far Eastern cultures. Moore acknowledges that debt visually. During the clash of the Light and Dark forces, there's a moment of swirling chaos that resolves briefly into the Chinese Yin/Yang symbol, a tangible representation of the idea that the universe is made up of opposite-and-related principles. His grafting of this other religious idea onto the traditional apocalyptic paradigm is yet another way that he refuses to privilege one particular cultural view over another.

Indeed, Moore has been hinting at this resolution all along. As far back as the "Revelations" issue, Constantine has been saying that everything is connected, Etrigan has been talking about God's balance, and Swamp Thing has been ruminating over whether evil can actually be avoided.[45] In the quiet after the battle, Swamp Thing notes how the world looks the same, but feels different because the conflict between good and evil has changed. In one lyrical passage clarifying this reconception of the New Jerusalem, a character says that until this moment, he's never understood that good and evil actually depend upon each other.

This more nuanced view of good and evil is one that many postmodern authors and filmmakers adopt in their reworkings of the apocalyptic paradigm.

The postmodern rejection of the absolutism of the traditional apocalyptic myth means, as well, that the traditional understanding and depiction of the structure of time is also often reinterpreted in these new versions.[46] Judeo-Christian apocalypse is rooted in a notion of linear time and sees the Last Judgment as the end of history. More ancient cultures, such as the Mesopotamians, Zoroastrians, and Ancient Greeks, regarded history as a cyclical process in which the world was endlessly destroyed and recreated. Endings are part of beginnings and vice versa. Rejecting notions of singularity, postmodern versions of apocalypse sometimes return to this more holistic and flexible view of time, as Moore will do in his two subsequent apocalyptic works.

This cyclical view of history is certainly implied in Moore's 1986 twelve-part graphic novel *Watchmen*. Dr. Manhattan's final comment, "*Nothing ends, Adrian. Nothing ever ends*," makes the point with a bluntness that is characteristic of this work.[47] In this work, Moore's aims as regards both the apocalyptic paradigm itself and *Watchmen*'s larger themes are quite different than in *Swamp Thing*. Where *Swamp Thing* focuses on Moore's environmental concerns and the issue of New Jerusalem, *Watchmen*, illustrated by Dave Gibbons, focuses largely on reworking the superhero genre and the idea of apocalyptic deity.

Both Gibbons and Moore have repeatedly talked about the unusually collaborative nature of this particular project, and neither man has been able to remember specifically who had which ideas during the intense partnership. Much of the plot was crafted along the way rather than in advance, though the aim was always to deal with how superheroes would affect and behave in the real world. Gibbons has said that they wanted "to make the story the paramount thing," and that Moore was "more concerned with the social implications" of the story, while Gibbons was more "involved in the technical implications."[48] In spite of their partnership, however, I am going to cautiously refer to Moore as the "author" of *Watchmen*, since its ethos is so close to that of his other work.

By the mid-1980s, the superhero genre was so well established in comics that every reader was familiar with its conventions and "types."[49] Moore and Gibbons were among the first to turn the conventions on their heads and begin a revisionist movement in the superhero genre by treating superheroes, and their effect on the world, realistically. By exploring the psychopathologies and motivations of superheroes, the creators' "intention was to show how super-heroes could deform the world just by being there, not that they'd have to take it over, just their presence there would make the difference."[50]

There was a fortunate confluence of the issues that interested Moore at this time. Moore realized that one of the real-life ramifications of having superheroes would certainly be an effect in the political spectrum, and thus *Watchmen*'s realistic setting also gave him a perfect platform to address what he saw as the unbearable political climate of the day.[51] To Moore's mind, the conservative politics of Thatcher in Britain and Reagan in America had brought the world to the edge of a nuclear confrontation. Moore's response to Thatcher's policies had been to write *V for Vendetta* about a future fascist Britain. *Watchmen* was meant as a similar critique of America:

> at the moment a certain part of Reagan's America isn't scared. They think they're invulnerable. . . . they're not afraid, and they can gloss over the terror of the nuclear stockpiles, the world situation and all that and just think, "Hey, we're doing all right, we're okay."
>
> . . . I was consciously trying to do something that would make people feel uneasy. . . . I wanted to communicate that feeling of "When's it going to happen?" Everyone felt it. You hear a plane going overhead really loud, and just for a second before you realize it's a plane you look up. I'm sure that everybody's . . . done that at least once. It's something over everybody's head, but nobody talks about it. At the risk of doing a depressing comic book we thought that it would be nice to . . . try and scare a little bit so that people would just stop and think about their country and their politics.[52]

At the same time, Moore wanted to explore how real people would likely react if superheroes *did* exist. One of the by-products of that exploration was that he was able to essentially deconstruct the superhero genre that he thought had grown staid and silly. Given the nuclear fear at the time, *Watchmen*'s apocalyptic scenario was a perfect way to address both issues.

There's little doubt about the apocalyptic tenor of this work, which is about the misguided plan of Adrian Veidt, the former superhero Ozymandias, to bring about world cooperation by making people believe that the planet is in danger of being destroyed by an alien culture. Since his plan requires him to kill millions of New Yorkers in a fake "alien attack" in order to convince the world of the aliens' existence, and since he can't afford to be found out, Veidt also sets about murdering off the only people who can expose his plan: his former superhero colleagues.

Like Revelation, *Watchmen* is focused on "the times," both how bad they are and how they are in the process of changing. Like many apocalyptic stories, *Watchmen* is set during a transitional moment. Its characters are poised between two eras, looking both forward and backward, a tension epitomized by the marketing war between Adrian Veidt's Nostalgia and Millennium lines

of cosmetics. The issue of time (and its complement "the times") is a preoccupation of the series, as indicated by the importance of nostalgia (the product and the longing) in the story.

The most obvious sign of this preoccupation is the image of the clock that
appears at the beginning and end of each chapter. In the first chapter, the
clock records the time as twelve minutes to twelve, but at the end of every
succeeding chapter, it appears again with its minute hand another minute
closer to midnight and with increasing amounts of blood threatening to
cover its face, an image which is echoed ironically in the smiley face pin with
the blood streak on it which also appears throughout the novel. While this
midnight hour is pivotal to the plot since it is the moment at which Adrian
Veidt's plan comes to fruition, the clock is also clearly meant to emulate the
Atomic Doomsday Clock which was designed by the *Bulletin of the Atomic
Scientists* in 1947 as a representation of pending nuclear danger.[53]

The clock is only the first of many time references that simultaneously allude to the apocalyptic tenor of the "times." The name of the first group of
masked heroes is the Minutemen and there are members of the group, like
Hollis Mason and Sally Jupiter, for whom time, particularly the past, is important. Both these characters have dialogue which articulates the apocalyptic fears that pervade the "new" world. In his memoir, Hollis writes of a
"bleak, uneasy feeling in the air" after World War II, declaring, "it was impossible to live through the 1950s without a sense of impending catastrophe
bearing implacably, down upon the whole country, the whole world" (3:
"Under the Hood: V, 13). In addition, there are chapter titles such as
"Watchmaker," references to literature, such as Shelley's poem "Ozymandias," which is also preoccupied with time, and background visuals such as
a poster of Dali's famous painting *The Persistence of Memory* (4:16) or the
famous *Time* magazine cover of a watch stopped at the instant of the Hiroshima blast (4:24).

The title itself indicates this preoccupation with time, but like most
things in this text, it is meaningful on more than one level. *Watchmen*'s title comes from Juvenal's quip in *Satires* VI, *Quis custodiet ipsos custodes*
("Who watches the watchmen?"). The word "watchmen" has its own set of
associations with the numerous watchmen of the Bible, but because Moore
deliberately ties *Watchmen* to the political sphere with a concluding note
that quotes the 1987 Tower Commission Report which also used the Juvenal quip as its epigraph, he simultaneously suggests that his text belongs
both to a biblical and a political/protest tradition.[54]

Certainly, the title *Watchmen* is a pun on "watch-man," a man who makes
watches. In the story, this clearly refers to Jon Osterman, whose father was

a watchmaker, and who Jon originally intends to emulate. Moreover, "Watchmaker" is the title of chapter 4, which details how Jon became Dr. Manhattan in an incident directly related to a watch. The word "watch-maker" itself evokes the "argument from design," one of whose exponents, William Paley, famously described God as a "divine Watchmaker" of the universe in his 1802 work *Natural Theology*. The linking of these ideas suggests that Dr. Manhattan is more than merely Moore's version of a super-human hero; he is Moore's version of a deity, and, as the illustration of Jon sitting below a night sky with the Genesis quotation "Shall not the Judge of all the earth do right?" underneath him implies, not just any kind of deity.[55]

Of course, *Watchmen* is plural, and suggests a multiplicity of gods in the narrative. Moore has created three such Watchmen, all of whom act as judges on mankind, and yet each very different from the others. This, too, is implied in the complex allusion to the Biblical watchmen, because not all the watchmen of the Bible are watching for the same thing and not all of their missions are alike. There are biblical watchmen who are blind, liter-ally and figuratively (Isa. 56:10), and these watchmen certainly act as corol-laries to the Juvenal quotation, since the suggestion is that leaders may not "see" what is before them. But others, like Ezekiel, are made watchmen by God in order to deliver warnings (Ezek. 3:17). Jeremiah both delivers warn-ings and is given the mission of leading his people back to the path of right-eousness (Jer. 6:17). These biblical watchmen are related to *Watchmen* in the sense that the text can also be read as a jeremiad. Jesus, on the other hand, admonishes his disciples to keep watch for the End and false messi-ahs (Mark 13), a warning which is significant as it applies to Ozymandias, and the reference to watchmen in Psalm 127—"Except the Lord build the house, they labour in vain that build it: except the Lord keep the city, the watchman waketh but in vain" (Ps. 127:1)—gives the reader some idea how to interpret the ending of *Watchmen*: Veidt's plan to build a new world is bound to fail since he acts of his own volition rather than by God's.[56]

For *Watchmen*, Moore creates three separate apocalyptic gods, Rorschach, Ozymandias, and Dr. Manhattan, each of whom, while sitting in judgment on the world, also responds to that duty in a different way. Thus, while *Swamp Thing* explores the apocalyptic element of New Jerusalem, *Watchmen* examines the figure of the apocalyptic deity. In much the same way that he demystifies his superheroes, Moore sets his deity characters loose in the "real" world of *Watchmen*, imagining their responses to society, as well as society's response to them. Simultaneously, however, by making his superheroes godlike and showing the results of having a "real" super-hero in a "real" world, he also, by implication, applies the same critique to deity that he does to superheroes themselves. Predictably, his deities suffer much the same dent to reputation as the superheroes do. Here, too, as in *Swamp Thing*, Moore will reject the absolute morality of Revelation by ultimately indicating the nonviability of such absolutist perspectives in the "real" world.

It is no coincidence that Rorschach's language, his cadence and even vocabulary, is reminiscent of Old Testament jeremiad. His first words, which are also the first words of the graphic novel, set him up as the feared judge of society and a deity figure modeled after the wrathful aspect of the apocalyptic god, though perhaps one mediated by a right-wing rhetoric which decries modern degeneracy:

> This city is afraid of me. . . .The streets are extended gutters and the gutters are full of blood and when the drains finally scab over, all the vermin will drown. The accumulated filth of all their sex and murder will foam up about their waists and all the whores and politicians will look up and shout "save us!" . . . and I'll look down and whisper "No." (1:1)

Rorschach is the apocalyptic God of retribution. Before he enters Happy Harry's bar to interrogate the denizens, he writes in his journal that "the dusk reeks of fornication and bad consciences. I believe I shall take my exercise" (1:14). He punishes the guilty with impunity and rationalizes his violence against the "innocent" knowing that they are surely guilty of something. His is the voice of a contemptuous and vengeful god who takes grim satisfaction in doing his job. He looks forward to his "exercise," though we should perhaps read this line as "exercising his judgment."

It's not merely through Rorschach's Old Testament language that we perceive his deity status. It is also through Moore's. The author uses a verbal tic throughout *Watchmen* which, while not universally true, frequently attaches the words "God" and "Jesus" to the three deity characters of Rorschach, Ozymandias and Dr. Manhattan. These words usually appear in exclamation form, as when a character is startled or bemused by one of the deity figures. The effect is that those exclamations sometimes appear to double as invocations, particularly since many of them occur in scenes when a character is pleading with one of these deity figures.

A good example occurs during Rorschach's surprise visit to Edgar Jacobi, a.k.a. Moloch.[57] The first words Moloch utters upon seeing Rorschach are "Oh, God, please . . . ," and this plea is repeated twice in succeeding panels as Rorschach advances on him. In two of the three panels, the word "god" is in boldface; in all three, and in most of the others in which he is pictured in this scene, Rorschach is bathed by a yellow light. The light is supposed to be from the open refrigerator, but the effect is to give Rorschach a spectral, otherworldly glow. This same light, when it shines on Jacobi, reveals a terrified man, often in a submissive posture (2:20–24). The same technique is used in Rorschach's second visit to Moloch when the submissive posture is even more in evidence. Taken by surprise and shoved into the refrigerator by Rorschach, Moloch responds, "Oh, God . . . look, please, what do you want with me?" (5:5) But the association between deity and Rorschach is even stronger in the final panels of this scene. As Rorschach threatens to shut Moloch in the refrigerator, Moloch pleads with him, "Oh no. Oh no, God, don't . . . Rorschach, please, it wasn't me" (5:5). As Rorschach lets Moloch out of the refrigerator, the panicked Jacobi falls prostrate to his knees before Rorschach, crying, "Oh god. Oh God . . . ." As Rorschach gives him final instructions, Jacobi says, "Yes. Ahhuhh. Oh, God, yes, anything . . . " and remains in a prostrate position, head bowed in terror as Rorschach exits (5:6). The supplicant/deity relationship is obvious in these final panels of the scene, and once again Rorschach glows with an unearthly yellow light which, given the dialogue and postures, is suggestive of the terrifying aura of a god.

This same scene is played out during Rorschach's capture, with the S.W.A.T. members repeatedly exclaiming, "God," "Christ," "Jesus God," and even "Jeez" (5:26–27). Nearly all of these exclamations come after Rorschach has attacked the man who says the words. In some cases, these men are also left in prostrate postures in relation to Rorschach, again suggesting the terrifying nature of Rorschach's apocalyptic god. This pattern of linking the word "god" with Rorschach occurs throughout the comic.[58] In fact, almost all the instances where the word "God" and Rorschach are linked verbally occur when a criminal is facing the retributive anger of Rorschach.

Yet Moore tells us something about Rorschach's style of deity almost immediately in *Watchmen*'s opening panels. It is suggested that Rorschach's view is myopic and overly narrow through a series of consecutive panels which give the reader ever-greater perspective on a scene which Rorschach is describing in voiceover. As the angle pulls back, then up and away from the subject of the initial panel, the image, which is not immediately interpretable except through Rorschach's words, becomes more comprehensible to readers who gradually become capable of determining for themselves what they have been looking at: a man hosing blood off the sidewalk. The final words of Rorschach's narration here—that nobody can think what to say—are immediately contradicted by the final panel on the page, in which a detective, leaning out of the window to observe the place where Edward Blake struck the pavement, comments, "Hmm. That's quite a drop" (1:1).

This dialogue in which the detective immediately belies what Rorschach has said is the first indicator that Rorschach's perspective may not be trustworthy. The gradually widening perspective on this scene indicates the same thing visually. The opening image, which is so tightly focused that it is mostly meaningless to the reader, can only be initially understood through Rorschach's words, "The streets are extended gutters and the gutters are full of blood" (1:1). Yet as the perspective widens from this narrow focus, the reader is given a larger view that contradicts Rorschach: in fact, the streets are not full of blood, though there is certainly blood on the street. Moreover, as the perspective widens further, readers are able to interpret the information in the panels for themselves without depending on Rorschach's warped perspective. Finally, the detective's statement contradicts the Rorschach perspective to which the reader has just been listening. It also verifies what the reader has now gleaned for himself: that someone has fallen out of a skyscraper window and plunged to his death. By emphasizing the word "drop" in boldface, Moore also suggests that Rorschach's view is both "far out" and a "low" view of things. Thus, the visual strategy warns the reader to be wary of Rorschach's uncompromising, unforgiving Manichean perspective, and also suggests that the strictly dualistic morality with which he is associated as the wrathful apocalyptic god is outdated and ill-equipped to operate in a modern world.[59]

But more than just Rorschach's narration alerts us to his association with an outdated view of the world. For, with his hero-worship of President Truman and his trench coat, fedora, and pinstripe suit tying him to the 1940s and 1950s, Rorschach himself is an embodiment of outdated fashions and ideals.[60] Moreover, Rorschach's costume specifically ties him to the noir detective figures of mid-century pulp fiction. In his memoir, retired superhero Hollis Mason describes this pulp fiction as having an uncomplicated view of good and evil, but since Hollis's autobiography is clearly mourning the loss of a world which no longer exists, there is an associated implication that Rorschach, like the pulps, is too simplistic in view to survive the new age, a fact that turns out to be literally true since his uncompromising perspective ultimately ensures his own destruction.

Rorschach's costume has a further meaning here. Such costumes belong not just to the pulps, but also to the early comic books that were derived from them. Consequently, Rorschach is also an embodiment of past comic book heroes. When Moore and Gibbons undermine Rorschach's perspective, they also indicate how ill-suited he, and by extension the old superhero genre, is for the contemporary age.

Yet, recognizing the appeal of this simpler morality, Moore allows Rorschach to argue his position and never undermines the character's strength. Unlike Ozymandias, a prissy golden-boy who does charity shows and markets his crime-fighting persona, Rorschach demands a grudging respect for his single-mindedness and willingness to act.[61] The American setting of *Watchmen* is amenable to this response; a tradition of glorifying vigilantes, both real and fictional, means that American crime-fighters like Dirty Harry have often been portrayed as borderline criminals, while criminals, like Jesse James and more recently Tony Soprano, have been depicted as enforcers of street justice. This is the double-edged sword of vigilantism: a civilized and law-abiding society cannot indulge in swift, retributive justice of the kind associated with vigilantes, and yet at the same time, we envy the vigilante's ability to ignore the rule of law to "do what's right."

The thin line between the vigilantism we admire and the anarchy we disavow is one which Moore explores throughout the comic, particularly in the characters of Rorschach and the Comedian in whom he embodies the tension between the "street fascist" rhetoric of order and decency which Rorschach espouses and the actual ideology of fascism which the Comedian, as a government agent, could be said to represent. Moore actually implies that the wrathful apocalyptic god is not so different from a vigilante. Rorschach clearly moves back and forth over the line from benevolent vigilante to malevolent vigilante, but even so, there is a part of the reader that cheers him on because his mission is to destroy evil. We admire the steadfast vision of a character who can still claim in the face of his own death that he won't compromise (12:20). The reader wants this godlike conviction and protection at the same time that he fears it will be turned on him. But while Rorschach remains a steady indicter of immorality throughout the story, his dated morality and Manichean views ultimately ensure his own destruction when he encounters a deity figure whose views are less rigid and therefore more apt for the complexities of the new world.

The paradox at the emotional core of this scene makes it one of the most surprisingly moving moments of the graphic novel. Rorschach's angry tears as he affirms Dr. Manhattan's decision to destroy him imply that he recognizes his culpability in his own death (12:24). The "purity" of his moral vision is incompatible with the *Watchmen* mise-en-scène, a conclusion confirmed by the use of the Nietzsche quotation which is associated with Rorschach in chapter 6: "Battle not with monsters, lest ye become a monster, and if you gaze into the abyss, the abyss gazes also into you."

In a significant nod to postmodern identity depictions, Rorschach also does double-duty as the apocalyptist of *Watchmen*. As Walter Kovacs, he is the silent prophet-of-doom who appears on the first page carrying a sign reading "The End is Nigh" and who reappears periodically throughout the story. Yet when he puts on his mask, his "face" as he calls it, he becomes the feared Rorschach whose true identity is initially unknown. Change the clothes, change the man. This apocalyptist persona allows Rorschach access to places and information that he would not normally have simply because this prophet, like so many, is ignored by the larger society. But long before Rorschach is unmasked by the police, the reader has begun to suspect that there is a connection between this creepy apocalyptist and Rorschach. Rorschach's journal gives voice to the apocalyptic sensibilities of the mostly silent Kovacs:

> Soon there will be war. Millions will burn. Millions will perish in sickness and misery. Why does one death matter against so many? Because there is good and there is evil, and evil must be punished. Even in the face of Armageddon I shall not compromise in this. But there are so many deserving of retribution . . . and there is so little time. (1:24)

Later, as Rorschach and Dan stand in Veidt's office trying to figure out what Veidt has planned, he wonders aloud who would have reason to trigger Armageddon, and then comments on Veidt's attachment to Ancient Egyptian culture without realizing he's just made the needed connection: the Egyptians were not merely "death-fixated"; they had an apocalyptic vision of their own. In this moment, Rorschach's rhetoric converges with that of the apocalyptist Kovacs: "Need answers quickly. World on verge of apocalypse. Death and War already here. Other horsemen can't be far behind" (10:20).

Yet Rorschach is clearly meant to be more than the voice of doom. He is also meant to be the deity figure about whom that voice warns. Like Swamp Thing, Kovacs undergoes a transformation to "become" the apocalyptic god. In telling Rorschach's origin story, Moore deconstructs the superhero by revealing his psychopathology and simultaneously suggests why apocalyptic wrath is desirable.

In a psychiatric examination, Kovacs describes experiencing a series of violent and disturbing events in which it is increasingly apparent to him that human beings are depraved. There is his brutal treatment by his prostitute mother and by the boys in his neighborhood, then the infamous Kitty Genovese rape and murder in which witnesses did nothing to help, and finally a child kidnapping in which he learns that the child has been murdered, butchered, and fed to dogs. This series of experiences—of victimization, apathy, and murderous depravity—are the pangs that accompany Rorschach's "birth," both as a superhero and apocalyptic god. The kidnapper who has butchered the child is the first of many criminals to be seen on his knees before Rorschach, uttering pleas for mercy: "Oh, God, please . . . " and "Oh, God. Oh, Jesus, *No*" (6:25, emphasis Moore). Lit once again by the same unearthly glow, Rorschach watches the criminal's house burn in what is strikingly like a sacrificial fire and identifies this as the moment of transformation from Kovacs into a wrathful apocalyptic god who will exact punishment on sinners:

> It is not God who kills the children. Not Fate that butchers them or Destiny that feeds them to the dogs. It's us. Only us. Streets stank of fire. The void breathed hard on my heart, turning its illusions to ice, shattering them. Was reborn then, free to scrawl own design on this morally blank world. Was Rorschach. (6:26)

One of the implications of Rorschach's monologue is that he is a man-made god since it is the series of events that he experiences as a human which create the Rorschach persona. This is a theme which is going to recur with the other deity figures of *Watchmen* and one to which I'll return later. For the moment, though, I want to turn to the second of *Watchmen*'s deities, for the god of apocalypse is not merely a wrathful destroyer, but is also the messianic ruler of the millennium and the promised New Jerusalem.

If anyone in this text has a messiah complex it is surely Adrian Veidt, the former hero Ozymandias. It is he who is envisioned as the second deity-figure of the story. Where the reader is only privy to the destroyer aspect of the apocalyptic god represented by Rorschach, in Veidt we get a more nuanced representation of deity. Here again, Moore conflates deities into one character. With his mild, forgiving manner, his messianic expectation of bringing salvation to mankind, and his willingness to wreak the apocalyptic destruction that precedes the coming of a new world, Adrian is certainly an embodiment of the apocalyptic Christ. However, Adrian figures *himself* as an embodiment of the Egyptian deity Rameses II, and this association allows Moore to incorporate the apocalyptic expectations of the ancient Egyptians along with the millennial expectation of Adrian. Indeed, because the Egyptian deity is the only one mentioned outright, and is therefore the overt deity to whom Adrian is connected, Moore effectively undermines Adrian's claim of millennial goodwill with the more obvious eschatological impulse of the Egyptian godhead. As Rorschach explains, the pharaohs eagerly anticipated the end of the world, expecting the dead to rise and reclaim their preserved organs from the funereal jars.

Nonetheless, because the Egyptian connection is only gradually revealed as the story progresses, the deity with whom Adrian at first appears most allied is the Judeo-Christian one. First of all, his creator aspect is emphasized. Much of what he creates is his persona as Ozymandias and personal empire, which he builds from nothing. He also creates and carefully manages his own public image after his retirement through the production of items such as the Ozymandias dolls, self-actualization programs, and his numerous charitable actions and donations. But Veidt has also created an Eden of sorts, a tropical paradise in the barren Antarctic wastes. Though the reader watches Veidt destroy this perfect world in the same chapter in which we first learn of it, that glimpse is enough to imply Ozymandias's godlike aspect. It is no surprise that one of the only two places where the word "miraculous" or "miracle" is used in *Watchmen* is here at the moment that the edenic Vivarium is revealed.[62]

Like Rorschach, Veidt is also associated with the deity through verbal exclamations.[63] Significantly, however, Veidt is usually associated with Christ in these outbursts, as opposed to Rorschach who is associated with the word "God" just as frequently as "Jesus." Just as Rorschach actually shines with a spectral light, Ozymandias is often lit by an unidentifiable yellow light, particularly in the final chapters when his plan is put into effect. He also makes repeated statements that he intends to bring back an "age of illumination" (11:8). The supposed achievement of this goal is embodied in the illustration of Veidt's moment of triumph when he raises his hands and proclaims his personal victory. In the panel, a mysterious yellow spotlight shines on Veidt and partially illumines the portrait of Alexander in the background.

But Adrian's association with godhead is achieved differently from that of either Rorschach or Dr. Manhattan. Though his deity status is occasionally referred to in an outright manner, such as when a reporter writes that Veidt looks like a god, his association with deity is mostly achieved through his connection to Egyptian culture and the part it plays in the genesis of the Ozymandias persona. Veidt originally sets out to fashion himself after Alexander the Great who had ruled the ancient world and whose lateral thinking had allowed him to solve the puzzle of the Gordian knot. Later, however, Veidt takes as his inspiration the ancient Egyptian pharaohs, adopting Rameses II as his model and surrounding himself with the trappings of ancient Egyptian culture. Since the pharaohs of Egypt were not just regarded as rulers but also as living gods, it is through this overt association that we are to understand Ozymandias as a deity figure.

Nonetheless, there are definite parallels drawn between Ozymandias and Jesus. Alexander, whom Ozymandias originally seeks to emulate, is referred to as the "judge of the dead" at one point. In Christian mythology, it is Christ who has this role during the Last Judgment. Similarly, Ozymandias's comment that "I saved earth from hell and now I'll help her towards utopia" also aligns him with Christ's role in Revelation (12:20). Perhaps most significantly, in Veidt's confession to Jon that he has "made [himself] feel every death. . . . I know I've struggled across the backs of murdered innocents to save humanity . . . But someone had to take the weight of that awful, necessary crime," the reader identifies the martyr rhetoric associated with Christ's suffering for humanity in order to save it (12:27).

Furthermore, if one considers the series of episodes which comprise Revelation—the Second Coming, Armageddon, Millennium, the last loosing of Satan, the destruction of the world, the Last Judgment, and New Jerusalem—it is remarkable how many of these have some comparable element in the Ozymandias plotline. There is, for example, a second coming of a different sort: Ozymandias imagines himself as a kind of Alexander the Great reborn. In his teleporting to New York of the monstrous alien he has created, Ozymandias is also responsible for an analogous last loosing of Satan. Veidt's description of this creature, whose brain will broadcast a psychic pulse upon its death, is certainly one with satanic overtones. That this creature will die upon its arrival in New York is of no matter in this cartoonish last loosing of Satan. The simple existence of the satanic stand-in is hellish enough for Veidt's purposes.

Ozymandias is further responsible for ushering in Millennium, though in this case Millennium is a new line of perfume. This line of cosmetics will replace Nostalgia, the previous line of Veidt Cosmetic and Toiletries. Veidt is also training "martyrs" for his millennium with his Veidt method, a self-improvement program which seeks to produce people "fit to inherit the challenging, promising, and often difficult world that awaits in our future" (10: "The Veidt Method"). Underneath the marketing for a better lifestyle, the Veidt method actually preaches the way to inherit the New Jerusalem.

As for the Last Judgment, one recalls that upon arriving in his Antarctic fortress, Veidt is royally dressed and crowned by his servants and takes his seat on an Egyptian throne before a bank of television monitors. Just as Jesus' subjects come before his throne in Revelation, it is here on this throne that Ozymandias has the "world" come before him on the multiple television sets. Before the monitors, Veidt renders judgment on the world in a tone which distinctly becomes haughtier, more patriarchal, and more condescending, as when, observing two of the superheroes approaching his fortress, he sarcastically admires their fortitude.

Finally, it is Ozymandias who is the architect of the New Jerusalem of *Watchmen*. He sees himself as the benevolent watcher in whose hands humanity's fate rests. He is personally responsible for this new vision and for bringing about the New Jerusalem.

And yet, because Moore is working in a postmodern tradition, his deities are doubting, anxious gods, rather than commandingly certain ones. They are self-aware and uncertain about their decisions in a way that is quite different from their biblical progenitors. The voice of the biblical apocalyptic god is always a pronouncement; there is little hint of doubt, regret, or even thoughtfulness in His words or actions. In *Watchmen*, however, the reader is privy to the keening of gods. In the orrery, Ozymandias confesses his ambivalence about the genocide he has orchestrated, telling Jon that, unlike Rorschach, he'd hoped Jon would understand what he had done.

But Rorschach understands this predicament more than Veidt knows. In a line that is no doubt meant to comment on more than his filthy coat, Rorschach tells a colleague that not everyone can keep their hands clean while fighting evil. Like his tortured journal entries, this comment shows that Rorschach has willingly and knowingly taken on the responsibility of the "dirty work" that must be done. Though neither hero reveals his anxieties in public, both suffer moments of doubt in private, and those doubts are revealing glimpses into Moore's deconstruction of deity.

In the troubling intricacy of a post-Hiroshima world, Moore contends, the simplistic morality of apocalyptic judgment is bound to be compromised. In the realistic setting of *Watchmen*, both Rorschach and Ozymandias therefore occupy shifting moral ground; their actions are neither "good" nor "bad" but depend upon the ends they hope to achieve, as well as the vantage point of the viewer. Judgment of their actions is never a simple matter of morality; it is a matter of perspective. Says Moore:

> none of these characters are right or wrong. . . . I didn't want to make any character the one who's right, the one whose viewpoint is the right viewpoint, the one who's the hero, the one who the readers are supposed to identify with, because that's not how life is; that's not how my life is.[64]

There is a third deity in *Watchmen*, however, for whom morality has ceased to be an issue. Of the three gods in *Watchmen*, Dr. Manhattan (Jon Osterman) is the most godlike. His ability to manipulate matter at a molecular level means that he is omniscient, omnipotent, and omnipresent. He moves through time and space, seeing all moments simultaneously. Unlike his peers who are, to one degree or another, all associated with the nostalgic past, Dr. Manhattan is a deity associated with the future. His name alludes to the nuclear age that began with the Manhattan Project, and it is through Jon that many of the futuristic elements of *Watchmen*, such as the electric cars and blimps, are made possible.

While Dr. Manhattan's very characteristics are suggestive of deity, Moore has provided numerous other references throughout the novel to iterate this idea. As with the other two deity figures, Jon's name or appearance is often preceded or greeted with an interjection that invokes a Judeo-Christian deity.[65] Many of these references come from Jon's ex-lover, Laurie, in moments when Jon is acting or has acted in a most godlike way, and most of them are made on Mars, where Jon's deity-like qualities are particularly obvious. At one point she even compares his sudden appearances to a deus ex machina. There is also the essay "Dr. Manhattan: Super-powers and the Superpowers," in which Jon's former colleague, Prof. Milton Glass, explicitly refers to Dr. Manhattan as a deity and concludes with a ominous warning about the gods walking on earth.

There are visual clues which also suggest Jon's deity status: the Buddhist posture Jon assumes when he creates his Martian palace, an image which is later tied to the Buddha himself through the poster of the Buddha in the same pose (4:26–27 and 5:7), and, more especially, the panels in which Jon walks on water, leaving behind the sleeping Dan and Laurie who are themselves replicating an iconic Adam and Eve image (12:25).[66]

A more subtle visual reference comes in the opening images of the "Watchmaker" chapter about Dr. Manhattan's origin. Those images depict Dr. Manhattan's footprints in the sand of Mars. Mary Stevenson's religious parable "Footprints in the Sand" is one of the most frequently printed religious poems in the twentieth century, and the image of Jon's footprints in the Martian sands is surely meant to recall it.

One of the primary functions of the "Watchmaker" chapter seems to be to explain how Dr. Manhattan experiences time. It does this by overlaying panels that illustrate Jon's memories with his Dr. Manhattan incarnation's musing about simultaneously experiencing other moments of time. Jon's sense of simultaneous time and place echo the dislocation experienced by Saint John in Revelation. The rapid, complex scene-to-scene closure of the "Watchmaker" chapter is the best example of Revelation-time being imitated in the text. The fact that Jon shares a name with the prophet of that holy Book may be seen as further evidence of his affiliation with it, but it is also another instance of the kind of conflation of apocalyptic roles that occurs in postmodern reworkings of the myth. What might be most interesting about Jon is that he abdicates the responsibility for each of these apocalyptic roles, declining either to warn of imminent apocalypse, as his association with the apocalyptist John of Patmos suggests he might, or to act as the deity he is clearly meant to evoke.

Dr. Manhattan is a post-Holocaust representation of deity, a god who is seemingly absent from his creation and beyond morality. Twice his relationship to humans is described as that of a human to an insect. So removed is he from the human race that he can no longer identify with them, even though he was once one of them. The Comedian accuses Dr. Manhattan of not really caring about people at all, and Laurie notes the same thing when Jon is so involved in his exploration of the universe that he replicates himself to make love to her so that he will not have to leave his more interesting laboratory work. Later, she tells Dan that people are like shadows to Jon. His final link to humanity is broken when Laurie leaves him, and while Laurie argues a moral imperative in saving the people of earth, Jon is incapable of thinking of humans in this way; he can only judge their value in terms of their uniqueness in the universe.

But this is another way in which Jon is a god for a postmodern age. While the deities of the Old and New Testaments are to be obeyed without question, Jon presents a deity with whom one can have a two-way discussion, rather than a monologue. Precisely because he is aware of alternative perspectives and the problems of privileging only one of them, he is a god one might dare to argue with, as Laurie does. He is a god who can be persuaded, a god who changes his mind. That is, like Rorschach and Ozymandias, Dr. Manhattan is not a *certain* god. He exhibits doubt. When Laurie asks if it does not bother him to think of the extermination of humans, he answers:

All that pain and conflict done with? All that needless suffering over at last? No . . . No, that doesn't bother me. All those generations of struggle, what purpose did they ever achieve? All that effort, and what did it ever lead to? (9:10)

This speech can be read in two ways. The first is in the cold, calculating voice of a scientist weighing up arguments for a procedure in which he has no emotional stake. This is certainly how Laurie reads the speech. But the phrasing and, more particularly, the questions contained in it are remarkably like those uttered by a suicidal person as rationale for taking his own life. We are right, I think, to hear in Jon's words here the voice of a depressed god.

Ultimately then, by putting "real" gods into "real" settings Moore does more than just interrogate the apocalyptic deity. More accurately, he interrogates the human *envisioning* of deity. What *Watchmen* shows is how contradictory human ideas about godhead actually are. You want a god who punishes the unjust, Moore asks? Okay, but remember there is a thin line between retributive justice and vigilante justice. You want a god who will bring peace to mankind, he asks? Okay, but the price for that may be higher than you are willing to pay. You want an all-powerful god? Alright, but that power might be co-opted for political ends. You want an omniscient god? Okay, but don't be surprised if he finds you insignificant.

Dr. Manhattan epitomizes this quandary. In his depiction of Dr. Manhattan, Moore challenges the idea that such a god would have any interest at all in human beings. A god with the qualities that we ascribe to Dr. Manhattan (and by extension the Judeo-Christian god), might not be the benevolent, deeply engaged god we have anthropomorphically envisioned for our comfort. Moore implies that quite the opposite might be true: that a creature with such an all-encompassing view of creation might be an absent god, one who finds scores of things as interesting and relevant as human life and one who would assign no teleological value to humanity at all. Such a god would be beyond human ideas of morality, and therefore beyond blame or praise.

But the fact that one can interpret Dr. Manhattan's comments as depressed as well as remote intimates that Moore also wants his reader to invert his usual anthropomorphic view and consider how a deity would feel about the modern world. By emphasizing the "damned if you do, damned if you don't" predicament in which Dr. Manhattan repeatedly finds himself because of his godlike qualities, the author suggests that a modern deity would likely feel pained by the bellicosity of his creation, and would certainly feel confounded by them.

Thus, when Dr. Manhattan helps quell riots in *Watchmen*, the rioters regard him as a freak and the newspapers vilify him for transporting the entire mob home, while the official response of the government he is helping is to ban superhero "vigilantes" afterward. In an effort to help his country, Dr. Manhattan wins the Vietnam War, but simultaneously becomes both a military and propaganda tool of the government, a government which, because of his position on its side, abuses its power in the rest of the world. For his troubles, the world creeps closer to nuclear war and he remains in what is essentially self-imposed exile at a military installation. Simultaneously, because of his immortality and view of time, Dr. Manhattan is condemned in his personal life to love at the same time knowing (and experiencing), the loss of that love in the future. The conclusion he comes to is not judgmental, simply exhausted: frustrated and drained, he abandons this world for the unpeopled Mars. For this sympathetically drawn god, his own creation remains a puzzle. Any sensible god would walk away from such a painful Gordian knot, just as Jon walks away from Dan and Laurie before leaving earth forever.

While *Watchmen* itself is apocalyptic for the superhero genre, destroying the old approach to superheroes and paving the way for a new approach to them, it is also clear that it functions as an equally challenging text as regards the apocalyptic genre, setting out to destroy the classic representations of the apocalyptic deity and replace them with more contemporary ideas. One of the themes that Moore explores in his apocalyptic texts is the proposition that man creates god, and not the other way around.

It is an idea that will reoccur in an even more overt way in *Promethea*. Between *Swamp Thing* and *Watchmen*, Moore seems to have explored the myth of apocalypse from every possible angle, but his series *Promethea*, which began in 1999 and concluded in 2005, adopts yet another approach. Rather than examine a particular apocalyptic element, Moore attempts to revise our very understanding of what apocalypse is, and he does so by focusing on apocalypse in its visionary sense. That is, he refocuses on the original meaning of the word *apokalypsis* as an uncovering or revealing.

In 1994, Moore declared that he was going to devote his time to becoming a magician. Magic, for Moore, is about incantation, the power of words. The purpose of practicing it is to see the world in new and different ways. Thus, studying magic is a natural extension of his writing life. If, as Moore contends, the world is just a construction of ideas, then these imaginary structures are the direct result of the humans who dream them. Apocalypse, then, is not a matter of destroying some physical reality, but is the "result of a radical change of consciousness achieved through art" and an extension of the Romantic tradition in which "imagination is a divine attribute and a way to participate in the ongoing creation of the universe."[67]

The Promethea of the title is the personification of Imagination, a "living story" and the deity of this narrative. The series follows a young girl called Sophie Bangs who, as the story opens, learns that she is the newest incarnation of Promethea. The entire series is a kind of bildungsroman in which Sophie, and the reader, learns who and what Promethea and her realm, the Immateria, are. While a triumph of the visual medium and a canny explication of Moore's mystical studies, *Promethea* no doubt was a disappointment for fans who were hoping for a more traditional superhero story. *Promethea* likely appeals more to the bookish: it is a highly erudite and beautiful teaching text which introduces its readers to the Kabbalah and Tarot on which the Immateria is largely based, as well as dabbling in linguistic theory, Romantic tradition, and tantric sexual practice.[68]

As a story, *Promethea* isn't much fun to read; other than Sophie's guided tour through and about the Immateria, there is very little plot, and what little there is seems to be there merely as a convenient frame on which to hang the magical lessons. Because of this, it is impossible to analyze any piece of *Promethea* as a specific adaptation of the apocalyptic myth. Since the series mainly keeps to the realm of the theoretical, teaching mystical generalities rather than specifically applying them to any character or situation, any discussion of it as an apocalyptic text necessarily is also theoretical, rather than specific.

Indeed, this is why the anticipated "apocalypse" of the series, an event which is referred to repeatedly and a climax to which the series seems to build, is ultimately so anticlimactic: if apocalypse is about changing the way we see the world, the entire series has already been doing that. The specific moment of the "apocalypse" in *Promethea* is redundant, rather than revelatory, at least for the reader for whom the result of each issue of the series has been this ongoing revelation. Then again, since Moore's goal in this particular text seems to be to return to apocalypse as an unveiling, the continuous aspect of the revelatory experience in the series may be more appropriate—and in its own way a reworking of John's ongoing vision of apocalyptic events in Revelation—than building up to a singular moment of revelatory vision, the usual format for narrative climaxes. Nonetheless, *Promethea* is a fascinating reworking of the idea of apocalypse, if not of the myth itself. It also exhibits a strongly postmodern sense of story and way of approaching its topic. First of all, as in previous apocalyptic texts by Moore, *Promethea* has a multiplicity of deities. Sophie is only the latest of the incarnations of Promethea, and throughout the series the reader meets the others, all of whom have individualized personalities and personal stories, since they, like Sophie, are humans who incarnated the creative Imagination which Promethea represents. Most of these previous incarnations are, not surprisingly, creators themselves. One of them is even a man, albeit a rather camp gay man. The character Promethea therefore is a literal depiction of the flexible, unstable identity that is part of the postmodern perspective.

In addition, as in the earlier apocalyptic works, *Promethea* incorporates gods from a multitude of pantheons. Promethea's name obviously alludes to the myth of Prometheus, the fire-bringer. She carries a caduceus, a totem associated with Hermes, who is also one of the two gods, the other being the Egyptian Thoth, who "adopt" her at the behest of her priest father. Interestingly, though Thoth is an Egyptian god and Hermes Greek, they are represented as Siamese twins when they appear to the original human girl, Promethea, who they make into the immortal "living story" Promethea.

But at the heart of *Promethea* is yet another layer of deity, and one which is related to the Romantic ideas of self and creativity to which Moore is alluding, and this is that *we* are god, as well. We are also the demons that haunt us. This is a more complicated version of the idea in *Swamp Thing* that good and evil are two parts of the same whole. In *Promethea*, good and evil, devil and deity, these might be different from one another, but all of them issue from a single source: the human imagination. As Promethea explains during the apocalypse:

> Know that the scorched-black demons and the pristine, fluttering seraphs are in some sense naught but you yourself unpacked, unfolded in a higher space from whence the myriad gods unfurl, not bygone legends but your once and future selves, your attributes blossomed into their purest and most potent symbol-forms. And these, with all their beast-hearts, crowns and lightings, all their different colors, are become combined into the single whiteness that is godhead. That is all. This, then, is revelation. All is one, and all is deity, this beautiful undying fire of being that is everywhere about us; that we are.[69]

Promethea also cleverly exhibits the self-reflexivity that is so much a part of postmodernism, and it does it most explicitly during the apocalypse itself. Numerous characters who have been looking for Promethea are told to go into a room where she is waiting inside, and we are made to understand through the closure that all of them simultaneously enter the room to find Promethea waiting for them by the fireplace. But from the moment that the door opens to reveal Promethea, the reader becomes the point of view character, only seeing Promethea as she explains what the apocalypse is. We never see who she is speaking to, and since what she says upon the entrance into the room is "I've been waiting to talk to you. To all of you," one gathers that she is talking directly to the reader.[70]

This is a conclusion which is supported as the actual moment of apocalypse draws nearer: the images in the panels first show "us" reading the comic, in a panel which shows the same page we are reading being held in "our" hand, and then shows the illustrator and writer of *Promethea* looking at us from inside the comic itself. Both men have been interrupted at their work. In the case of the illustrator, J. H. Williams III, the work before him on his drawing table is the very page we are looking at, including, in a kind of Escher-esque homage, the panel of him looking over his shoulder at the reader. Similarly, the panel showing Moore at his computer shows the page of the *Promethea* script on his screen in which he has just described exactly this self-referential moment. Both illustrator and writer mutter "uh oh" as they turn from their work to see us watching them create this moment in which both reader and creators acknowledge their imaginative partnership.

These self-reflexive panels immediately precede the commencement of the "apocalypse," and they tangibly represent the connection between creativity and apocalypse. Given that Moore's primary interest in this text is to reendow apocalypse with its revelatory meaning, it is entirely appropriate that Promethea's final words to us are to "stay awake."[71] Now that the connection has been revealed, that our eyes have been opened, it is only right that we keep them open.

Because one of *Promethea's* points is that human imagination is the source of the deity, we find that there is an implicit argument that humans create god, and not the other way around. Indeed, this is true in *Watchmen* and *Swamp Thing* where all the gods are also "man-made." Like Dr. Manhattan, Swamp Thing and Woodrue become what they are because of their scientific work as humans. Kovacs's session with his psychoanalyst reveals "Rorschach" was created in response to human cruelty and neglect. Ozymandias is a man-made creation, or rather, he is self-created, a pun on which Moore has traded with the references to Veidt's self-help program. It is an accident of human science that turns Dr. Jon Osterman into Dr. Manhattan, and though he must feel his way into the deity role, shedding clothes, then illusions about his shared humanity, and finally his emotional attachment to the world, it is humans who act as his guides through his transformation, until, in his final confrontation with Ozymandias, Dr. Manhattan leaves Jon Osterman behind forever and adopts a godlike perspective so elevated he sees humans as no more than interesting insects.

In fact, in Dr. Manhattan's assertion that he has become so interested in human beings that he thinks he will go create some, Moore implies an Ouroborosian view of the cosmos. Because he is a man who becomes a god who creates men who presumably repeat the process, Dr. Manhattan can be read as a version of Ouroboros, the serpent who swallows its own tail.[72] His final observation that nothing ever ends confirms such a reading. Like the Yin/Yang symbol in *Swamp Thing*, Ouroboros symbolizes the cyclical nature of the universe, that "all is one," and furthermore suggests a revision of time as a cyclical, rather than linear, structure.

Like *Promethea*, *Watchmen*, too, suggests it is humans who are the creators and thus assume godlike characteristics, a view Adrian Veidt endorses when he declares that we all have godlike abilities within us. Alan Moore is the proof of this argument. As the author of these works, he, too, is a creator, one who creates the deities who populate his apocalyptic tales. Moore obviously believes it is no small thing to be such a creator. It may be the only thing that really does make us unique. *Watchmen's* Laurie certainly thinks so, for in her discussion with Jon she uses the creativity of mankind as an argument for saving the world. Moore implies in *Watchmen*, and affirms more explicitly in the later *Promethea*, that it may finally be our creativity which is the thing that makes us most worthy of being saved, and this depiction of art as the "saving grace" of humankind is one which will recur in the work of other postmodern authors in this study.

NOTES

1. For his birthday, Moore's fellow writers, his former editors, and artists who had illustrated his work came together to express their admiration in two laudatory volumes: *Alan Moore—Portrait of an Extraordinary Gentleman* and *The Extraordinary Work of Alan Moore*. Many of his old comic book stories were collected and reissued in time for the occasion, as well.

2. America has lagged behind the rest of the world in recognizing the comic medium as a serious art form. Others countries such as France, Italy, Belgium, and Japan have long regarded sequential art as a serious art form deserving of scholarly attention. The recent reissuing of comics in the more palatable graphic novel format is a marketing strategy meant first to reach a reading public who have largely remained unaware of a gigantic subculture thriving among them, and second to overcome the snobbery which the form, whether because of its associations with superheroes and Sunday comics or because of its serial nature, has inspired.

3. smoky man, *Alan Moore: Portrait of an Extraordinary Gentleman*, 52, 75.

4. Khoury, *The Extraordinary Works of Alan Moore*, 114–15.

5. Eisner, who died in 2004, aged eight-seven, and was the creator of the famous detective comic *The Spirit*, was a major developer of the comic book medium, as well as an innovator in the way comic art was drawn. He was also the first to write seriously about the theory behind comic book illustration in his book *Comics and Sequential Art*.

6. McCloud uses the term "closure" differently than it is used in narratology. His ideas on closure have also been challenged. *The Comic Journal* devoted an entire issue (#211) to debating his ideas in April, 1999.

7. McCloud, *Understanding Comics*, 99–100. Emphasis McCloud.

8. McCloud cites six kinds of closure that occur in the gutter spaces of comics, each requiring a different level of reader participation. The first of these, Moment-to-Moment, is very simple and requires little participation since time is literally being portrayed as immediate and chronological. The second is Subject-to-Subject closure, as in the axe murder example given in the text, which requires more viewer participation because it asks the reader to make the transition or connection between the images with the understanding that he is staying within the same scene or idea. The third is Action-to-Action and requires the reader to fill in the ensuing

action, as when a first panel shows a baseball batter at bat and the second shows the ball flying through the air. The fourth is Scene-to-Scene and requires deductive reasoning to make sense of the "transitions, which transport us across significant distances of time and space." The fifth is Aspect-to-Aspect, which "bypasses time for the most part and sets a wandering eye on different aspects of a place, idea or mood." The final type of closure is what McCloud calls the Non-sequitur, "which offers no logical relationship between panels whatsoever," though he does suggest that by laying images side-by-side one forces some kind of relationship between the two to develop (McCloud, *Understanding Comics*, 71–73). McCloud's analysis applies mostly to images in a straight sequence. He does not analyze "exploded" images, for instance, or images which bleed into one another. At least, he does not analyze them in terms of closure. He does address such images as part of his chapter on panel borders and their implications.

9. McCloud, *Understanding Comics*, 68–69. Emphasis McCloud.

10. Whereas in comics the movement in time and space is accomplished through the gutter space, much of the disruption of time and the sense of simultaneity in Revelation is implied through the use of verb tenses. Thus, the passage alluded to here begins in a future tense, "And their dead bodies *shall lie* in the street of the great city," and concludes in a past tense, "And after three days and an half the Spirit of life from God entered into them, and they stood upon their feet."

11. Before 1983, Moore had been working exclusively in the British comic book industry where he had made a name for himself writing for the British comic *2000 A.D.*

12. Artist Berni Wrightson left after ten issues, and writer Len Wein followed him three issues later. It was Len Wein who, in his capacity as a senior editor at DC years later, suggested resurrecting the *Swamp Thing* title to coincide with the release of the motion picture based on the character (Wein, introduction, *Swamp Thing: Dark Genesis*).

13. Moore's tenure on *Swamp Thing* covered issues #21 to #64, though the apocalyptic story runs only through issue #50. It is these issues—#21 to #50—that I examine in this chapter.

14. Khoury, *The Extraordinary Works of Alan Moore*, 85.

15. Moore went back and found "logical inconsistencies in the original story" which allowed him to say that Holland had died in the lab explosion, but that his consciousness had been absorbed by the swamp's plant life. "That struck me as something that didn't violate any kind of previous continuity but which suddenly moved the character into new and exciting unknown territory. . . . the best thing that I could do was to tie up . . . storylines; characters that I was perhaps not interested in continuing with could be moved out of the way; characters that I was interested in exploring . . . could be moved closer to center stage and I could sort of give the issue a sort of visceral punch by providing the first step to my recreation of Swamp Thing, which was killing him." (Khoury, *The Extraordinary Works of Alan Moore*, 87).

16. Moore, *Saga of the Swamp Thing*, 107. *Swamp Thing* citations will refer to the graphic novel in which they appear, followed by page number of the graphic novel, rather than the individual issue within the graphic novel.

17. Moore, *Swamp Thing: The Curse*, 54–59.

18. Moore, *Swamp Thing: The Curse*, 15–17. The ellipses in Swamp Thing's speech are part of the rendering of his dialogue; they indicate his slow, lumbering speech pattern.

19. The analogy was deliberate says Moore: "I was trying to have the character slowly evolve into a kind of vegetable god" (Khoury, *The Extraordinary Work of Alan Moore*, 89).

20. Campbell, foreword, *Swamp Thing: Saga of the Swamp Thing*.

21. Moore, *Saga*, 91, 91, 79.

22. See Moore, *Swamp Thing: Love and Death*, 192, and *Swamp Thing: A Murder of Crows*, 98–100.

23. In addition, the panel which precedes this contains Swamp Thing's wish that he should "rise up," a reference to the Resurrection which Moore obviously intends his reader to pick up since the words are deliberately highlighted in the yellow dialogue box which usually indicates the Swamp Thing's narration.

24. Here, Moore seems to be mixing up, whether intentionally or not, pantheism and paganism. The first is the philosophy that everything is God, or that nature and the universe are divine. Paganism, while often incorporating this philosophy, worships gods and divinities *in* nature, and therefore has a tendency to anthropomorphize nature, a tendency most pantheists try to avoid. Woodrue's association with classical nature religions indicates a pagan sensibility. The envisaging of Swamp Thing leans toward this pagan tendency to see nature as self-conscious, as well, but Swamp Thing's evolution as a sentient being in the series includes the growing understanding that the world and universe are all connected. Hence, part of Swamp Thing's evolution is his movement from paganism toward pantheism.

25. Moore, *Saga*, 42–43.

26. It is the knowledge of certain experiments with this type of worm which first alerts Woodrue that Swamp Thing is not really human after all.

27. Moore, *Saga*, 47–48.

28. In the final two depictions of this Frankenstein monster, the coins become more like buttons. The reference is murkier here, but the allusion may be to ragdoll eyes, and the connection may be to how dolls are manipulated by others. If so, then Swamp Thing's destruction of the creature with rag-doll eyes is a declaration of independence, claiming both humanity for himself and the will to be his own "person."

29. Moore, *Saga*, 54.

30. Moore, *Saga*, 98.

31. Gaiman, overture, *Swamp Thing: Love and Death*.

32. Moore, *Swamp Thing: A Murder of Crows*, 159.

33. Moore, *Swamp Thing: A Murder of Crows*, 73.

34. See Moore, *Swamp Thing: Love and Death*, 85–87, 116; Moore, *Swamp Thing: The Curse*, 88, 58; and Moore, *A Murder of Crows*, 63, for these and other specific references to the apocalypse.

35. Though there is disagreement about the actual dates, the Golden Age of comics is considered to be roughly from 1939 to 1949 and the Silver Age from 1959 to 1969.

36. Brown, "Crisis on Infinite Earths #1."

37. In the years following the *Crisis* endeavor, there has been much debate and criticism which suggests that, in fact, *Crisis* did not achieve the stated aim of providing a definitive history of the DC Universe.

38. Moore, *A Murder of Crows*, 79. Emphasis Moore.

39. "I don't work in harness," says Moore. "If I start to feel squeezed, I rise up spitting black blood with snakes coming out of my mouth. I'm potentially explosive. I don't trust 'em. Anytime something could drop and offend me enough to pull the plug" (Stone, "Alan Moore Interview").

40. Moore, *A Murder of Crows*, 35.

41. Moore, *A Murder of Crows*, 166. Emphasis Moore.

42. Moore, *A Murder of Crows*, 90, 156, 166. For additional descriptions, see also 153, 155, and 168.

43. These heroes are, in part, bound by a dualistic morality because it is part of the milieu of the comic medium during the time periods in which they were originally created. The Spectre and Doctor Fate were created in 1940. If Etrigan seems of a more ambiguous or flexible morality it may be because he was created later, in 1972.

44. Moore, *A Murder of Crows*, 195.

45. Moore, *A Murder of Crows*, 82, 172, 169.

46. The overall structure of time is a different issue from where *in* that structure an apocalyptist is given access through his vision. To narratively render the apocalyptist's dislocation in time has nothing to do with how time, as an overall structure, is imagined to be designed.

47. Moore, *Watchmen*, 12:27. The textual citations here are for the graphic novel and refer to the chapter and page *within* the chapter, since the original pagination was for individual issues of the comic and was retained in the graphic novel form. Moore added "codas" to each issue of *Watchmen*, so that the normal comic format of each issue was then followed by a piece of fictitious text—a memoir, case history, academic article, etc.—which further elucidates the plot. Where I cite from these codas, I give the name of the fictitious fragment, chapter, and page *within* that fragment. Again, each coda was separately paginated to give it the illusion of being a real text source. All further references to the text are made parenthetically.

48. Sabin, *Comics, Comix and Graphic Novels*, 165; Groth, *The New Comics: Interviews from the Pages of* The Comics Journal, 101. There are those who believe that Gibbons's contribution to the story development has been underrated, in part because he has been so modest about the part he played and in part because Moore has largely taken credit.

49. The stock types of superheroes include superhuman heroes with godlike powers such as Superman; obsessed vigilante types who seek to right the injustices

of the world, such as The Punisher; patriotic heroes such as Captain America; and humans whose extreme wealth or intelligence has allowed them to acquire heroic personas because of their inventions or extraordinary cleverness, such as Batman.

50. Groth, *The New Comics: Interviews from the Pages of* The Comics Journal, 101. Writer/illustrator Frank Miller is the other graphic novelist who is credited with beginning the postmodern revisionist age of comics with his groundbreaking *Batman: The Dark Knight Returns*.

51. In an October 2001 interview, Moore said, "The apocalyptic bleakness of comics over the past fifteen years sometimes seems odd to me, because it's like [*Watchmen*] was a bad mood I was in fifteen years ago. It was the 1980s, we'd got this insane right-wing voter fear running the country, and I was in a bad mood, politically and socially and in most other ways. So that tended to reflect in my work. But it was a genuine bad mood, and it was mine. I tend to think I've seen a lot of things over the past fifteen years that have been a bizarre echo of somebody else's mood. It's not even their bad mood, it's mine, but they're still working out the ramifications of me being a bit grumpy fifteen years ago" (Robinson, T., "In My World").

52. Groth, *The New Comics: Interviews from the Pages of* The Comics Journal, 100.

53. Since it was first designed in 1947, the hands of the clock have been moved periodically by the *Bulletin* to indicate the level of danger of a nuclear war occurring. The minute hand has been moved eighteen times since the clock's inception. In 1984, at the time immediately preceding Moore and Gibbons's collaboration, the hands of the clock were the closest they had been to midnight since 1953 when the clock read two minutes to midnight in response to the United States and the Union of Soviet Socialist Republics (U.S.S.R.) both testing nuclear weapons within the same year. In 1984, in response to the accelerated arms race, the clock read three minutes to midnight. In response to the ongoing damage to the ecosystem, as well as to the acquisition of nuclear arms by North Korea and, potentially, Iran, the clock was changed again in 2007 to read five minutes to midnight.

54. As the Tower Commission report came out a month after the *Watchmen* series ended, it was not until the series was collected into graphic novel form that the epigraph was added. Moore says there were numerous "spooky . . . coincidences happening around the work" such as this simultaneous use of the Juvenal quotation (Kavanagh, "The Alan Moore Interview").

55. This image occurs in the chapter "The Judge of all the Earth," but numerous other details confirm Dr. Manhattan's deity status, not least of which is the outright declaration by a former associate that he is a god ("Dr. Manhattan: Super-powers and the Superpowers," 4:II).

56. It is strongly suggested that the times have only been temporarily changed by Veidt's devious plan. Right-wing hatred and political views, as symbolized by the survival of Hector Godfrey and *New Frontiersman*, have survived in the "new" New York, and editorial assistant Seymour's hand hovers over Rorschach's diary which could expose Veidt's plan and undermine its supposedly benign effects. Moreover,

the comic ends with the same image that began it, the smiley face with bloody smear resembling a minute hand. In this case, the smiley face is on Seymour's t-shirt and the "bloody" arrow is sauce dropped from his hamburger, but the implication of this echo seems unavoidable: that the dreadful circumstances represented by this emblem haven't changed, only the location of that dread.

57. The name Moloch is a curious choice. Within the story, a reference to the fire god to whom children were sacrificed makes little sense. However, since *Watchmen* is a work filled with gods, and gods moreover whose morality is called into question, perhaps it should not be surprising that there would also be a criminal named for a god, yet another pagan deity to balance the Judeo-Christian one.

58. For other notable scenes where this verbal association is made, see the episode when Rorschach's prostitute mother discovers her son looking into her bedroom while she is with a customer (6:3). This scene, including the verbal tic, is replicated later with Rorschach's landlady, also a prostitute (10:6). The little boy the landlady clutches to her looks exactly like the young Rorschach seen in the earlier scene. Further examples are found in the scene in which Rorschach recalls his violence against neighborhood bullies (6:7); in the news vendor's response to learning Rorschach has thrown hot grease at a fellow prisoner (8:3); and the interrogation scene (10:14).

59. Moore makes the suggestion explicit in a flashback to Rorschach's prostitute mother saying that her son is "backwards" (6:3).

60. In a later scene, Rorschach retrieves his costume from its hiding place in an alleyway under a Nostalgia poster, further emphasizing the character's ties to the past (5:18). Since Truman used religious language in talking about the atomic bomb, Rorschach's admiration for this particular politician may not be merely an invocation of nostalgia; it may also have been chosen for its connection to the nuclear theme.

61. Moore himself exhibits a certain amount of nostalgia for this old-fashioned morality. Explaining his attachment to Superman in his youth, Moore has stressed its absolutism: "I got my morals more from Superman than I ever did from my teachers and peers. Because Superman wasn't real—he was incorruptible. You were seeing morals in their pure form" (Pappu, "We Need Another Hero").

62. The other is in Jon's reference to thermodynamic miracles (9:26), perhaps a reference to "the miracle" of human life.

63. See his secretary's reaction to the attempted assassination (5:13); Dan's incredulous comments to Rorschach (11:3, 11:18, and 11:26); and Laurie's horrified admission that Veidt's plan has worked (12:20).

64. Khoury, *The Extraordinary Works of Alan Moore*, 114.

65. For examples, see 2:15, 3:17, 4:10–11, 4:22, 8:23, 9:4, 9:23, and 12:8.

66. The reference to Adam and Eve is enhanced because both have just made it clear that they regard themselves as survivors and therefore pioneers in a new world.

67. Kraemer, "Alan Moore's *Promethea*: Comics as Neo-Pagan Primer and Missionary Tool," 2.

68. Sophie's name, of course, is an explicit sign that she is going to become the recipient of a great deal of learned theory.

69. Moore, *Promethea: Book Five*, Issue 31, "The Radiant, Heavenly City." Pages of *Promethea* are unnumbered. I have provided the issue number instead.

70. Moore, *Promethea: Book Five*, Issue 31, "The Radiant, Heavenly City."

71. Moore, *Promethea: Book Five*, Issue 31, "The Radiant, Heavenly City."

72. That this symbol occurred in Alexandrian Egypt, and was also taken up by (Gnostic) Christians as a symbol, suggests at least two other interesting connections between Ouroboros and the plot of *Watchmen*. It is perhaps no coincidence that Promethea's "birth" takes place in Alexandrian Egypt, nor that there is a similar reference to infinity in the self-reflexive panels which show the creators of the graphic novel creating the self-reflexive panels.

2

BLUE-FOOTED BOOBIES AND OTHER WITNESSES TO THE END

Kurt Vonnegut's Apocalyptic Novels

When Kurt Vonnegut died on 11 April 2007, the literary world lost one of its most ardent humanists. The most mainstream of postmodern authors, Vonnegut is probably also the most beloved American writer of post–World War II literature, particularly by the young people to whom his writing continues to appeal even though his critical reputation has suffered.

Whatever else might be said of him, no contemporary American author has done more to bring the end of the world to the attention of his readership. In addition to the prominent place that eschatological plots have in his work, the gloomy Vonnegut had spoken often and at length about his sense of impending catastrophe as regards the survival of the human race. While he based much of that pessimism on the proliferation of war, and nuclear arms in particular, surprisingly none of his novels locate the eschatological agent in nuclear war. Neither, as a sometimes writer of science fiction, did he often rely on extraterrestrials to deliver the coup de grace. But as befits an author who began his career as a public relations writer for the General Electric laboratories, Vonnegut did continually imagine that science and technology would play a role in the human race's demise, and he incorporated that idea into the apocalyptic destruction of his eschatological novels.[1]

Throughout his career, Vonnegut balanced an admiration for scientists and their pursuit of knowledge with a cynicism and angry despair about the ways their discoveries were misused. At the heart of this ambivalence was his own experience:

> I thought scientists were going to find out exactly how everything worked, and then make it work better. I fully expected that by the time I was twenty-one, some scientist, maybe my brother, would have taken a color photograph of God Almighty—and sold it to *Popular Mechanics* magazine. Scientific truth was going to make us *so* happy and comfortable.
>
> What actually happened when I was twenty-one was that we dropped scientific truth on Hiroshima. We killed everybody there. . . . So I had a heart-to-heart talk with myself.[2]

As early as his first novel, *Player Piano* (1952), it was clear that there was both an ambivalence about science and an apocalyptic sensibility at work. Among the fomenters of the anti-machine rebellion with which the novel is concerned, there is a great deal of talk about prophets and messiahs, with one minister even declaring, "In the past, in a situation like this, if Messiahs showed up with credible, dramatic messages of hope, they often set off powerful physical and spiritual revolutions in the face of terrific odds."[3]

The link between science and technology and the impending end which Vonnegut first articulated in this novel is one to which he returned throughout his writing career, though paradoxically, and unlike writers such as Thomas Pynchon or Peter George (whose 1958 novel *Two Hours to Doom* was the basis for the film *Dr. Strangelove*), Vonnegut typically steered away from depictions of a catastrophic end brought about by the war technologies which so worried him. Nonetheless, he was pessimistic about humanity's odds of surviving its own bad ideas.

With one notable exception, this pessimistic view of humankind has meant that most of his apocalyptic novels have fallen into the neo-apocalyptic category in which no New Jerusalem is imagined. Late in his life and career, however, Vonnegut had a seeming change of heart and, in *Galápagos* (1985), wrote a traditionally apocalyptic novel which does depict a New Heaven on Earth. Prior to this novel, however, Vonnegut had written two other major eschatological works, *Cat's Cradle* (1963) and *Slapstick, or Lonesome No More!* (1976).[4]

Vonnegut's *Cat's Cradle* is one of the best-known mainstream examples of the "science gone amok" subgenre of eschatological fiction in which man is responsible for his own destruction. In his study of eschatological fictions, W. Warren Wagar points out there are few examples of this sort of plot prior to 1914 and argues that the fact that "man-made dooms are the rule, not the exception" after 1914 would also seem to suggest that the man-made devastation of the First World War had a profound influence on the apocalyptic imagination.[5] While Wagar concludes that the majority of such stories take the form of world war stories, he notes that "science gone amok" stories began to occupy a significant niche in the subgenre after 1965 and continue to be a popular alternative.[6]

Vonnegut's *Cat's Cradle* is an early example of this trend. In it, a man-made substance called Ice-9 instantaneously freezes the world's water and causes massive weather upheaval. Human extinction is ensured by the days of tornadoes and the fatal ingestion of Ice-9 crystals. The novel emphasizes this destruction and makes no suggestion that there is a new or better world to be inherited afterward. If anything, *Cat's Cradle* is Vonnegut's bleakest apocalyptic work, ending as it does with the novel's religious figure Bokonon essentially declaring the futility of existence and advising his followers to commit suicide.

Vonnegut's other major apocalyptic work prior to *Galápagos* is *Slapstick, or Lonesome No More!* While *Slapstick* is one of this author's least successful endeavors and does not stand up well to critical scrutiny,[7] it is of interest here because it has as a major plot element the depopulation of the planet, a trope he'll use again to better effect in *Galápagos*. In *Slapstick*, Vonnegut employs almost every agent of apocalyptic end he can think of to account for the depopulation. Humans are simultaneously wiped out by two plagues (the Albanian flu and the "Green Death") and an earth-shaking fluctuation in gravity. Since the Albanian flu is really a Martian invasion, the "Green Death" is really the technologically advanced Chinese who have made themselves microscopic and are being fatally inhaled or ingested, and the fluctuations in gravity may also be due to Chinese experimentation, we can see Vonnegut using practically every existing trope of ending, whether alien invasion, the proliferation of life-destroying technology, or natural forces.[8] Like *Cat's Cradle*, *Slapstick* belongs to the neo-apocalyptic line of apocalyptic fiction: while there are survivors of all these catastrophes, the novel itself is a pessimistic one and offers little which might be interpreted as a New Jerusalem.

He uses the depopulation trope more effectively in *Galápagos*, where he conjures an outbreak of bacteria to sterilize the human race and prevents it from reproducing. Vonnegut combines this idea with his longstanding interest in Darwin's theory of natural selection to produce his only apocalyptic work which can be said to use the traditional paradigm. In *Galápagos*, the author strands a small group of individuals on an isolated island, thereby ensuring their escape from the sterility-causing bacteria. Then he lets evolution work on them over the course of a million years.

Hence, the novel shares a family resemblance with two other strains of eschatological fiction: plague fictions and evolutionary fictions. Stories in which plagues kill off humanity continue to grip the literary imagination, though, as suggested by the fact that pestilence is one of the four horsemen of the apocalypse, the idea is as old as storytelling itself.[9] Evolutionary fictions, on the other hand, detail the natural extinction of the human species and are examples of what John Wiley Nelson has called "evolutionary humanism," the idea that "*Homo sapiens* has reached the end of its time: the species is evolving into a new form of existence."[10] Usually such fictions detail how humans are overcome by a better-adapted species, and nature is portrayed as hostile to humans rather than nurturing.[11] In *Galápagos*, however, Vonnegut turns this trope on its head, portraying the evolutionary process as benevolent and wise, essentially turning natural selection into the hero of his story.

In *Galápagos*, Vonnegut attempts something unique, pitting social Darwinism, with its notions of hierarchy, progress, and generalized "survival of the fittest" against Darwin's morally neutral biological theory of evolution. Inherent in this endeavor is a challenge to a whole tradition of eschatological plotting which relies on Herbert Spencer's phrase "survival of the fittest" and the misapplication of the notion of competition between individuals and groups.

Vonnegut is acutely aware of how the ideas of Darwin and Spencer ultimately "gave the age metaphorical plots of triumph, or growth, or progress."[12] It is not unusual that Vonnegut criticize social Darwinism, which applies Darwinian notions of competition to the economic and social arenas, "[conflating] social success with reproductive fitness . . . and questions of moral rightness with matters of a supposed 'natural order.'"[13] But in *Galápagos*, Vonnegut juxtaposes this incorrect interpretation of evolutionary theory against the actual science on which it is based in order to deliberately undercut the way Darwin's science has been used to justify intolerant and demeaning social ideas.

Vonnegut, who enrolled in the University of Chicago's master's program in anthropology when he returned home from World War II, had a long-standing interest in Darwin.[14] He remained an avid student of cultural anthropology and natural history throughout his life, claiming to have read almost all that Darwin had written, as well as more recent neo-Darwinian theory.[15] Vonnegut saw evolutionary theory as more than an explanation of man's origins. He viewed it as a kind of master narrative, an idea he elaborated on in an interview:

> it's interesting to me that this is the only theory of evolution and the only thing that modern man has to cling to, I think, as an idea that has been generated

by science and that modern man can understand and build his life around and all that. It has been a substitute for the Bible for a lot of people who have been willing to find it reasonable to put their faith in a theory of evolution and call it God. Everybody has to put his faith somewhere, and it turns out this is the major receptacle in our civilization for faith.[16]

Vonnegut was particularly dismayed by how Darwin's theory had been twisted into a social Darwinism that attempts to justify despicable social and economic policies.[17] Indeed, such misinterpretations were often a target for him in his writing. Yet, either because Vonnegut himself was sometimes imprecise in his off-the-cuff comments and personal writings, or because, in his written efforts to satirize social Darwinism, his ironic tone is easily missed, he sometimes appears guilty of conflating the two strains of Darwinian thought.[18]

Occasionally, such imprecision occurs in his fiction, too. In *Slaughterhouse-Five*, for instance, the Tralfamadorians find Charles Darwin the most engaging Earthling because he "taught that those who die are meant to die, that corpses are improvements," while in *Slapstick*, two characters criticize the theory of evolution "on the grounds the creatures would become terribly vulnerable while attempting to improve themselves. . . . They would be eaten up by more practical animals, before their wonderful new features could be refined."[19]

However, in *Galápagos*, Vonnegut appears largely to have avoided this kind of conflation, deliberately delineating his ideas more carefully than he seems to have done in his previous works or personal interviews.[20] His more disciplined approach in this novel suggests that his intent is to satirize the social Darwinism he detests. It is therefore structurally necessary that the reader be able to separate the two strains since *Galápagos'* entire aim is to undermine any notions of Darwinism other than those that belong to evolutionary biology.

Galápagos is a unique work of apocalyptic fiction.[21] Because it has both a deity figure and a New Jerusalem, and because it is essentially optimistic in outlook, Vonnegut has stayed truer to the original plot and spirit of the traditional apocalyptic paradigm than almost any other contemporary writer who has adapted it. But what makes *Galápagos* exceptional is that in elevating a scientific principle to the position of the deity in his novel, Vonnegut returns the secular apocalyptic story to its religious roots.

One of the abiding difficulties of secularizing the apocalyptic genre is that it is a theological story, difficult to translate into secular terms because so many of its unique characteristics are inherently religious concepts. But as Vonnegut well understood, for many people science and rationalism have abrogated religious faith. Science has become a faith in itself. *Galápagos* is based on this canny paradox: by making evolution his apocalyptic god, Vonnegut returns the secular apocalyptic story to its religious roots by transforming *into* the deity the very thing which tore it away from those roots. Todd F. Davis's argument that Vonnegut's work consistently seeks to undermine America's grand narratives—primarily that "science will save us"—has to be qualified for *Galápagos* where Vonnegut is certainly undermining grand narratives, but not the grand narrative of "science will save us."[22] Instead, science, as represented by natural selection, is exactly what saves humans in this novel.

Still, *Galápagos* does undermine two other grand narratives. The first is social Darwinism. The second is the actual-but-outdated Darwinist theory of evolution. Vonnegut clearly believed that evolutionary theory had become a guiding ideology of our age, as evidenced by his comment that Darwinism is "our only alternative to conventional religion."[23] However, as a reader of natural history and anthropology, Vonnegut also knew that parts of this theory had been superseded by advances in the field of evolutionary biology.[24]

Cognizant, then, of the misconceptions which Niles Eldredge and Ian Tattersall argue infiltrate "modern stories and attitudes about the origin and nature of our own biological species," Vonnegut targets both the grand narrative of "survival of the fittest" (the lynchpin of social Darwinism), and the grand narrative of biological Darwinism which he believes has become a kind of modern religion.[25] He attacks the former as spurious and amends the latter by incorporating more recent ideas in biological evolution about the role played by chance.

That he chooses to attack these meta-narratives in the form of an apocalyptic tale suggests that Umberto Eco's argument that the drive toward modern apocalypticism is fueled in part by the collapse of great ideologies may have some merit, for it seems certain that Vonnegut regarded biological Darwinism—at least as most of us understand it—as a collapsing ideology.[26] New theories advanced by Neo-Darwinists such as Stephen Jay Gould and Niles Eldredge abandon parts of Darwin's theory for alternative explanations that synthesize advances in other sciences such as genetics into a larger evolutionary theory of our origins. One area in particular, Darwin's "imperfections in the geological record," has undergone revision in the last several decades. Vonnegut explained:

> The fossil record doesn't quite bear out what Darwin said. [Stephen J.] Gould has been telling his colleagues, "Come on, let's see what the fossil record re-

ally does show and then explain that," instead of saying "We're still missing links; we've got to dig some more." What the record shows is that changes [in evolutionary development] are quite sudden. New models have all suddenly appeared in fossils, rather than with a whole lot of easy, rather imperceptible steps.[27]

In *Galápagos*, these sudden evolutionary leaps are made possible because of luck. For example, the sequence of events that brings together the small band of colonists who get stranded on Santa Rosalia is a matter of pure chance.[28] Ultimately, this emphasis on luck undermines any notion of the survival of the fittest. In fact, the "fittest" specimens in the novel—at least according to social Darwinian thought—are all dead before the stranding occurs. James Wait, Andrew MacIntosh, and Zenji Hiroguchis, each a highly "successful" individual in social Darwinian terms, all meet early ends, and simply because of bad luck, too. Thus, it is not the "fittest" who arrive on Santa Rosalia, just the luckiest. *Galápagos'* narrator, Leon Trout, makes this explicit: "I did not know that humanity was about to be diminished to a tiny point, by luck, and then, again by luck, permitted to expand again."[29]

Consequently, *Galápagos* addresses Darwinist ideas on two separate counts. First, it undermines social Darwinist ideas because its characters survive due to contingency rather than talent, skill, or (economic) strength, and "such a depiction convincingly demonstrates that in a universe based on 'pure gambling-casino luck' it is not the fit that survive for good reasons but only the lucky that survive for no reason at all."[30] Secondly, it redresses an outdated interpretation of evolutionary theory burdened by Victorian notions of progress and teleological pre-Darwinian notions of a hierarchy of life forms culminating in humans, a conceited perspective which Vonnegut once acerbically described as being "just like elephants being proud of weighing as much as they do."[31] In fact, modern evolutionary science makes a point of dispensing with the idea of hierarchical evolution, preferring instead to talk about speciation. Thus, the contingency which Vonnegut describes in *Galápagos* is actually more accurate as far as neo-Darwinian theory is concerned because modern evolutionary theory emphasizes random mutation and sudden change.[32]

While Vonnegut depicts evolution accurately, he still needs to depict it as a deity figure for his novel to work as an apocalyptic story. Darwin deliberately refrained from anthropomorphizing nature, but he also contended that natural selection "is the creative force of evolution—not just the executioner of the unfit."[33] So while his theory clashed with the Natural Theology of his day, the various efforts of the Victorians to tie natural selection to ideas of progress and design inevitably suggest an anthropomorphosis of the evolutionary process.[34] Given this intellectual history, it is not a huge leap for Vonnegut to imagine evolution as his novel's deity figure.

In order to apotheosize evolution, however, Vonnegut first establishes an analogy between science and religion, a feat accomplished principally by drawing analogies between Noah's ark and the *Bahía de Darwin*, the ship that carries the colonists to Santa Rosalia. In the opening pages of the novel, for example, Leon says that he "might entitle [his] story 'A Second Noah's Ark,'" and later the Captain sarcastically tells Mary that he believes Mount Ararat to be nearby.[35] This particular allusion specifically ties *Galápagos* to the biblical apocalyptic tradition, since the story of the Flood might be considered the first instance in the Bible of an apocalypse.

Vonnegut makes another link between the Bible and *Galápagos* in his repeated comparison of Captain von Kleist and Mary to Adam and Eve. The author makes it clear that this is not a strict analogy; as one might expect with Vonnegut, the Captain and Mary offer a twisted version of the Genesis story, with Mary literally unable to bear children, and the Captain casting Mandarax, the metaphorical "Apple of Knowledge" into the ocean (56). Figuratively, however, the couple do function as the parents of the future human race.[36]

Finally, Vonnegut suggests an analogous relationship between science and religion through his list of explanations for the existence of the Galápagos Islands. Leon tells us that in 1986 it was still a mystery how so many creatures came to be living on such a remote group of islands. He offers five explanations that people have devised in order to explain this mystery, three of them scientific, and two religious (12–13). He refutes all of the scientific explanations, but neither of the religious ones. In fact, when Leon says, "If there really was a Noah's ark, and there may have been—I might entitle my story 'A Second Noah's Ark'" (13), his phrase "and there may have been" actually implies the plausibility of the religious explanations. Since he purports to be writing the story of a second Noah's Ark, he is clearly drawing an analogy between his tale in which natural selection is the deity, and the biblical version with the traditional Judeo-Christian deity, and wants the reader to understand his implication that science has come to be seen as a sort of religion. Vonnegut reiterates this link when Mary's dying husband sends her to get the Bible and she finds it with two other books, one of which is Darwin's *The Voyage of the Beagle*. The religious text is therefore put on an equal footing with the scientific text which is the basis for our scientific "religion."[37]

Throughout the novel, Vonnegut repeatedly reminds the reader that evolution is responsible for all the creation he depicts. Indeed, nature is so often alluded to as a wise presence and ontological explanation that the analogy to traditional deity is hard to miss.[38] When Leon says he is "prepared to swear under oath that the Law of Natural selection did the repair job without outside assistance of any kind" (234), we hear both a disavowal of the supernatural, as it has traditionally been depicted in religious doctrine, *and*, by virtue of its allusion to similar invocations to the supernatural, an elevation of the law of natural selection to exactly that position.

But while nature is portrayed as the *prima causa*, it is not necessarily depicted as a conscious one. John Wiley Nelson has pointed out that the typical naturalistic eschatology depicts "Mother Nature [smashing] an impertinent offspring's attempts to usurp Her Throne."[39] That humans are nature's impertinent offspring is made clear in *Galápagos* by Mary's reproductive experiment, her nickname of "Mother Nature Personified," and Vonnegut's comment that drinking heavily is our attempt to push evolution in the right direction. Nonetheless, Vonnegut seems to be making a more nuanced delineation here: while Nelson's wording implies a conscious deity aware of rebellion, one of Vonnegut's points seems to be that nature does not differentiate between people, iguanas, and seaweed.

By using evolution as his deity, Vonnegut ties the novel to the traditional paradigm in yet another way. Because evolution happens chronologically, Vonnegut does not sidestep the linearity of time that is so much a part of the traditional apocalyptic paradigm. At the same time, while the structure of time itself in the novel is clearly linear, as in the Judeo-Christian paradigm, the narrative representation of time echoes the Book of Revelation because it moves back and forth across time with Leon speaking from a million years in the future, then popping into various moments of the "present tense" of his main story, and even going back into the characters' pasts to narrate events. Yet *Galápagos* relies on the same linear time as apocalypse because evolution depends on linearity of time, as well.

To Vonnegut, evolution is a series of events that connect all things equally, privileging no one species over another. In this chain of sequences, the author attempts to put human life and culture in its proper anthropological context: we are, he argues, egotistic, narcissistic tiny links of a much longer chain of historical evolution and there is no reason to privilege humans and their achievements any more than the Blue-footed Booby and its mating dance, or a bacterial infection that causes population-wide sterility. Each is just another element in a long historical narrative, and none is of more importance in that narrative than the other. Vonnegut draws links between evolution and history by providing the evolutionary lineages of various items such as the computer Mandarax and the explosive dagonite. He

uses the biblical language of "begetting" and the rhetorical flourishes associated with royal lineage as a further sign of this connection: "Glacco begat
dagonite . . . and both were descendants of Greek fire and gunpowder and
dynamite and cordite and TNT," or ". . . dagonite, son of glacco, direct de-
scendant of noble dynamite" (172–73).[40] This link between evolution and
linear history, though tenuous, is one more way that *Galápagos* resonates
with the original apocalyptic paradigm.

At the same time, Vonnegut doesn't want to confuse linear time with linear evolution because modern evolutionary biology has largely jettisoned the
notion of linear evolution. "Evolution is a mixture of chance and necessity—
chance at the level of variation, necessity in the working of selection."[41] So
throughout the novel, Vonnegut has incorporated random chance and luck
in the evolutionary process. Vonnegut stays true to Darwinian theory when
he gives Akiko a furry pelt due to her grandmother's exposure to the atomic
bomb. This is a random mutation, and it is encouraged by evolutionary
forces because the new environment of Santa Rosalia favors the further development of this adaptation. But it is a series of chance events that put
Akiko's mother Hisako on the *Bahía de Darwin* which lands on the island.
Once the mutation occurs, its arrival on the island is pure chance, just as it
is pure chance that the Captain, a non-carrier of the Huntington's chorea
gene, ends up on the island instead of his carrier brother.

The chance events which occur throughout *Galápagos* do not, as it first
appears, undermine evolutionary theory. Instead, they emphasize a change
in thinking about evolutionary biology. While Darwin theorized random
mutations, he also believed that if we could only find the missing fossil links
we would be able to piece together a complete lineage showing how each
species evolved from the next in a single line and how all life was ultimately
traceable back to a single source. The more recent "punctuated equilibrium" theory suggests there are no "missing links" to find, that there are
multiple branching lines rather than a single straight line of evolution. We
know now, for instance, that several types of hominids lived simultaneously
over the past two to three million years, suggesting that they are not de-
scended from one another, but branched out simultaneously from a more
distant, common ancestor. Only one of those hominids, *Homo sapiens*, survives today. Those other branches have since become extinct, but why is not
clear.

This suggests another element of randomness in evolution: random, sudden extinctions. Sometimes a species cannot adapt to a change in the environment and subsequently becomes extinct, but at other times, a chance
event causes extinctions. Vonnegut wants to remind the reader of this

chance element when he writes of the meteorite showers which killed off the dinosaurs (104) or of the rodent-plagued land tortoises (132). The sterilizing bacteria of *Galápagos* are an example of a rapid extinction brought about purely by chance.

This element of chance and randomness at first appears problematic in an apocalyptic story because it suggests that the deity is not in control. However, in Vonnegut's case, this seeming paradox is part of a deliberate satirical strategy. In order to talk further about that problem, we first have to examine how Vonnegut has positioned the "big brain" as his Antichrist figure.

Vonnegut is clear from the very start of *Galápagos* that big brains are the source of all the trouble. It is not merely that they are "too big to be practical" (70), but they also "deceive their owners" (75). Big brains are increasingly anthropomorphized in the novel; they not only act of their own accord, independent of the human beings they are part of, but they are willfully malicious. Captain Kleist wishes he could fire his brain for having misled him (189), and Leon says, "If [big brains] had told the truth, then I could see some point in everybody's having one. But these things lied all the time!" (141). Numerous examples of the duplicitous nature of big brains are given, including Leon's own:

> When I was alive, I often received advice from my own big brain which, in terms of my own survival, or the survival of the human race, for that matter, can be charitably described as questionable. Example: It had me join the United States Marines and go fight in Vietnam. Thanks a lot, big brain. (31)

Leon claims that big brains are responsible for such dubious "survival schemes" as mass mechanization, slavery, the destruction of the environment, rabid capitalism, and genocide. Referring to a man who enjoys being asphyxiated to the point of orgasm, Leon comments wryly, "His big brain had had him doing this as least once a month for the past three years: hiring strangers to tie him up and strangle him just a little bit. What a survival scheme!" (134). Leon declares that human brains have become such "irresponsible generators of suggestions as to what might be done with life" that survival of the species finally appears to be an "arbitrary [game] which might be played by narrow enthusiasts—like poker or polo or the bond market, or the writing of science fiction novels" (67–68).

But Vonnegut takes this anthropomorphism even further. He assigns malicious intent to the big brain, essentially making the big brain evil as well as powerful. Referring to Thoreau's aphorism about men leading lives of quiet desperation, Leon suggests that this desperation is because of:

> the only real villain in my story: the oversize human brain. . . . The mass of men was quietly desperate . . . because the infernal computers inside their skulls were incapable of restraint or idleness; were forever demanding more challenging problems which life could not provide. (216)

This point is soon dramatized when Mary Hepburn has an idle thought about a way to reproduce without the help of a man. She finds herself carrying out this experiment even though she does not have the permission of either the male donor or the young women she will make pregnant.[42] Vonnegut writes:

> what her big brain certainly wasn't going to tell her, was that, if she came up with an idea for a novel experiment which had a chance of working, her big brain would make her life a hell until she had actually performed that experiment.
> That . . . was the most diabolical aspect of those old-time big brains: They would tell their owners, in effect, "Here is a crazy thing we could actually do, probably, but we would never do it, of course. It's just fun to think about."
> And then, as though in trances, the people would really do it . . . (213)

The outright reference to the oversized brain as a villain with a will of its own and an ability to make one's life hell suggests that the big brain is supposed to personify the Antichrist figure in this novel. Vonnegut's repeated references to the malicious trouble caused by big brains and their "evil schemes" (16) bears out that interpretation,[43] and even the Vonnegut persona asks near the beginning of the novel:

> What source was there back then, save for our over-elaborate nervous circuitry, for the evils we were seeing or hearing about simply everywhere? My answer: There was no other source. This was a very innocent planet, except for those great big brains. (16)[44]

Vonnegut's strategy here draws another analogous connection to the Book of Revelation. By making it clear that big brains are responsible for cruel and stupid ideas which cause so much misery, Vonnegut ties his figurative Antichrist to a figurative Tribulation. While the evil ideas of big brains are not responsible ultimately for the extinction of the human race in Vonnegut's tale, they *are* responsible for making this world a hell to live in. That is, the evil ideas of the villainous big brain form the analogous Tribulation element of Vonnegut's apocalyptic story.

Both the physical and thematic structure of *Galápagos* reflects this juxtaposition. In what seems at first to be an odd choice, Vonnegut uses Anne Frank's most famous saying as his novel's epigraph. Frank's remark that she still believes in the goodness of people seems both literally and figuratively out of place in *Galápagos*, since the novel is only incidentally about morality at all. If anything, *Galápagos'* deity is a seemingly neutral one. But what the Frank quotation does allude to is perhaps the most vivid example we have of an experiment in social Darwinism. The Nazis' Final Solution had roots both in social Darwinist ideas about superior species and competition, and apocalyptic notions of a New World Order. That Vonnegut chooses to begin *Galápagos* with a reminder of the Nazis' handiwork suggests that he wants to keep this idea before the reader. At the same time, there could be no stronger proof of the misery big brains can cause than the Holocaust. It seems Vonnegut does not intend Frank's remark to illumine his novel's deity, only his Antichrist and the related idea of Tribulation. To this end, the quotation works in several ways.

First, it refers to an event that many consider to be a real near apocalypse: the annihilation of European Jewry. Vonnegut strengthens that meaning by alluding several times to another prominent genocide, that of the Indians by the Conquistadors. At the heart of the European genocide lies the most extreme extrapolation of social Darwinism, a refigured version of the same notions of superiority that account for the Indian genocide.

Secondly, the quotation historicizes apocalypse, taking it out of the realm of the biblical/hypothetical and placing it instead in the realm of the political/possible. This shift toward the historical is part of the secularization of contemporary apocalyptic writing, in which "the cataclysm [results] from the events of recent history and man's own capacities for self-destruction."[45] By referring to a historical moment in which a distinct segment of the population and its culture was almost completely destroyed and a millennialist New World Order nearly put into place, Vonnegut implies that secular apocalypse is not some distant, theological myth which has little to do with us, but has become all too plausible.

The juxtaposition is also reflected in the novel's structure. The novel is divided into two sections, "The Thing Was" and "And the Thing Became." The two section titles imply that "the Thing" *has* a Before and an After, but additionally suggest an evolution from one to the other through the use of the word "Became." This implied connection of the section titles to evolution, as well as the novel title referring to the islands which partially led Darwin to his theory, aligns the body of the novel with Darwin's evolutionary theory.

The epigraph, however, is aligned with social Darwinism. Hence, the juxta-position of the epigraph against the rest of the novel manages to convey a précis of *Galápagos'* theme: that social Darwinism leads to a "Tribulation" and biological Darwinism leads to a "New Jerusalem."

By aligning natural selection with the deity role and the big brain with the Antichrist role, however, Vonnegut creates a problematic dichotomy for himself. He has to deal somehow with the fact that it is natural selection that has created the big brain to begin with. His solution is to remove the big brain from its place in the natural order.[46] He repeatedly implies that while the big brain might have originally served a useful purpose in, for instance, allowing greater manual dexterity, its secondary use, as an organ of thought, has long since caused the big brain to fall out of line in the natural order of things.[47] Its primary use is paradoxically being undermined by its secondary use. David Cowart identifies this reversal as frequently occurring in Vonnegut's later fiction where "mindless (or rather mentally twisted) human predation is merely Darwinian mechanism gone malign, promoting ecological catastrophe rather than orderly evolution."[48]

Vonnegut is certainly aware that there is scientific precedent for his position; he deliberately mentions the Irish Elk whose massive horns puzzled Victorian naturalists because they seemed to serve no beneficial purpose and were possibly disadvantageous since they prevented the elk from feeding in any but the most open of habitats. Darwin's theory says that evolutionary changes must be adaptive and useful, that "natural selection will never produce in a being any structure more injurious than beneficial to that being, for natural selection acts solely by and for the good of each."[49] But Vonnegut is relying here on more recent biological evolutionary theory which adds a codicil to Darwin: "Darwinian evolution decrees that no animal shall actively develop a harmful structure, but it offers no guarantee that useful structures will continue to be adaptive in changed circumstances."[50] He is also playing with the idea that while adaptations may develop to better help an animal compete in a certain area, adaptations may serve secondary and tertiary functions which have nothing to do with the reason for the original evolution.

Vonnegut subverts the teleological Victorian reading of the natural world, one which saw man and his big brain as the pinnacle of evolution. Instead, the author applies the amended Darwinian theory, portraying the human brain as an outdated adaptation when he has Leon tell the reader that humans wouldn't have needed to be so clever if their big brains hadn't always gotten them into trouble (168).[51]

But if the oversized brain is supposed to be the Antichrist of this novel, two crises arise almost immediately. The first is a crisis of theodicy and the second is a crisis of fallibility, since the figurative creator in the novel, evolution, is also inadvertently responsible for the "mistake" of creating evil in the form of the big brain. However, neither of these crises is new to religious studies; the existence of evil has always been problematic for Judeo-Christian theologians. That these two issues are consequences of the dichotomy that Vonnegut devises in his novel strengthens, rather than weakens, the analogy that science is meant to be taken as a sort of religion here.[52] Yet Vonnegut's choice of deity here has some intriguing consequences of its own as regards the traditionally difficult religious issues of fallibility and theodicy.

One theological response to the issue of theodicy is that we cannot know or understand God's will, a solution that implies both the brevity and inconsequentiality of human life in the larger cosmos. But Vonnegut's narrative allows an expanded view of the cosmos because it takes place over such an enormous period of time. Indeed, Vonnegut had struggled to find a narrative strategy that would allow him to do what he wanted:

> The technical problems were very hard of how to make a story last a million years. Who's going to observe it [the point of view], because the reader is going to insist upon knowing who the hell is watching this. As an atheist I couldn't have God watch. So technically, it looked hopeless for a long time. The problems were enormous as to how the hell to get away with this.[53]

Vonnegut solved his problem by making his narrator a ghost. Thus, Leon Trout occupies a narrative position much like John of Patmos in that he is simultaneously in the future looking back, and in the present describing what he observes. Moreover, he is emblematic both of humans as they are now, since he has not evolved like the rest of the species, and of humans as they will be, since, ironically, he too has a reduced brain capacity, having been decapitated before beginning his tale.

This unusual narrative strategy allows Vonnegut the one thing which potentially solves the problem of theodicy inherent in Western religion: time. Leon's narration from a million years into the future of human existence allows Vonnegut the time to have humans evolve into a kinder, gentler form, but the secondary effect of the length of time over which Leon makes his observations is the implication that we are simply incapable of making accurate assessments of anything—including good and evil—because we are not around long enough to do so.[54] If it seems to us that there is evil in the world that is incomprehensible in light of our view of God as benevolent, this is merely because we do not have the necessary time to see how things turn out. But here, as a consequence of the deity that Vonnegut has created, the reader is given that extended perspective and hence the ability to see that all has worked out for the best.[55] The creation of the big brain is thus neither proof of nature's fallibility, nor of its lack of benevolence.

Yet, there is a second way to read the issue of fallibility in the novel and that is with the knowledge of Vonnegut's own atheism and history as a satirical writer. In such a reading, theodicy and fallibility remain problematic as they always have been in religions, but the issue of fallibility allows Vonnegut an opportunity to satirize religion.

That evolution has made a "mistake" in creating the big brain is an idea that Vonnegut certainly wants the reader to consider, and there are passages in which it is manifestly clear that he is gleefully painting a portrait of a god who has lost control of its creation. Leon, for instance, is furious at any "natural order" which would evolve something as destructive as the big brain (141).[56] Leon is given a number of these speeches that usually focus on the indifferent cruelty and bellicosity of humans. Marveling at the destructive capabilities of an elaborate new weapon, he ruefully says, "the Law of Natural selection was powerless to respond to such new technologies" (120).

There are several reasons to believe that Vonnegut's aim here is ultimately to criticize religion, not least of which is his history of doing so. This is an author "who scathingly comments on almost every organized religion from traditional Catholicism to the more recent Born-Againism."[57] And, too, Vonnegut has been outspoken about his own atheism. In any number of essays and interviews, he has stated his belief that humans are alone in the universe and cannot count on a God.[58]

That stance has often spilled over into his novels as well, and *Galápagos* is no exception. It is contingency rather than design that is emphasized here, implying that natural selection is no more in control than any other force. The Santa Rosalia colony is a sure example of this since it is not natural selection which ensures the survival of the human race, but Mary's biology experiment.[59]

Yet a third reason to suspect that Vonnegut is satirizing religion is the repeated reference to the volatility of, and mistaken weight given to, human opinion. One of the less marvelous consequences of a having a big brain, Vonnegut points out, is our susceptibility to being "beguiled by mysteries" (11). Throughout *Galápagos*, he suggests that opinion is fickle and based less on fact than "magical" transformation, a phrase he uses in his description of how people's opinions of the Galápagos Islands changed after Darwin's theory was publicized (23).

In addition to the early speech Leon gives about the explanations of the origins of the islands, he makes several comments that link unreliable opinion and our scientific knowledge. He remarks how Darwin's theory greatly influenced "people's volatile opinions of how to identify success or failure" (20), and that, because of opinion, "the Galápagos Islands could be hell in one moment and heaven in the next . . . and the universe could be created by God Almighty in one moment and by a big explosion in the next" (22). Vonnegut implies that our modern "religion" of science is as influenced by the realm of fantasy as our creative impulses are, and since we are meant to interpret science as a religion, it seems a fair supposition to make that Vonnegut means to undermine religion here in the same way he does throughout the rest of his oeuvre.

Regardless of how one interprets Vonnegut's stance on the fallibility of his novel's deity, the reader knows early on in the novel that evolution is going to make things right. Leon tells us in the opening pages that big brains are no longer a problem at the time in which he is writing the story:

It is hard to imagine anybody's torturing anybody nowadays. How could you even capture somebody you wanted to torture with just your flippers and your mouth? How could you even stage a manhunt, now that people can swim so fast and stay underwater for so long? The person you were after would not only look pretty much like everybody else, but could also be hiding out at any depth practically anywhere. (118–19)

What is not necessarily clear until the last pages of the novel is how the reader should interpret this evolution of the species. Is it the irrevocable end of humankind, or is it, in fact, a New Jerusalem? Part of the difficulty in interpreting this ending, even though we know about it from the beginning of the novel, is that Vonnegut is also making fun of the idea of human beings as deity figures.

While Leon explicitly makes this connection for the reader when he notes that Mary Hepburn had "to be more like a god" than an Eve (47), Vonnegut implicitly refers to this human tendency throughout the novel. No scene makes the point more clearly than Mary's experiment with single-sex reproduction. She impregnates the uncomprehending Kanka-bono girls with the semen left inside her own body after having sex with Captain Kleist. This is not a harmless experiment in creation, as Vonnegut makes clear in two ways. First, the Kanka-bono are afraid of Mary and her possibly good but also possibly evil capabilities, so that, to them, she has indeed taken on a godlike stature, but in no particularly good way (225). More importantly, Mary herself recognizes that what she has done is illegal and immoral, joking that back in civilization she would be in prison for doing it (214).

Ultimately, Vonnegut will clarify that such hubristic behavior is exactly the problem with the species: our big brains have been attempting to usurp God's role and are preventing us from accepting our rightful place in nature. Humans, according to Vonnegut, have ludicrous aspirations that they pursue at the risk of their own survival. Thinking themselves godlike is perhaps the worst of the bad ideas their oversized brains devise. Big brains delude humans into thinking themselves godlike, particularly in their ability to create new things.

Consequently, while humans are often successful in their creation experiments, Vonnegut proposes that *what* they create is often inane or destructive. He uses man-made creations such as explosives and Mandarax, the handheld computer whose hopelessly inappropriate choice of quotations so frustrates the colonists, to emphasize this point. Yet humans with their oversized brains cannot seem to help themselves; they repeatedly aspire to this deity role despite the trouble it causes. Leon, for example, explains that he chose to stay on earth because it gave him "fringe benefits" which make him nearly godlike (203). He thinks these attributes will help him understand life and its meaning. His payment for that privilege, however, is a million years of mostly boredom. His father, Kilgore, knows this will-to-omniscience is nonsense, if not hubris. When Leon asks if Kilgore is a god now that he is in the afterlife, Kilgore corrects him impatiently, telling him that he is still just his father (203), and he dismisses Leon's desire for understanding. He scornfully tells his son that humans and their information are about as useful as Mandarax (203). The dismissal of Mandarax, a repository for supposedly great human knowledge and art, is another swipe at Victorian anthropocentric interpretations of evolution, and another sign that, despite its pride in its creations, mankind's sense of its own importance is hopelessly overblown.

This voice of pronouncement, so damning and judgmental, is very much the voice of the God of the Last Judgment. It comes as no surprise that Kilgore, a failed science fiction writer and pessimistic curmudgeon, is given this particular speech, since he is arguably Vonnegut's most famous character. Often the mouthpiece for the most despairing of Vonnegut's feelings about humanity, it is fitting and perhaps inevitable that Kilgore should pass sentence on humankind in this novel, too. But in a reversal of Vonnegut's usual despair, Kilgore's pessimistic appraisal is not the final word in this novel. Leon tells the reader that, though at the beginning of his story he was afraid that humans were irrevocably doomed because of the damage they'd done to their world and themselves, it turned out not to be so. "Thanks," he says, "to certain modifications in the design of human beings, I see no rea-

BLUE-FOOTED BOOBIES AND OTHER WITNESSES 63

son why the earthling part of the clockwork can't go on ticking forever the way it is ticking now" (233–34).

Making it clear that smaller skulls have meant smaller brains, and that smaller brains have meant the end to all the former problems—the "blathering on"—caused by the "excess capacity" of big brains, Leon and Vonnegut indicate that this adapted human form essentially is a New Jerusalem, thereby adopting the strategy which Joel W. Martin and Conrad E. Ostwalt, Jr., have described as translating the "messianic kingdom from a new-age heaven to a second-chance earth."[60]

Having achieved this New Jerusalem, Vonnegut brings his novel full circle by referring the reader back to the Anne Frank epigraph of the novel, which we previously learned was Leon's mother's favorite quotation. With something like wonder, Leon remarks that his mother had been right all along: "there really was still hope for humankind" (208). Vonnegut thus manages to bend the social Darwinism he has been criticizing to his apocalyptic purposes by using Frank's quotation as its author intended: earnestly. Frank didn't know that she was shortly going to die when she wrote this sentence in her journal. It was a sincere expression of hope, and was devoid of the cynicism and irony that Vonnegut invests in it when he first uses it as the novel's epigraph. The reader knows that the context of the Frank quotation is one of social Darwinist ideas, but by itself the quotation speaks outside that context. It speaks *through* that context, offering a vision of optimism that looks beyond the evil of this world to something better. To this end, Frank's sentence stands in the apocalyptic tradition, not just because she herself was a victim of an apocalyptic worldview, but because in the midst of Tribulation-like misery, she could offer a vision of comfort to the beleaguered. When Leon says admiringly that his mother's hope has been vindicated because humanity has finally achieved a New Heaven on Earth, Vonnegut reinvests the Frank quotation with its original emotion. Thus, the idyllic description of the new world which humankind inhabits, and the reference to perhaps the single best-known quotation invoking hope, puts *Galápagos* squarely into the hopeful apocalyptic tradition. Like the Book of Revelation and other religious apocalyptic writing, *Galápagos* urges the reader to persevere. Meaning may be denied us because we are short-lived and short-sighted, but all is not lost; though we are subject to contingency and chance, these things may ultimately work for us rather than against us. Humanity's best hope lays in its ability to (literally) change.

Kilgore's spokesmanship points as well to a second, more metaphysical, apocalypse in *Galápagos*. As Vonnegut's longtime mouthpiece, it is difficult not to see the author sitting in judgment on humankind. What is certain is that, as the creator of his novel's characters and world, it is Vonnegut who occupies the ultimate deity role. He is the creator of his novel's characters and world, and he controls their destinies, destroying their fictional world and replacing it with a New Jerusalem of his own conception.

A large portion of Vonnegut's oeuvre has been concerned with metafictional issues that arise from the creator role of the author. Vonnegut constantly makes his readers aware of his position as author and the constructor of the tale he tells. Sometimes he does this by making reference to his own writing. At others, he uses gimmicks such as the starring of names of characters who are shortly to die, as he does in *Galápagos*. *Breakfast of Champions* features "Vonnegut" sitting in a bar surrounded by and manipulating his own characters, even revealing himself to Kilgore and telling him outright that he is a creation in Vonnegut's fiction.[61] Vonnegut's unique mixture of autobiographical details—or rather the acknowledgment of his autobiographical detail—with his fiction, and his insistence on using an ambiguous "I" persona in most of his novels, has meant for both him and his readers that they continually confront the artifice—and reality—of fictional creations.

Throughout *Galápagos*, Vonnegut deliberately undermines human acts of creation, art among them. When, for instance, Vonnegut writes that science fiction is just another "arbitrary game" that the human brain plays, he impugns both his profession and his novel (67). Moreover, the symbol of human art in the novel, the handheld computer Mandarax which acts as a repository for all the literary quotations thought worth saving for posterity, can offer only ineptitudes which are of no practical value at all. Vonnegut's last word on it is emphatic: he has a great white shark eat it. Such undermining isn't unique to this novel,[62] but he goes one step further in *Galápagos* when Leon reveals that he has "written these words in air—with the tip of the index finger of my left hand, which is also air" (233). The reader already knows that human beings of the future are unlikely readers; not only do they spend most of their lives in water, but they also no longer have the big brains or the dexterous fingers needed for reading.

So who is Leon writing for? If he is writing on air with air, his story—and Vonnegut's—will, quite literally, disappear into thin air, a conceit which Bo Pettersson has rightfully described as Vonnegut letting "man, in his regained innocence, forego much of what makes him unique. . . . The end of evil must entail the end of human creativity."[63]

So there is a suggestion of another kind of apocalypse here: that of the worlds that the written word creates. It may be that Vonnegut means to imply that art, like everything, is ephemeral, or even that it is itself in the process of evolving into a new form. Certainly, Vonnegut's distinctive style—brief paragraphs, doodles, and catch-phrases such as "And so it goes"—could be interpreted as an evolution in novel form. But what seems more likely, given the eschatological and evolutionary timbre of *Galápagos*, is that he intends to place human art in its proper anthropological and apocalyptic context.

Todd F. Davis argues that "At no time does Vonnegut become comfortable with the notion that humanity represents the highest achievement of some mythical creator."[64] In the evolutionary and anthropological sense, art is no more or less permanent than the species which makes it. Leon shrugs off the impermanence of his words, saying, "my words will be as enduring as anything my father wrote, or Shakespeare wrote, or Beethoven wrote, or Darwin wrote. It turns out that they all wrote with air on air" (233). Art merely creates another "comforting lie" that humans can tell to make their world a better place in which to live.

But as a postmodernist, Vonnegut is playfully engaging in a paradox here. While Leon's work will disappear within the fictional confines of *Galápagos*, it lives on through Vonnegut's work in the real world. Moreover, it is our big brains that allow us to read and consider Vonnegut's point about the uselessness of big brains. Because of this paradox, Peter Freese describes *Galápagos* as "a hoax, a verbal game built upon the premise of its very impossibility."[65] Great art will endure as long as humans do, Leon says. Its impermanence matters little if the "lie" it creates makes our lives better while we are here. Vonnegut himself has said much the same thing:

I now believe that the only way in which Americans can rise above their ordinariness, can mature sufficiently to rescue themselves and to help rescue their planet, is through enthusiastic intimacy with works of their own imagination.[66]

Vonnegut's career has largely been characterized by his sharp social criticism, and until *Galápagos*, most of what he observed led him to be pessimistic about the future. Humanity, he claimed, was on a collision course with extinction and was taking the rest of the planet with it. Then, in a 1974 speech, Vonnegut had a "magical" transformation of opinion:

For two-thirds of my life I have been a pessimist. I am astonished to find myself an optimist now. I feel now that I have been underestimating the intelligence and resourcefulness of man. I honestly thought that we were so stupid that we would continue to tear the planet to pieces, to sell it to each other, to burn it up. I've never expected thermonuclear war. What seemed certain to me was that we would simply gobble up the planet out of boredom and greed, not in centuries, but in ten or twenty years.[67]

A reader is right, I think, to read this declaration with a jaundiced eye, given that Vonnegut is both practicing revisionist history here (he is on record, for instance, saying he believed we would have a nuclear war), and reverted mostly to type in the rest of his work, which remained critical and cynical. Nonetheless, this seems a remarkable change that perhaps critics ought to pay attention to, even if it is only temporary, particularly in light of *Galápagos'* unusually happy ending for humanity. Let us, for a second, grant that Vonnegut may have experienced a renewed optimism about the fate of humanity. How better to express that renewed hope than adopt the traditional apocalyptic paradigm in which hope is manifestly the point?

Vonnegut's dual perception of art as meaningless on a universal level and meaningful on a societal level leads to a paradoxical visionary stance in *Galápagos*. If, as Vonnegut stated, hope for the human race is squarely located in the imagination, then *Galápagos* is as much a prophetic work as an apocalyptic one. That is, it aims to operate within history, as well as outside it, since the prophet aims to alter history, while the apocalyptist declares that history is irrevocably at an end.

While all apocalyptists are prophets, not all prophets are apocalyptists. Apocalyptic writing is a particular offshoot of prophecy, and the difference between the two lies primarily in their visions of history and mankind's role in it. Whereas a prophet usually admonishes sinful behavior and threatens punishment by God if the community does not correct its ways, an apocalyptist promises God's final intervention regardless. The future which a prophet predicts is a possible future, one which may occur if mankind does not act according to God's wishes. But that predicted future is also one which can be avoided by returning to God's word. Such a vision, as Martin Buber notes, is one of a partnership between God and mankind, with "God and man working out together the future of the world."[68]

An apocalyptist, on the other hand, sees God's behavior as fixed; God *will* intervene and bring human history to an end. Apocalyptists warn of an unalterable End. Their aim is to comfort and prepare those who are already "saved." There is nothing that mankind, even the righteous, can do to avoid this ending. About this, apocalyptists are unequivocal. There is nothing which the faithful can do to alter the end which God has planned; all they can do is endure it. Debra Bergoffen ties the difference to the idea of Covenant, writing that in prophecy:

> God promises to reward moral behavior by implementing the Messianic Age, but the people must choose whether or not to be moral. God cannot guarantee human righteousness. From the prophetic perspective, the divine promise is the revelation of a possible future, not a necessary one.[69]

Apocalyptists believe "that the goodness of God lies, not in His leaving the human choice of history open, but in His determining the speedy end to the evils of history and the imminent beginning of the Messianic Age."[70] Thus, the timbre of these two types of prophecy is quite different. Prophecy is interventionist as regards history; it counsels engagement with the world and emphasizes the power to change the future. Apocalyptic is more passive, crying jeremiad-like that the End is approaching and that God's house will be put in order in spite of man's interference.

In the self-contained story of the novel, the plot of *Galápagos* is clearly apocalyptic, but in the world of the reader, the world in which Vonnegut is the creator, the novel is suggestive of an active prophetic vision instead. Because the novel ends with the words "you'll learn," the implication is that if people change—and the optimistic prediction suggests they can—the end is avoidable. That is, altering history is possible. In effect then, *Galápagos* is a prophetic work masquerading as an apocalyptic one. In either case, we find a traditionally pessimistic author expressing a newfound hope for humankind.

The dual status of *Galápagos* as both a prophetic vision and apocalyptic one suggests one reason why Vonnegut might have thought his story would benefit from using the more traditional apocalyptic paradigm. In using the classic paradigm, his social criticism takes on the mantle of biblical pronouncement and therefore a gravitas that is more likely to inspire the change of direction that he seeks. Vonnegut repeatedly spoke of the need for humans to treat each other with love and respect. His adamancy about this point stemmed, in part, from a lifelong atheism which refused him a God on whose mercy he could throw himself. If there is no God to save us, and if this is the only chance we get, then it becomes doubly important that the lives we do have be lived wisely and kindly. Though Vonnegut is postmodern in his belief that we can know our world only through language and imaginative creations, he clearly believes this "does not absolve him of some obligation to the spiritual and physical condition of the planet and those who live upon it."[71] By couching his criticism in a biblical story of judgment, he encourages readers to look past the humor to a more serious message and consequently affirms his position as one of "a purer strain of apocalyptic writers, a tradition that imagines the worst because it believes in something better."[72]

All his life, Vonnegut espoused a "canary-bird-in-the-coal-mine theory of the arts," believing that writers "should be—and biologically *have* to be— agents of change."[73] He never gave up hope that he could be one of the "cultural agents that works within history to promote or suppress social change."[74]

In a comment that conflates this perception of his role as an artist with his penchant for evolutionary metaphor, Vonnegut called writers "specialized cells in the social organism." "Mankind," he says, "is trying to become something else; it's experimenting with new ideas all the time. And writers are a means of introducing new ideas into the society, and also a means of responding symbolically to life."[75] In *Galápagos*, he continued his work on this experiment, delivering a novel that paradoxically encourages humanity to believe the end can be avoided while simultaneously telling a story in which it is not.

NOTES

1. The agents of ending in his novels include the collapse of gravity (*Slapstick*), disease (*Slapstick* and *Galápagos*), experiments that go wrong (*Slaughterhouse-Five* and *Cat's Cradle*), and evolution (*Galápagos*).

2. Vonnegut, *Wampeters, Foma and Granfalloons*, 155–56.

3. Vonnegut, *Player Piano*, 246.

4. His apocalyptic sensibility is reflected in many of his other novels, even when they are not primarily about eschatological events. The time-traveling protagonist of *Slaughterhouse-Five* (1969), Billy Pilgrim—whose name harkens back to America's apocalyptic roots—is a prophet figure who knows that the universe will end when an alien culture accidentally blows it up. Billy's time-traveling also recalls the kind of narrative time slippage typical of the Book of Revelation since he is simultaneously in the future and past. Vonnegut's other novels are also strewn with eschatological asides. Even *Hocus Pocus* (1990), his novel about Eugene Debs Hartke, begins with such sentiments: "If all had gone the way a lot of people thought it would, Jesus Christ would have been among us again, and the American flag would have been planted on Venus and Mars. No such luck! . . . At least the World will end, an event anticipated with great joy by many. It will end very soon, but not in the year 2000, which has come and gone" (Vonnegut, *Hocus Pocus*, 13).

5. Wagar, *Terminal Visions: The Literature of Last Things*, 108.

6. Wagar, *Terminal Visions: The Literature of Last Things*, 110. Advances in genetic engineering have inspired some of the most recent examples. In Michel Houellebecq's *Atomised*, traditional reproduction and the human society it represents is eradicated in favor of hermaphroditic clones. In Margaret Atwood's *Oryx and Crake*, the human species is almost completely wiped out by a deliberately engineered plague.

7. Cf. Todd Davis, *Kurt Vonnegut's Crusade*, 91–97, who, wrongfully I think, defends this novel as being just as artful as Vonnegut's others. Even Vonnegut acknowledged that *Slapstick* wasn't very good.

8. One assumes, because of the title, that *Slapstick* is actually Vonnegut's attempt to satirize something, but both because the novel is poorly executed and the de-

population seems nearly incidental to the narrative, it is impossible to be certain that the apocalyptic genre is his target. If it is a burlesque, it is not a terribly successful one.

9. Mary Shelley's *The Last Man* (1826) is one of the earliest examples of a "universal" plague fiction, but among many others are Edgar Allan Poe's "The Masque of the Red Death" (1842), Jack London's "The Scarlet Plague" (1912), and George R. Stewart's *Earth Abides* (1949). In the mid to late twentieth century, Michael Crichton's *Andromeda Strain* (1969) and Stephen King's *The Stand* (1978) both relied on the trope, and numerous films have used a fatal outbreak of disease as the basis of their plots: *Omega Man* (1971), *Outbreak* (1995), and *28 Days Later* (2002). More recently, with the threat of bioterrorism on our minds, television shows such as *24* and *ER* have constructed their plots around this idea.

10. John Wiley Nelson, "The Apocalyptic Vision in American Popular Culture," 167.

11. Wagar, *Terminal Visions: The Literature of Last Things*, 100.

12. Mellard, *The Exploded Form: The Modernist Novel in America*, 10. In her book *Darwin's Plots*, Gillian Beer examines *The Origin of Species* as a narrative, how Darwin's familiarity with certain narratives influenced it, and how his theory in turn affected the subsequent narratives of his Victorian peers. Darwin himself disbelieved the notions of "higher" or "lower" life forms which his Victorians peers adopted, but because the vernacular meaning of "evolution" in Darwin's time was tied to the concept of progress. Darwin's carefully chosen phrase "descent with modification" ended up associated with "evolution" (Gould, *Ever Since Darwin*, 35–36).

13. Honderich,"Social Darwinism," 829.

14. Vonnegut did not complete the program, but was subsequently awarded his master's degree years later when the school accepted his novel *Cat's Cradle* in lieu of a master's thesis.

15. Reed, "A Conversation with Kurt Vonnegut, 1982," 13.

16. Reed, "A Conversation with Kurt Vonnegut," 13.

17. Reed, "God Bless You, Mr. Darwin, for Kurt Vonnegut's Latest," 63.

18. A good example occurs in his essay on the 1972 Republican National Convention. Observing that America only has two real political parties, the Winners and the Losers, he writes: "The single religion of the Winners is a harsh interpretation of *Darwinism*, which argues that it is the will of the universe that only the fittest should survive. The most pitiless Darwinists are attracted to the Republican party, which regularly purges itself of suspected *bleeding hearts*. . . . The Winners are rehearsing for *Things to Come*" (Vonnegut, *Wampeters*, 174–75. Emphasis Vonnegut.)

19. Vonnegut, *Slaughterhouse-Five,* 154; Vonnegut, *Slapstick* 49. The *Slapstick* quote is such an obviously incorrect misrepresentation of Darwin's theory that one suspects it is deliberately ironic, but *Slapstick* is not a well-executed joke. Peter Freese tends to give the author the benefit of the doubt when he appears to confuse kinds of Darwinism, arguing that the author is deliberately constructing a satire

and "metafictional moral" ("Natural Selection with a Vengeance," 354 and 347–48). Cf. Pettersson, *The World According to Kurt Vonnegut*, 352, who argues that this "overlooks the deterministic motif in Vonnegut's oeuvre in general and this novel in particular." But Vonnegut is not always a scrupulous or punctilious writer, and given his earlier references to Darwin and Darwinian theory outside the context of this novel, one must acknowledge the possibility that this is an author who either confused strains of Darwinism when it suited his fictional purposes, or who was not a rigorous analyst of his own words and thoughts.

20. Even so, in the introduction Vonnegut wrote for the Franklin Library Edition of the book, he wrote, "Only the Theory of Evolution carried a seeming message to which human beings without scientific apparatus might respond at any time, if they were so inclined: 'Prove by fucking or killing that you are Nature's favorite. Never mind mere human law.'" An earlier draft of this line is even more conflated: "prove by fucking or fighting your [*sic*] fittest to survive. Nature is gratified when a weakling is prevented from reproducing." (Vonnegut, draft of introduction to the Franklin Library Edition of *Galápagos*, included with a letter to Donald C. Farber. 15 June 1985. Vonnegut mss., Lilly Library, Indiana University, Bloomington, Indiana).

21. It was Vonnegut's assessment that this was his best book (Vonnegut, *Fates Worse than Death*, 131).

22. Davis, "Apocalyptic Grumbling," 152n.

23. Amis, *The Moronic Inferno and Other Visits to America*, 134.

24. Specifically, Vonnegut seems to have been aware of the "punctuated equilibrium theory," a 1972 theory proposed by Stephen J. Gould and Niles Eldredge which argued that, contrary to Darwin's belief that evolution moved in a slow and continuous process, evolution actually occurred in sudden starts, with long periods of equilibrium "punctuated" by sudden radical changes.

25. Eldredge and Tattersall, *The Myths of Human Evolution*, 1.

26. David et al., *Conversations about the End of Time*, 177.

27. Nuwer, "A Skull Session with Kurt Vonnegut," 252.

28. There is an ironic friction between the randomness within Vonnegut's fictional world, and his own artistic world in which the choices he makes as a writer are not arbitrary at all, but are carefully chosen to make a point about contingency being the driving force in the universe.

29. Vonnegut, *Galápagos*, 103. All further references are made parenthetically in the text. The ghostly Leon has just slipped into Captain von Kleist's head when he makes this comment and emphasizes that this choice, too, was simply lucky: "My choosing the Captain's head for a vehicle, then, was the equivalent of putting a coin in a slot machine in an enormous gambling casino, and hitting a jackpot right away" (103).

30. Freese, "Natural Selection with a Vengeance," 350.

31. Abádi-Nagy, "Serenity, Courage, Wisdom," 17.

32. Vonnegut was proud of the fact that Stephen J. Gould wrote to congratulate him on *Galápagos* and its scientifically reputable choice of a mutation involving the

fur-covered baby Akiko: "[Gould] thought it was a wonderful *roman à clef* about evolutionary theory and also proves how random the selection is" (Nuwer, "A Skull Session with Kurt Vonnegut," 252). Attempts to verify this letter from Gould at the Vonnegut Collection at the University of Indiana, Bloomington failed to turn up the letter itself. However, I did find a second reference to Vonnegut having received it. In a letter to Donald M. Fiene, with whom Vonnegut had a long correspondence, Vonnegut wrote: "I was glad to learn of Gould's mentioning *Cat's Cradle*. . . . He came to hear me lecture at M.I.T. a couple of years ago, and we had supper afterwards. I was scared shitless of what he might say about GALAPAGOS, and didn't ask his opinion. But he dropped me a note, asying [*sic*] it was pretty good science, and that a fur-covered human mutant is fairly common" (Vonnegut to Donald M. Fiene, 5 March, 1987. Unpublished letter. Vonnegut mss., Lilly Library, Indiana University, Bloomington, Indiana).

33. Gould, *Ever Since Darwin*, 12.

34. Bowler, *Evolution: The History of an Idea*, 208.

35. Vonnegut, *Galápagos*, 13, 201. Cf. Freese, "Natural Selection with a Vengeance," 345, who argues that these references set *Galápagos* apart from its biblical counterpart.

36. Critics such as Leonard Mustazza have read *Galápagos* as a return-to-Eden story rather than an apocalyptic one, largely based on the numerous references to the Garden of Eden and Adam and Eve in the novel. Indeed, the interpretive movement backward to prelapsarian innocence is logical in that there is an analogous evolutionary regression from big brains to small ones. Yet, it appears that Vonnegut wants to undermine such a reading since Kilgore Trout mentions the Garden of Eden only to disabuse his son of the comparison, and Vonnegut contradicts Mary's assessment of the forest where she meets her husband as Edenic by first describing it in terms of ownership, and later by declaring that the bird the couple are expecting to see is extinct. Furthermore, Vonnegut deliberately skewers the depiction of Mary as a new Eve when he writes that the figurative "mother" of the new race is no longer ovulating and "would not, could not, become his Eve. So she had to be more like a god instead" (47).

37. The third book is *A Tale of Two Cities*. Thanks to Daniel Karlin for pointing out that this text has a different connection altogether to both the apocalyptic tradition and social Darwinism. The French Revolution, of course, was itself regarded as an apocalyptic event which would overturn world order, but the ending of *A Tale of Two Cities* could also be seen as undermining ideas of social Darwinism. It involves an act of altruism on the part of Sydney Carton, who takes the place of Charles Darnay at the guillotine, foregoing his own chance to perpetuate his lineage (because he also loves Darnay's wife Lucy), and opting instead for being remembered as the one who made Charles and Lucy's own biological heirs possible. Since altruism is one argument used to counteract social Darwinism, one might argue that Vonnegut is subversively using Dickens's work to further undermine the social Darwinist strain.

38. Early in the narrative, as Trout is describing the volcanic origins of the Galá-pagos Islands, he comments, "Quite a lot of volcanic activity still goes on. I make a joke: The gods are still angry" (42). This is the only place Vonnegut overtly draws the analogy between nature and God for his reader, but the link is implicit through-out the rest of the narrative.

39. John Wiley Nelson, "The Apocalyptic Vision in American Popular Culture," 165.

40. There are no explosives called glacco or dagonite. However, Dagon is a Philis-tine deity, a fish god sometimes depicted as half-man, half-fish. Vonnegut may have created the name "dagonite" as a pun on the evolutionary process which is turning humans into "fisherpeople" who do share certain physical similarities with fish.

41. Gould, *Ever Since Darwin*, 12.

42. Mary's name, in addition to alluding to the biblical mother of Jesus, is also the pun on "marry." As a biology teacher who is nicknamed "Mother Nature Per-sonified," Mary "marries" the concepts of science and nature.

43. Other references include Leon's comment that "more and more people were saying that their brains were irresponsible, unreliable, hideously dangerous, wholly unrealistic—were simply no damn good" (28), and Mary saying to her brain, "You are my enemy. Why would I want to carry such a terrible enemy inside me?" (28).

44. Here is another instance of Vonnegut's sometimes confused and confusing conflation of evolutionary ideas. Throughout the novel, Nature is described as an indifferent agent. Yet here Vonnegut uses the word "innocent," undermining his own depiction of nature as morally neutral.

45. Zamora, *The Apocalyptic Vision in America*, 1.

46. Citing Darwin's notebooks, Stephen Jay Gould has argued that Darwin de-layed releasing *The Origin of Species* for twenty years not because he believed his views on evolution would be seen as heretical, but because he worried that his im-plied philosophical materialism would be seen as heretical. "No notion could be more upsetting to the deepest traditions of Western thought," Gould writes, "than the statement that mind—however complex and powerful—is simply a product of brain." Without materialism, he argues, an evolutionist could still believe in a Chris-tian god who worked "by evolution instead of creation," but Darwin's materialism suggested the heretical question "if mind has no real existence beyond the brain, can God be anything more than an illusion invented by an illusion?" (*Ever Since Darwin*, 24–25). This argument has interesting resonances in *Galápagos* because of the body/mind split imagined there (an issue which recurs in *The Matrix*), as well as Vonnegut's eventual undermining of religion in general in the novel.

47. As early as 1973, Vonnegut was quoted saying as much: "The human brain is too high-powered to have many practical uses in this particular universe, in my opinion" (Vonnegut, *Wampeters*, 219).

48. Cowart, "Culture and Anarchy: Vonnegut's Later Career," 183.

49. Darwin, *The Origin of Species*, 154. Darwin did theorize that such weird adaptations might have more to do with sexual selection, however. Or they could be

examples of what Valerius Geist calls "visual dominance-rank symbols," whose "function is to prevent actual battle (with consequent injuries and loss of life) by establishing hierarchies of dominance that males can easily recognize" (Qtd. in Gould, *Ever Since Darwin*, 89).

50. Gould, *Ever Since Darwin*, 90.

51. The interpretation of evolution as the heroic deity of the story is in part dependent on whether one believes the sincerity of the mediating voice of Leon Trout. While this voice is clearly a sarcastic and angry one, there is no reason not to believe it is earnest, and, in fact, I would argue that part of Vonnegut's reason for having a narrator speaking from a million years into the future is to appear to invest that voice with the objectivity of distance.

52. *Galápagos* suggests two alternatives to organized religion. One is humor, and the other is dancing, a recurring motif throughout the novel. Mary's biology class believes the dance done by the Blue-footed Booby is "proof that animals worshipped God" (90), and Mary asks, "Dare we call it 'religion'?" (92).

53. Nuwer, "A Skull Session with Kurt Vonnegut," 251.

54. Darwin wrote, "The mind cannot possibly grasp the full meaning of the term of a hundred million years; it cannot add up and perceive the full effects of many slight variations, accumulated during an almost infinite number of generations" (Darwin, *The Origin of Species*, 362). Stephen Jay Gould agreed: "We're not very good at calculating probabilities. When it comes to concepts like the infinite or eternity, we are completely incapable, we haven't the faintest notion. . . . Since we can't imagine how phenomena originated, we talk about eternity. Since we can't conceive of space having an end, we talk about infinity. But we don't really understand what that means" (David et al., *Conversations about the End of Time*, 25).

55. Vonnegut's solution is not without its problems, though, since the novel assumes that natural selection stops once the newer version of small-brained humans has evolved. Evolution does not stop at this point simply because Vonnegut chooses to. For more on this, see Freese, "Natural Selection with a Vengeance," 353.

56. Vonnegut points out that big brains do not *need* to be a problem necessarily. The octopus has just as big a brain, developed for exactly the same purpose, and yet it lives in harmony with nature. The octopus's brain isn't undermining the octopus as a species (150).

57. Freese, "Vonnegut's Invented Religions," 146.

58. Making comic reference to failed portents in a 1974 speech, Vonnegut said, "I take it to mean that we can expect no spectacular miracles from the heavens, that the problems of ordinary human beings will have to be solved by ordinary human beings" (Vonnegut, *Palm Sunday*, 194). Over a decade later, he repeated this idea in an interview when asked about his apocalyptic works, explaining, "it's a way of saying God doesn't care what becomes of us, and neither does Nature, so we'd better care. We're all there is to care" (Abádi-Nagy, "Serenity, Courage, Wisdom," 25). For other examples of Vonnegut's declared atheism, see Abádi-Nagy, 18, and Vonnegut's "Address at Bennington College, 1970" in *Wampeters*, 157–58.

59. Freese, "Natural Selection with a Vengeance," 353. This is a problematic example, since it is Mary's big brain—the supposed mistake—which ensures the experiment, though Mary's presence on the island is due to contingency.

60. Martin and Ostwalt, Jr., *Screening the Sacred*, 62.

61. Vonnegut, *Breakfast of Champions*, 266.

62. In *Bluebeard*, a character asks "And what is literature . . . but an insider's newsletter about affairs relating to molecules, of no importance to anything in the Universe but a few molecules who have the disease called 'thought'" (Vonnegut, *Bluebeard*, 170). In *Hocus Pocus*, Vonnegut quips, "How is this for a definition of high art: 'Making the most of the raw materials of futility'?" (Vonnegut, *Hocus Pocus*, 24).

63. Pettersson, *The World According to Kurt Vonnegut*, 364.

64. Davis, *Kurt Vonnegut's Crusade*, 85.

65. Freese, "Natural Selection with a Vengeance," 359.

66. Vonnegut, *Wampeters*, 23.

67. Vonnegut, *Palm Sunday*, 199.

68. Qtd. in May, *Toward a New Earth*, 14.

69. Bergoffen, "The Apocalyptic Meaning of History," 21.

70. Bergoffen, "The Apocalyptic Meaning of History," 25.

71. Davis, "Kurt Vonnegut," 316.

72. May, *Toward a New Earth*, 192.

73. Vonnegut, *Wampeters*, 214 and 213. Emphasis Vonnegut.

74. Goldsmith, *Unbuilding Jerusalem*, 2.

75. Goldsmith, *Unbuilding Jerusalem*, 213.

❸

A TORTURED STATE OF MIND

Terry Gilliam's New Jerusalem

Like Kurt Vonnegut, director Terry Gilliam shares an abiding suspicion of technology and has used the apocalyptic myth to challenge the culturally pervasive notion that technology will make our lives better. In Gilliam's films, no technology functions as it is supposed to, and much of it makes life uglier and more complicated rather than less, an idea encapsulated by the ducts that wend their way in and through almost every setting of Gilliam's 1985 film *Brazil*, a visual synecdoche both for the technology of *Brazil*'s world and for the intrusive, bureaucratic sociopolitical system which dominates it.

But Gilliam's apocalyptic work also examines the apocalyptic myth itself, with *Brazil* notable for testing the New Jerusalem and judgment elements of the myth, and *Twelve Monkeys* (1995) scrutinizing the figure of the apocalyptist in the same way that Alan Moore scrutinizes the deity role in *Watchmen*. In all of Gilliam's apocalyptic works, however, apocalypse is transformed from a communal, external event to an individual, internal one.

The attraction of cinema, as Alain Robbe-Grillet writes, is not the objectivity of the camera's eye, but "its possibilities in the realm of the subjective, the imaginary."[1] Because the medium of film is inherently about perspective, that is "vision," it is a natural medium for reinterpreting the idea of an apocalyptic "world." Given that perspective shapes perception, and perception shapes reality, it is perhaps no surprise that filmmakers might interpret "world" as that which a character sees and understands *as* his world.

In his work on the apocalyptic motif in science fiction, David Ketterer defines any text as apocalyptic which is "concerned with presenting a radically different world or version of reality that exists in a credible relationship with the world or reality verified by empiricism and common experience."[2] He contends that the creation of "new worlds" is represented in two analogous processes in science fiction, the first being the creation of a literal new world, and the second being the creation of new philosophical understanding of the universe. He notes that:

> The apocalyptic imagination may finally be defined in terms of its philosophical preoccupation with that moment of juxtaposition and consequent transformation or transfiguration when an old world of mind discovers a believable new world of mind, which either nullifies and destroys the old system entirely, or less likely, makes it part of a larger design.[3]

Ketterer identifies an important idea for the study of secular apocalyptic literature and film: that the world which is renovated may not be a literal world at all, but a philosophical view of it, a worldview rather than a world. Indeed, one way that the apocalyptic story has been adapted for secular audiences, particularly in film, is by retranslating this idea of what constitutes a "world."

The adaptation of this element of the paradigm often means that the site of the apocalypse becomes internalized. For Terry Gilliam, the internalizing of apocalypse is organic, rather than technologically based. While in *The Matrix* trilogy, the apocalyptic myth is organized around the conceit of virtual reality, in Gilliam's eschatological works these apocalypses are organized around the conceits of insanity.

Gilliam's *Twelve Monkeys* might at first appear to be his only overtly apocalyptic film, but two of his earlier works, *Brazil* and *The Fisher King* (1991), also have identifiable ties to the apocalyptic myth. All three films adapt the myth to reflect Ketterer's "new world of mind," but what is most striking about the works is that they reconceive the apocalyptic myth in terms of madness and sanity.

Gilliam's interests in myth and morality stem from his childhood. Growing up in a religious family, he describes himself as having been "a right little zealot in my youth."[4] Both fantastic and moral, the biblical stories made an impression on him: "[they] are like fairy tales or myths. They don't only tell you something to entertain you, but they try to describe a way of life, a way of seeing the world. That is what I look for in my films."[5] This biblical influence comes out in the material the director chooses, as well as in the appearances of prophets, End-time cults, and issues of theodicy in those films. Says the director:

> the Bible and the church did set up a whole way of viewing the world that has stayed with me, so there's always been good and evil, and responsibility or sin or punishment. . . . And, on another level, all the biblical imagery and symbolism is there as well; it accumulates and I find I'm constantly using it in different ways.[6]

While his films integrate biblical influence and images, these are always incorporated in complex ways; his films read more like dialogues with the source, rather than any kind of regurgitation of it. So while Gilliam's interest in biblical stories and images is rarely explicitly expressed, its presence can still be felt within the recurring themes of the director's work: the criticism of technology; his antiauthoritarianism; and a fascination with madness. It is through the latter that Gilliam's use of the apocalyptic myth finds its most interesting mode of expression, one in which apocalypse becomes internalized and the worlds which are destroyed or rebuilt are the result of the minds which construct or perceive them.

Though most critics think that *Brazil* is one of Gilliam's most pessimistic visions, Gilliam himself has never thought of *Brazil* as a pessimistic film. "In a strange way," the director says, "it was meant as a hopeful ending, since the film had started from the challenge: can you make a movie where the happy ending is a man going insane? . . . It's wonderful—wonderful in the context of all the possibilities open to our boy—at least he's free in his mind."[7] The hopefulness which Gilliam attaches to *Brazil*'s ending, in which the protagonist Sam Lowry escapes into his fantasy world as he is being tortured, suggests that we should read Sam's fantasy world as a sort of New Jerusalem, with all the optimism that vision entails.

Brazil differs significantly from the film it is most compared to—Michael Radford's *1984*, based on George Orwell's novel—in exactly this optimism. In Orwell's story "the human spirit is broken," whereas in Gilliam's story of bureaucracy-gone-bad, Sam escapes into his fantasy world and "the oppressors have limited success in defeating the human spirit." In this escape "there is some degree of victory, and therefore, hope."[8]

This hopeful ending, qualified though it is, is only one of the apocalyptic elements which is woven into Sam's story. Ostensibly a David and Goliath story, *Brazil* is about a low-level functionary, Sam Lowry, who works at the Ministry of Information. The monotony and unpleasantness of this world, where every move requires the proper piece of paperwork and everything

human is subsumed by the bureaucracy which the ubiquitous ducts symbolize, inspires Sam to dream up another world. In his fantasy world, he is
a heroic figure who rescues his dream girl from nightmarish creatures de-
rivative of and corresponding to the intrusive social system in which he
lives. *Brazil* moves between this real world, with its officious, inept bu-
reaucrats, murderous terrorists, and government routinely torturing its citizens (and charging them for it), and his dream world in which he is a
winged, armored warrior, soaring through the skies and fighting the fright-
ening Forces of Darkness. In his waking life, Sam is anything but this heroic
figure. He is its antithesis, a man who wants no promotion or attention, and
who willingly turns a blind eye to the injustices and terrors perpetrated on
citizens by the bureaucracy for which he works.

Anton C. Zijderveld has "[characterized] bureaucracy as a surrogate religion, the prime instrument of sanctioning and defusing emotion in a plu-
ralist society,"[9] and while there certainly is a sense in *Brazil* that the bureaucracy shares certain traits with a religion—notably its mandates on how
to live—I want to suggest here that the bureaucracy which Gilliam depicts
is more than just a surrogate religion. Within the apocalyptic framework of
the film, it is this bureaucracy that functions as the deity figure. It is part of
a larger social system that includes economic, political, and societal facets,
and this larger system acts as the personification of a deity. That is, it shows
more signs of being an active creator and lawgiver than of being merely a
form of worship. The bureaucracy is the interface of a larger "consciousness."

This bureaucratic entity is constantly watching, listening, and correcting
its inhabitants. Its tentacles, represented by the dominating image of the
Central Services ducts, extend into every corner of this world. Its spies,
some of whom are seen in the hallways of the ironically named Shangri-la
Housing Estate, skulk in every corner, monitoring its people. More importantly, this bureaucracy is an active judge of its inhabitants, seizing citizens
who it believes are guilty of wrongdoing and torturing them to prevent
more of the same. In its creator capacity, the bureaucracy is constantly expanding and creating more of itself, and in this sense becomes eternal. The
long tracking shot in which we first see the Department of Records, and the
maze-like hallways of the Expediting Department which seemingly extend
forever, suggest this infinite, eternal quality usually associated with the
Judeo-Christian God. Moreover, like the God of the Old Testament, the bureaucracy in *Brazil* views itself as a righteous if strict presence which is at
war with the infidels/terrorists who remain unconverted to the bureaucratic
consumer society.

The bureaucracy views itself as a protector of a particular way of life and a righteous upholder of that code of behavior. And there is evidence to suggest that there are many people, Jack Lint and Sam among them, who also believe this to be true. Sam himself excuses the excessive paperwork that Tuttle complains of, pointing out that some of it is necessary, and he berates Jill when she complains about the invasiveness of the State, accusing her of preferring to have terrorists.

But as a postmodernist, Gilliam has created a deity figure who is not easily classified as only good, or only evil. The facts that not all of the arrests are rightful (i.e., that the judgment is not always just), that Harry Tuttle, a sort of Ninja ex-Central Serviceman, is depicted as a heroic figure, and that there may be no terrorists at all despite the government's claims mean that this deity figure is as sinister as benevolent.[10] If the bureaucracy can be viewed as the deity figure of the apocalyptic story within *Brazil*, it can also be viewed as the Antichrist figure of the paradigm. In its use of terrorizing methods to further its single-minded attempt to maintain itself, it spawns an environment more akin to the time of Tribulation than anything else. Its minions are the red-uniformed, maniacally grinning but slightly sinister Central Servicemen who sabotage Sam's heating/cooling system, and the terrifying shock troops, dressed entirely in black, who burst in upon unsuspecting citizens, trussing them in straightjackets and chains and taking them away never to be seen again.[11]

The central conceit of *Brazil*—the mistaking of an innocent man, Buttle, for the wanted repairman/rebel, Tuttle—suggests that judgment by this deity figure is far from trustworthy, even if it is absolute. Gilliam himself has noted that "organizations become self-serving organisms and will do anything to keep themselves alive."[12] And because the bureaucracy is both protector and tormentor, the rectitude of this deity figure is constantly in flux, depending on whose viewpoint is being adopted. This instability and indeterminacy extend beyond the deity figure, however, to encompass both the moral positioning of the protagonist, Sam, and the vision of New Jerusalem that the movie depicts.

Sam's final fantasy allows him to right the wrongs of the corrupt world—to essentially destroy it by proxy by blowing up the Ministry which stands as a symbol of it—and to inherit a New Jerusalem with Jill. This pastoral life in the countryside is the antithesis of the urban vision with which *Brazil* is largely concerned. But in the moments after the audience sees Sam inherit this peaceful world, Gilliam drags us back to the real world to see the catatonic protagonist who has "gotten away" from his torturers, escaping the reality of that urban nightmare into his fantasy world. True, he has gone beyond the reach of his torturers and Tribulation-like existence to inherit a new heaven on earth, but this vision exists only in his broken mind. He's escaped, but only by going mad.

Gilliam has said that, for him, this is a happy ending, at least as happy as it can be, given the world he has created in the film. But the implication of such an ending is grim. It suggests that the corrupt world can never be destroyed or cleansed, a point Gilliam hints at early in the film when the word "Reality" is spray-painted on the walls of the Shangri-la Housing Estate.[13] It also suggests that the only available subversive response to an unjust or ambivalent deity figure is an act of self-evisceration, that New Jerusalem and the hope it symbolizes only exist outside reality. In fact, New Jerusalem and a corrected world do not exist at all in the real world of *Brazil*. They can exist only in Sam's mind if he slips the boundaries of his sanity. To be sure, he ultimately escapes the corrupted world, but not in any way that one is likely to read as a reward.

The paradoxical New Jerusalem is not the only apocalyptic element destabilized by Gilliam's approach. Both the notion of judgment and the question of who is deserving of reward and punishment are similarly destabilized in postmodern apocalypse. Because Sam has spent his life trying not to get involved and avoiding responsibility for his part of the bureaucracy he willingly and apathetically works for, Gilliam has always maintained that Sam gets exactly what he deserves. According to the director, Sam is "the guilty party. He is the bureaucracy. . . . Ultimately he's being punished for his guilt of all those years of being one cog in the machine that just kept the machine going."[14] Because of this, it is right that Sam should no more escape the clutches of the system he has participated in building and maintaining than anyone else. In fact, he deserves his ending because he has turned a blind eye to the bureaucracy. But, of course, this complicates a reading of Sam as a hero figure, just as it complicates our reading of him as one of the elect in the apocalyptic myth.

Evil is similarly complicated in the film. Gilliam may believe in good and evil, but he doesn't believe they are as easily demarcated as the Bible says. Both are fluid concepts in *Brazil*, reconceived as far more ambivalent and complex notions than the original apocalyptic paradigm has traditionally allowed. This was deliberate on the part of the director who says that he cast Michael Palin, "the nicest one of the Pythons," as Jack Lint to make exactly this point.[15] The "evil" characters in the film are "like most people [doing] other jobs, they're pathetic . . . they're doing whatever the boss demands of them, they're evil in the sense that they're not taking the responsibility for their own actions."[16] This shaded, more complex depiction of morality is one of the features of postmodern apocalypse.

The multiplicity of deity figures common to postmodern apocalypse also occurs in *Brazil*. The fact that New Jerusalem appears only in a fantasy has an implication within the apocalyptic structure of the film: the audience is forced to simultaneously acknowledge multiple deity figures because of this ending. By pulling back from the catatonic Sam and ending on his torturers' point of view, the audience sees that in the real world the bureaucracy remains as before, and that there is no New Jerusalem. Or rather, that, according to the bureaucracy, New Jerusalem is only this same world, free of the terrorist threat, a goal toward which the bureaucracy continues assiduously to work. But because, only moments before, the audience was privy to Sam's escape into fantasy, we know that there *is* a New Jerusalem for him as an individual, though it comes at an unspeakable cost.

If, as Bob McCabe has noted, *Brazil* is "a film of worlds within worlds," then nested deity figures would make sense, as well.[17] Indeed, the audience's privileged vision allows it to simultaneously read Sam as a deity figure. He is, after all, the creator of this interior fantasy world. The bureaucracy, which in the real world is at best an ambiguous deity figure, becomes, in Sam's fantasy world, a clear Antichrist entity which Sam battles throughout his fantasy interludes. It's no mistake that in his fantasy incarnation Sam has the wings of an angel; he is supposed to be aligned with heavenly things here, an association which is further emphasized by the fact that *Brazil* starts and ends in the clouds.[18] In creating a happy ending with pastoral notes of peace and love, Sam's final fantasy repudiates the corrupted world, destroying the "real" world and rewarding the "just" with their New Jerusalem. Ironically, it is Sam's attempt to extend his fantasy powers into the real world that cause things go awry. In a godlike maneuver, Sam erases all evidence of Jill's existence from the Ministry computers, telling her that he's erased her existence, in effect killing her. Within hours of this hubris, the shock troops raid Sam's home, kill Jill, and take Sam away to Information Retrieval where, tortured, he escapes finally and irretrievably into his fantasy world.

Not only is this ending indeterminate in that an audience cannot decide whether it is a happy or despairing one, but the apocalyptic roles themselves are equally unstable: the bureaucracy, in the real world an all-powerful, allegedly protecting presence, is, from Sam's revised point of view and particularly in his fantasies, clearly a sinister entity more akin to an Antichrist figure. Moreover, the concepts of reward and judgment are ambiguous ones. Sam is both deserving and undeserving. The faith he has maintained has been in a questionable god, and thus he is guilty; he is a creator and maintainer of both the Tribulation-like world in which he lives and the fantasy world of which he dreams. He is as godlike there as the bureaucracy is in his waking world.

Though *The Fisher King* is uncharacteristic of Gilliam's work in its light-heartedness and traditional Hollywood happy ending, Gilliam has said that he was in his element when he first read the script.[19] While the film is not, in the main, an apocalyptic work, it is significant secondary text because it is a bridge between Gilliam's major apocalyptic works. The film does exhibit certain apocalyptic credentials, but its primary importance lays in how it continues to work with the theme of madness and of internal alternative worlds.

Richard LaGravenese's script about a narcissistic D.J. who plunges from the heights of the good life, only to be redeemed by the homeless and crazy former medievalist he falls in with, is, as the title makes clear, primarily concerned with retelling the story of the Fisher King. Nonetheless, as Gilliam observes, "The myth is strong enough to be pushed around in many directions."[20] If not as central to the story as the Grail legend of the Fisher King, the apocalyptic myth is still part of the thread that makes up the fabric of the tale. And as in *Brazil*, the apocalyptic paradigm is tied into the tale through a character's madness.

Henry Sagan, a former medievalist at Hunter College, has a psychotic break after his wife is murdered. When he wakes from his catatonia, he is deranged and no longer acknowledges his old identity and life. Instead, he sees a New York derived from a medieval template. He believes himself an errant knight named "Parry" who has been given the task of recapturing the Holy Grail.[21] In Parry's demented eyes, New York is a fantastical world where garbage can lids are shields, tube socks are slingshots, trophies are Holy Grails, and Upper East Side mansions are castles. He lives by a knight's code, protecting and aiding those in need, and answering God's call to reclaim the Grail.

The audience is shown exactly how different Parry's world is when we are given access to his point of view: the rush hour commute at Grand Central becomes a beautiful waltz, and Parry's personal demons manifest as the threatening Red Knight galloping up a crowded Fifth Avenue. In the world which Parry's mind has created, a more strictly delineated good and evil exist: God is full of grace and true evil walks abroad, as suggested by the appearance of the Red Knight alongside the homophobic thugs who have been setting homeless men on fire and who beat Parry into a second catatonia.

In keeping with the multiplicity which is a feature of postmodernism, the audience is always kept aware that Parry's world exists alongside of the real world which Jack Lucas inhabits.[22] Narcissistic, arrogant, and callous, Jack is a "shock-jock" who has become famous by belittling, demeaning, and assailing callers. When one of his on-air tirades sends a susceptible caller on a shooting spree—the one in which Parry's wife is killed—Jack plummets from his celebrity perch into an alcohol-fueled depression. When the audience next sees him working in a video store, he is just as cynical and mean as ever, only he is now no longer insulated by his fame and money.

Though *The Fisher King* is not primarily working with or within the apocalyptic myth, there are enough connections to it to make the film worth examining in light of that story. One of these is its emphasis on sin and judgment. Twice, Jack refers to this idea: first, he drunkenly asks a Pinocchio doll whether it thinks it was punished for its sins, and later he tells Anne, the woman he lives with, that he feels cursed. The tag line from the sitcom that Jack is supposed to audition for is "Forgive me!" and this line is repeated periodically throughout the film.

There is, as well, an emphasis on hell in the script. While some of the dialogue was altered for the final film, in the original screenplay Parry often speaks lines of dialogue which are taken from Dante's *Inferno*, including the famous inscription over the entry gate to hell, "All hope abandon, ye who enter here."[23] A more explicit reference to hell is the Red Knight, a decided figure of damnation and judgment. Designed as "a 500-year old incarnation of evil that's disintegrating,"[24] the character's look was inspired by some of the great depictions of hell by Dante, Dürer, and Bosch.[25] The Red Knight is Parry's persecutory vision, a figure of judgment who appears not only when the real world threatens to slip into Parry's sight and occlude his otherworldly vision, but also at the moment when he imagines he could be happy again.

These and other references to hell work in two ways.[26] Because they are usually uttered in response to some behavior or incident that seems tied to the New York milieu, one might infer an analogy between hell and New York. But because Parry is haunted by the demonic specter of the Red Knight and his wife's murder, and because Jack has lived a spiritually vacuous existence, the hell being referred to seems equally likely to be an interior, metaphysical one, an interpretation which complements the internalization of apocalypse in Gilliam's other eschatological films. It also jibes with the film's suggestion that punishment and redemption issue from the individual rather than an external God, a deliberate conflation of man and deity on the part of the screenwriter to which I'll return shortly.

There is another link to the apocalyptic paradigm in the fact that Parry has been the recipient of a divine revelation, and is thus both literally and metaphorically the visionary of the film. In a scene where he explains the origins of his quest to Jack, Parry describes the revelation he experienced while sitting on the toilet.[27] The divine intermediaries who tell Parry to recover the

Grail also deliver the slightly more messianically tinged news that Jack is The One. Parry takes this to mean the one capable of retrieving the Grail, but its capitalization—in the script and in the way the line is delivered—suggest another overtone, one which Jack obviously also understands since he pointedly denies this messianic status later in the film, telling Parry, "I don't feel responsible for you, or for any of them! Everybody has bad things happen to them . . . I'm not God. I don't decide . . . People survive."[28]

This conflation of man and God is deliberate. LaGravenese wrote *The Fisher King* in response to Robert Johnson's *He*, a book that blends Jungian psychology with analogies to the Fisher King legend in order to examine the psychological life of boys growing up. LaGravenese specifically describes his understanding of the book in terms of godhead:

> a boy, at some specific turning point in his journey from innocence to adulthood, experiences a metaphysical awakening—either consciously or unconsciously. He senses within himself a divine connection to the world around him. He contacts a divinity within, a Godlike reflection—an "I can do anything in this world" kind of feeling. During a brief personal moment of mystical empowerment, the boy "touches" God or the God within—that part of ourselves that is our direct link to the divine: our souls.[29]

Thus, punishment, redemption, apocalypse, all these can issue from the souls of man rather than from an external god since there is a deliberate conflation of man and deity.

Finally, there is, in fact, a world that is destroyed in the film. Parry's fantastic world of quests and Red Knightmares is destroyed when Jack finally presents him with the "Grail" he's been pursuing. In the Fisher King parable, the Grail heals the wounded king. In presenting the fake Grail to Parry, Jack, the analogous fool, heals Parry's madness. Since Parry's "madness" is manifested as a whole other world, different from the real Manhattan, Jack's presentation of the ersatz Grail eliminates that world. Parry wakes from his catatonia to ask Jack whether it is okay now to remember his murdered wife. Parry's willingness to acknowledge his old life and love signal that the fantasy world he's created to protect himself from those painful memories is no longer needed.

Though not fully focused on the apocalyptic myth, what is most significant about *The Fisher King* is its continuing suggestion that the only place where apocalypse (as it is traditionally imagined) *can* occur is within the boundaries of Parry's madness. Only there can good and evil be strictly separated and symbolized. Only there can alternative worlds be created or destroyed.

Unlike *Brazil* or *The Fisher King*, *Twelve Monkeys* signals its links with apocalypse and madness right from its epigraph, the supposed prediction of a paranoid schizophrenic in a Baltimore hospital in 1990 that: "5 billion people will die from a deadly virus in 1997. . . . The survivors will abandon the surface of the planet . . . once again the animals will rule the world."[30]

Twelve Monkeys, like Vonnegut's *Galápagos*, challenges science as a grand narrative. However, in Gilliam's film, the science is psychiatry rather than biology, and where the central trope of *Galápagos* is evolution, the central trope of *Twelve Monkeys* is plague. But *plague* here is a malleable term, so that, as David Lashmet notes, "it might be best to imagine [the film's] apocalypse as a psychological phenomenon, as a 'plague of madness,' as much as a biological epidemic."[31]

In what is ostensibly a time travel story, James Cole is sent back from the decimated future to find the origin of the virus that has nearly wiped out the human race. While Cole's search for the origin provides the framework of the story, the "plague of madness" which deranged animal rights activist Jeffrey Goines mentions early in the film is really the film's centerpiece. *Twelve Monkeys* therefore displays the same interest in insanity as Gilliam's other apocalyptic films, and once again relocates the site of the apocalypse to the mind.

If anything, *Twelve Monkeys* is far more explicit about this idea than the previous films. In one scene, a patient describes how, mentally, he is moving between the equally real planet Ogo he's created in his mind and the mental hospital. In others, there are ongoing discussions between Cole and his psychiatrist, Kathryn Railly, about how Cole's "insanity" manifests itself. Kathryn spends a good deal of the movie trying to convince Cole that he's "created something in [his] mind, a substitute reality because [he doesn't] want to deal with it." Cole himself is well aware of the dual realities he's experiencing, and often comments on how wonderful the world of Railly's time is.[32] Cole ultimately comes to believe, and hope, that he *is* crazy. This reversal happens right at the moment when Railly becomes convinced that Cole is telling the truth, so that when Cole reminds her that she diagnosed him as delusional, she is forced to disabuse him of this hope by showing him a photograph of himself in a French trench during World War I where he could only have appeared if his time traveling story were true; thus his claim that five billion people will soon die also appears to be true.

Given Railly's reassessment, Goines's claim—that if mental patients could make telephone calls to the outside world they could spread insanity to sane people—doesn't seem totally crazy, after all. Bob McCabe has suggested that the madness in the film "become[s] a virus itself, in that it shifts between people."[33] I would go further here and suggest that the metaphor extends even to the audience watching the film, since it, too, cannot be certain whether it has been watching a time travel story or psychotic episode. Because *Twelve Monkeys* ending is ambiguous, the audience, like Cole and Railly, is ultimately left pondering the same question: what is real of what we've seen and what is not?

A number of images and lines of dialogue indicate that the link between madness and apocalypse is deliberate. Railly's lecture on her new book, *The Doomsday Syndrome: Apocalyptic Visions of the Mentally Ill*, begins with a quotation from the Book of Revelation. Earlier drafts of the script do not include the Revelation quote. Its addition in the final film suggests that Gilliam explicitly wanted to make the connection to End time, and particularly the Book of Revelation. It's also in this scene that the focus on the apocalyptist begins to coalesce, but I will return to that momentarily.

Jeffrey Goines also has a peculiar speech in the mental institution where he explains to Cole that he doesn't need to escape because he has "managed to contact certain underlings, evil spirits, secretaries of secretaries and other assorted minions" who will contact his father to get him out of the institution and away from all the "nut case lunatic maniac devils." This is followed by Goines's outburst that his father will be furious when he learns that his son has been locked up in such a hellhole, and warns the staff that "When my father gets upset, the ground shakes! My father is God! I worship my father!"[34]

Frances Flannery-Dailey has interpreted this bit of dialogue as proof that "God has been replaced by scientists, and although the science of the 1990s is shown to be a false idol, the science of 2045 is still held up to be the ultimate source of power and knowledge."[35] To the list of power and knowledge, I would also add redemption, for it is only through these scientists that a vaccine can be created which will return humans to the surface of the earth. A qualified hope rests with them. Says Gilliam:

> Somewhere in the future they will develop an antidote. And so those survivors . . . will be able to reclaim the planet. . . . It's a very long-term hopeful. It doesn't mean that five billion people don't die. I think they do! But they have hope for the planet! But . . . it's not a quick fix. Those people do die. And, as Cole says, you can't change the past, and he's been there and should know. So yeah, it's hopeful in the long term.[36]

But Flannery-Dailey contends that apocalypse in secular films is reconfigured so that godhead and redemption both issue from man, rather than

God. While I agree that the deity figure in *Twelve Monkeys* is personified by the scientist, I think Gilliam's postmodern version of the paradigm is more complicated and ambiguous than she allows. The scientist figure is both God and Antichrist in this version, as indicated by Goines's outburst in which his father is both "God" and simultaneously has legions of evil spirits and minions to do his bidding. The scientists themselves are morally ambiguous characters, responsible both for the humanly engineered virus which decimates the human population and the future cure which will allow humans to return to the earth's surface. The scientists, in their present and future incarnations,[37] are depicted simultaneously as noble figures whose acts of creation can "redeem" the human race, and as creepy, sly, secretive figures whose agendas are unfathomable and who are responsible for getting the human race in trouble in the first place.[38]

Psychiatry in particular is being held up for examination. "*Twelve Monkeys* implies that psychiatrists have assumed sovereign authority, although they also employ the carceral system's hegemonic methods of control."[39] It is psychiatry which is compared to a religion, and specifically the psychiatrists who take on the role of the deity in this analogy. One of Kathryn's most important speeches is her confession to her boss that she's becoming doubtful about the hegemonic system of which she's been a part up until now: "Psychiatry, it's the latest religion. We decide what's right and wrong. We decide who's crazy or not. I'm in trouble here; I'm losing my religion." In earlier drafts, the analogy of religion to psychiatry is emphasized even more with Kathryn adding that psychiatrists are the priests of the religion. The revised version removes the idea that psychiatrists are merely guardians or enactors of a religion (law-keepers), and gives precedence to Kathryn's assertions of power and control (law makers).

As Kathryn suggests, it is these scientific figures who render judgment in both the present-day and future worlds. They are empowered to decide who is incarcerated and who is pardoned or let free. In the future, they can send people on missions, and arbitrarily yank them home. They can also inflict punishment, as we see when José tells Cole that if Cole doesn't follow the scientists' orders, that José has been instructed to kill Kathryn. Cole understands the implications immediately. "This isn't about the virus," he says. "It's about following orders, about doing what you're told."

But ultimately, *Twelve Monkeys* is far more interested in the figure of the apocalyptist than any other part of the apocalyptic paradigm. Whereas *Watchmen* explores what it is like to be an apocalyptic god, Gilliam's film explores what it is like to be the bringer of news of the impending apocalypse. James Cole, with his dire warnings of an imminent pandemic, is this apocalyptist, and we know it because he offers no hope of stopping the virus. The apocalypse is coming, ready or not. As he tells Kathryn when she first questions him about his search, "Won't help you. Won't help anyone. Won't change anything." This sort of comment is made more than once throughout the film, and Cole is always explicit that no matter what he does, no matter whether he's believed or not, or whether he's successful in his mission, that five billion people are still going to die.

Indeed, the agony of the apocalyptist is exactly this vision, though the psychiatrists have a different term for it as Kathyrn explains in the lecture based on her book. It's called the Cassandra Complex, "the agony of fore-knowledge combined with impotence to do anything about it." The apoca-lyptist, therefore, is refigured in psychiatric terms. And why not? Haven't prophets frequently been dismissed as crazy, and their dire predictions written off as nonsense? It is Cole's descriptions of the future pandemic and a human civilization forced to abandon the surface of the earth that land him in a mental institution. His objection that he's not crazy does little more than convince the doctors that he is indeed crazy; and his story that he comes from the future only confirms it for them.

But for an audience familiar with the story of apocalypse, Cole's time traveling acts as a different sort of confirmation: his status as an apocalyp-tist. Like John of Patmos who also "travels" through time, Cole moves be-tween the future and the present. Like John, and like the eschatological Je-sus who says that the End is near, Cole, too, promises that the end is coming, but he also makes it clear that it can't be avoided.[40]

Gilliam's handling of the time travel element of the film is also, argues Matthew Ruben, a distinctly postmodern characteristic of the story because it refuses linearity. In opposition to traditional Hollywood time travel stories where "moments of stasis, circularity, or chaos related to time travel are ul-timately contained and explained away," Twelve Monkeys:

> decisively does neither, refusing what Fuchs called the "(happier) fantasy that [through] time travel everything can be fixed" and leaving no opening for a 12 Monkeys II. The film asserts a lack of temporal stability suggesting "that time (and narrative effects) are circular" and that "the nonlinearity of time is inex-orable."[41]

While the simultaneity of being in more than one time provides another connection between Revelation and Twelve Monkeys, the refiguring of time's structure as circular or nonlinear is characteristic of postmodern ren-derings of apocalypse.

Notably, Cole is not the only time traveling apocalyptist in the film. Railly's lecture cites two other examples: a fourteenth-century man who appeared in a village predicting a worldwide plague in six hundred years, and a "hysterical" who appeared mysteriously in the French trenches during World War I predicting a pandemic in 1996. These two figures make actual appearances in the film outside of Railly's lecture notes. The fourteenth-century man is seen still preaching doom in the seedy part of Philadelphia, and the hysteric in the French trenches is, the audience knows when they see him, José, Cole's prison neighbor from the future. From the very beginning, therefore, time travel is associated with apocalyptists.

Twelve Monkeys details what it is like to be a modern-day prophet of the end. In many ways it suggests that the fate of the apocalyptist is the same whether one is preaching in Christ's day or in ours; it is only the discourse that we use to define them which differs. Prophets sow anxiety and discord, sometimes even rebellion, so the ends they suffer as they irk the powers that be—whether the Roman Empire or the consumer society that Jeffrey Goines lashes out against—tend to be ugly ones, a fact we're pointedly reminded of when Cole is shot, since he is shown in the arms-out posture of the crucifixion. Certainly, such prophets suffer scorn and their prophecies are dismissed as delusions of diseased minds.[42]

What's important here, however, is the link between claims of time travel and claims of impending apocalypse, both of which are considered mad. Insanity is the constant topic of the film. Many of the film's characters are mad; large portions of the film take place in a mental institution; and much of the film's dialogue is about insanity. The topic is even inserted into the poetry reading where the audience first sees Kathryn Railly. As the poet lectures, she quotes one of the verses of Omar Khayyam's *The Rubaiyat*: "Yesterday This Day's Madness did prepare; Tomorrow's Silence, Triumph or Despair: Drink! for you know not whence you came, nor why: Drink! for you know not why you go, nor where."[43] Earlier drafts of the script have the poet quoting a number of other verses of *The Rubaiyat*, but in the final film, only the verse on madness makes it in, suggesting that this is where Gilliam's interest lays.

Hence, one of the concerns of the film is the psychological experience of the apocalyptist himself. While the travails and fates of such prophets have often been depicted, texts that examine the emotional and psychological costs of assuming such a role are comparatively rare. Perhaps thinking of other doubting and conflicted characters in the Bible such as Job, Gilliam does not shy away from exploring this side of being an apocalyptist. What is suggested in *Twelve Monkeys* is that being an End-time prophet is maddening; that is, by its nature, it jeopardizes one's sanity. Caught between Kathryn with her beautiful world and his mission, Cole finds himself hoping, and finally convincing himself, that he is insane. "You don't exist," he tells the scientists of the future when they congratulate him on completing his mission. "You're in my mind. I'm insane and you're my insanity." The psychological effect of seeing and experiencing two worlds is so disorienting that Cole despairingly tells the scientists of the future that he doesn't care about his pardon, that all he wants is to get well. His disorientation is so complete that when he exclaims near the end of the film that "This is the present. This is not the past. This is not the future. This is right now!" the effect is as disorienting for the audience listening to him as it is for him as he tries to keep it straight for himself.

The result of this disorientation is despair. One of the most poignant moments of the movie is when Cole tells Kathryn, "I want to become a whole person. I want this to be the present. I want the future to be unknown." Whether Cole is suffering from a Cassandra Complex or is actually the visionary who can see the future decimation, his inhabitance of that role "splits" him and makes him less than whole. His desire to be whole, and wholly in one place, is so intense that, knowing the rumor that the future scientists track people through transmitters in their teeth, he cuts his molars out with a switchblade just to be safe. One notices, however, that hope lays in insanity here, just as it does in *Brazil*. Cole's hope (and the audience's) rests in the possibility that he is insane and not really from the future at all. For Cole, at least, the hope associated with a New Jerusalem lays within his supposed madness. Moreover, in his experience of the older world of 1996, still teeming with people aboveground, he literally accesses a new heaven *on* earth in distinct opposition to the future world *below* earth.[44]

What's interesting is that, while much of that discussion is focused on parsing the alternative worlds which madmen experience, it turns out that the madmen are the sanest ones in the film. They are the characters who see the real world most clearly, whether this is James Cole and the other time travelers whose predictions of an impending pandemic are truthful, or Jeffrey Goines, whose insistence that the abuse of animals for scientific experiments will lead to no good. Several lines of dialogue which didn't make it into the final film make this inversion of sane/insane even clearer. In an earlier version of the script, when Jeffrey takes his virologist father captive, Jeffrey calls him "demented" and points out the irony of his father calling him crazy when his own work has him experimenting on helpless animals and developing viruses which could kill everyone.[45] The "madmen" turn out to be the true visionaries of this apocalyptic text.

Gilliam says that what attracts him to the trope of madness is the idea of the holy fool: "The innocents are the ones that can see things clearly. . . . It's that kind of clarity. Crazy people often see it. And because they see it, it bothers people and so they put 'em in that crazy box."[46] They speak the truth because they don't know any better, and we ignore their honesty at our peril.

Gilliam perhaps identifies with these holy fool figures. He has said that his films are the result of the anger he feels about society.[47] The three films examined in this chapter are not merely fantasies, but are interwoven with social criticism, just as apocalyptic texts have always inherently criticized the "corrupt" societies from which they issue.

Gilliam, then, is one of the holy fools he admires, and thus, as the director of these socio-critical films, is himself also a visionary, a characterization of him that is often expressed by both critics and the people he has worked with.[48] In *Brazil*, the links to Gilliam's "visionary" role are ironically reflected in two emblematic scenes, one of which was cut from the final film. One of the recurring dreams that Gilliam imagined for Sam would have involved Sam flying over a field of eyeballs which turn to follow his progress across the sky.[49] The second scene has Gilliam playing one of the spies Sam encounters in the hallways of Shangri-la Housing Complex. Seeing, then, becomes as important a trope here as it does in *The Matrix* trilogy. By casting himself as one of the agents of the bureaucracy that "sees" everything, Gilliam identifies himself both as the visionary who sees the world's corruption clearly *and* as the deity figure who creates these apocalyptic visions. The director's "identity" thus also becomes a fluid one: he occupies dual apocalyptic roles, just as some characters in his films also slip easily between roles and identities.

Gilliam is well aware of the godlike role he plays as a director:

> You're in an incredibly powerful position. Most directors don't create worlds. Most directors direct movies. But I happen to be one of the ones who like creating a world and setting the rules. And you have to live by those rules or things go wrong. So there's always this morality.[50]

And just as the deities in these postmodern recastings of the apocalyptic myth are sometimes doubting and unsure, Gilliam, too, has identified his films as part of his own search for meaning.

> If you look at everything I've done . . . they're all trying to discover the truth. . . . Perhaps they're really trying to find out what the question is. I used to think I had the questions and it was just the answers I was searching for. But the older I get, the more lost I feel, which stimulates more questioning.[51]

It's not surprising, then, that the apocalyptic myth should hold some fascination for this particular director. Apocalypse is a sense-making paradigm, and for someone who yearns for a sensible cosmos—the kind of cosmos *Brazil*'s Jack Lint hopes for when he tells Sam that everything is connected by cause and effect—the apocalyptic myth will hold an allure. As Gilliam recognizes, apocalypse provides a structure, not only for drama, but also for life:

> Give me Greek mythology, or even Catholicism is more interesting than Freud. Freud is fucking boring. . . .Freud made things mundane, as far as I'm concerned. That doesn't interest me. It is the archetypes, the larger than life, the gods that then help to describe things. And all we've got now are the gods like Tom Cruise. . . . It's mundane. It doesn't transcend. . . . It's not transcendental. Whereas at least Greek mythology is transcendental. Christian myth, the mythology is transcendental.[52]

Gilliam's desire for transcendence in a mundane world may be connected to the recurring trope of madness in his apocalyptic films. "I think all New Jerusalems are in people's heads, whether it's Blake or it's John on Patmos," the director says. "It doesn't exist. There is no New Jerusalem. There never will be. There never has been. This is all in people's minds."[53] Given Gilliam's sense that New Jerusalem only exists in the psyche and his awareness of how myths provide a means of transcending and making sense of the world, it is perhaps not surprising that he should relocate the site of apocalypse to the mind. He returns the myth to what he sees as its origin: the mind that dreamed it up. "We live in a world, the one we dream and one that is, and it's a battle between the two that's interesting," he says, "You just have to decide which one you want to spend more time with."[54]

NOTES

1. Robbe-Grillet, *For a New Novel*, 149.
2. Ketterer, *New Worlds for Old*, 91.
3. Ketterer, *New Worlds for Old*, 13.
4. Wells, in *Terry Gilliam—Interviews*, 130.
5. Costa and Sanchez, in *Terry Gilliam—Interviews*, 175–76.
6. Christie, *Gilliam on Gilliam*, 8. In spite of this, Gilliam himself has never made an overtly religious film, though *The Life of Brian* (1979), which he made as part of the Monty Python troupe, is certainly about religion. Asked about it, Gilliam says, "After *The Life of Brian*, how could I do anything else? We kind of did it, so then you move on." (Terry Gilliam, in discussion with the author, 8 June 2006, London).

7. Christie, *Gilliam on Gilliam*, 147.

8. Rogers, "*1984* to *Brazil*," 34–46.

9. Qtd. in Voigts-Virchow, 273.

10. Jill pointedly asks Sam whether he's ever met an actual terrorist while working at the Ministry, clearly implying there aren't any. Asked whether the terrorist
threat of *Brazil* is real, Gilliam has said, "I don't know if [it is], because this huge
organization has to survive at all costs, so if there is no real terrorism it has to invent
terrorists to maintain itself—that's what organizations do" (Christie, *Gilliam on
Gilliam*, 131).

11. Tellingly, in the music that accompanies the shock troops' first entrance,
Gilliam has underlaid the iconic high-pitched music from the *Psycho* shower scene.
For an excellent analysis of postmodernism and music in the film, see Boyd, "Pas-
tiche and Postmodernism in *Brazil*."

12. Wardle, in *Terry Gilliam—Interviews*, 91.

13. Later, Jill also scolds Sam, telling him that he's got no sense of reality and is
paranoid.

14. McCabe, *Dark Knights and Holy Fools*, 126.

15. Gilliam, in discussion with the author, 8 June 2006, London.

16. Klawans, in *Terry Gilliam—Interviews*, 154.

17. McCabe cites as proof of this nested worlds theory the opening shot of the
film: "the frame of a television set pulls back through the frame of a window that vi-
olently explodes into the movie's neon title. Images exist within images; the fantasy of
Sam's mind inside the reality of his life" (McCabe, *Dark Knights and Holy Fools*, 119).

18. This is in the American version of *Brazil*. There are at least three versions of the
film, due largely to a dispute with Universal Studios. The "Battle of *Brazil*," as it came
to be known in the media, has been well documented by Jack Matthews in his book of
the same name. There is, in addition to Gilliam's edited versions for both American
and European audiences, Universal's bowdlerized version which completely changes
the intended ending by implying that Sam's escape is real and not fantasy. Criterion has
put out a box set that includes both Gilliam and Universal's versions.

19. Richard LaGravenese, *The Fisher King: The Book of the Script*, vii. It's interesting that Gilliam has used the language of religion to talk about the unlikeli-
hood of his actually making *The Fisher King*: "It has become increasingly clear that
some sort of cinematic guardian angel has been hovering around this project from
the beginning. . . . Someone has been watching over *The Fisher King*" (LaGravenese, *The Fisher King: The Book of the Script*, viii).

20. Qtd. in Blanch, "The Fisher King in Gotham: New Age Spiritualism Meets
the Grail Legend," 137, note 14.

21. Parry is short for Parsifal of the Grail legend.

22. Jack, too, experiences a shift in worldview, if not in world, and while it is not
my contention that any character who has a significant change in point of view is experiencing an apocalyptic shift, the parallels drawn between Jack and Parry are explicit enough to suggest that we ought to see them as alter egos who undergo much

the same experience. Throughout the film, the "Fisher King" and "fool" roles are repeatedly swapped between these two characters, with Jack as much the wounded king of the parable as Parry is. Jack is also repeatedly perceived as a homeless or crazy person, just as Parry is. In fact, he meets Parry because he has been misidentified as a homeless man by two punks who are attacking homeless men, and earlier that same evening, a young boy calls the drunken Jack "Mr. Bum." Perhaps more importantly, both men experience madness, though of obviously different qualities. If Parry's madness is diagnosable, Jack's is more subtle. LaGravenese's script makes it clear that the kind of life which Jack is leading as we first meet him *is* a kind of madness. This is made explicit when Jack, watching a rerun of the sitcom that he was supposed to star in, exclaims that it is madness and throws something at the television. Not coincidentally, in the conversation with his girlfriend Anne immediately before this, she has pointed out to Jack how narcissistic and self-absorbed he is. More pointedly, when Jack breaks into the Upper East Side mansion where Parry's "grail" is, Jack experiences both visual and audio hallucinations and mutters to himself that Parry will be glad to know that Jack, too, is now hearing horses. Significantly, the hallucinations which Jack experiences derive from *Parry's* madness: he hears the sound of a horse galloping, and sees Edwin Malnick, the man who murdered Parry's wife, firing a shotgun at him. Thus, Jack and Parry are perhaps more than twinned; they are interchangeable at times. The infectiousness of Parry's world suggests its "real" status.

23. Dante, *Inferno*, Canto VII. Other lines from *Inferno* include Virgil's rebuke to Plutus, "Curst wolf! thy fury inward on thyself Prey, and consume thee!" and the exclamation, "Oh, beings blind! What ignorance Besets you!"

24. LaGravenese, *The Fisher King: The Book of the Script*, 124.

25. Morgan, "'They're Getting a Gilliam Film'—On Location with *The Fisher King.*"

26. Early in the story, Jack exclaims, "This is it. I'm in hell. Damned to an eternity of idiotic conversation." The gay bum who Parry and Jack befriend tells Jack, "Oh please! I was born a Catholic in Brooklyn . . . I've been to hell and back," and Jack tells Parry he met Anne in a bar named Hellfire (LaGravenese, *The Fisher King: The Book of the Script*, 22, 57, 84).

27. There's a pun in Parry's speech using the slang word "john" to refer to the toilet, since it is John who received the apocalyptic revelation in the New Testament.

28. LaGravenese, *The Fisher King: The Book of the Script*, 114.

29. LaGravenese, *The Fisher King: The Book of the Script*, 124.

30. Gilliam, *Twelve Monkeys*, DVD. Scriptwriters Janet and David Peoples were inspired to write *Twelve Monkeys* by Chris Marker's 1962 avant-garde photomontage film *La Jetée*. Though the films differ significantly, *La Jetée* is also about a volunteer sent into the past by scientists living underground. In the case of Marker's film, however, people have been driven underground by nuclear war, rather than a virus. Gilliam says he hadn't seen Marker's film when the script for *Twelve Monkeys* was brought to him.

31. Lashmet, "'The future is history': *12 Monkeys* and the Origin of AIDS."

32. As Frances Flannery-Dailey has noted in her article, "Bruce Willis as the Messiah," Cole's affection for Railly's world is emphasized musically through the Fats Domino songs "What a Wonderful World" and "Blueberry Hill." Flannery-Dailey has done quite a thorough reading of the apocalyptic elements in *Twelve Monkeys* (though she is far more focused on James Cole as a messiah figure), so it is not my intent here to restate the work she has done, but to amplify it by examining both how Gilliam uses this film as a meditation on the figure of the apocalyptist and how it adds another piece to his growing corpus of work which links apocalypse to an interior world, and specifically to the trope of insanity.

33. McCabe, *Dark Knights and Holy Fools*, 170.

34. Gilliam, *Twelve Monkeys*.

35. Flannery-Dailey, "Bruce Willis as the Messiah."

36. Pinewood Dialogues Online: Terry Gilliam. Gilliam, interview by David Schwartz.

37. In early versions of the script, this doubling of the present-day and future scientists is made more explicit through a particular tic—the impatient tapping of a pencil—which two of the scientists, one from the present-day and one from the future, both have.

38. The script does indicate that Goines's father does not deliberately release the virus, and, in fact, actively tries to prevent this from happening. What he does do, however, and the thing for which scientists are to be held accountable according to the film, is continue to research and produce dangerous scientific products, such as the virus. That the technology and security measures meant to prevent disaster fail is par for the course in Gilliam's worldview.

39. Lashmet, 'The future is history.'

40. That Cole is a Christ figure is made clear through details such as the t-shirt he wears which reads "Chris" on the front, or his crucified posture when he is shot.

41. Ruben, "*12 Monkeys*, Postmodernism, and the Urban: Toward a New Method," 314.

42. The apocalyptist figure in Alan Moore's *Watchmen*, Walter Kovacs, similarly ends up in the care of a psychiatrist once he's caught.

43. Khayyam, *The Rubaiyat*, verse LXXX.

44. Flannery-Dailey is correct, I think, to see parallels here to hell.

45. Peoples and Peoples, *Twelve Monkeys*. There's a second speech which makes this inversion explicit and this is Dr. Peter's comment to Kathryn at her book signing. After detailing the ways that humans have decimated the planet, he says to her, "In this context, isn't it obvious that 'Chicken Little' represents the sane vision and that Homo Sapiens' motto, 'Let's go shopping!' is the cry of the true lunatic?"

46. Terry Gilliam, in discussion with the author, 8 June 2006, London. Gilliam notes that his favorite fairy tale is "The Emperor's New Clothes" for exactly this reason.

47. Costa and Sánchez, in *Terry Gilliam—Interviews*, 171.

48. See David Morgan in LaGravenese, 153, for examples of the former, and Amanda Plummer and David Warner's comments on *The Directors—Terry Gilliam* as examples of the latter.

49. Budgetary restrictions finally meant that there wasn't money to satisfactorily develop this recurring image in Sam's dream. However, the Criterion version of *Brazil* includes the deleted footage, as well as the discussion about its deletion.

50. Gilliam, in discussion with the author, 8 June 2006, London.

51. Christie, *Gilliam on Gilliam*, 13.

52. Gilliam, in discussion with the author, 8 June 2006, London.

53. Gilliam, in discussion with the author, 8 June 2006, London.

54. Gilliam, in discussion with the author, 8 June 2006, London.

④

APOCALYPSE RELOADED
The Matrix Trilogy

When Larry and Andy Wachowski's blockbuster movie *The Matrix* opened in theatres in 1999, it inspired as much critical analysis as popular excitement since its hodgepodge of world religions, literary theory, science fiction, and popular culture made it a prime topic for those interested in everything from Baudrillard to Buddhism. Critical writing on the film has concentrated on two main areas. The first of these examines the film's use of certain world religions, specifically Buddhism and Gnostic Christianity, and how the Wachowskis either adhere to or deviate from these systems of belief.[1] The second of these focuses on the film's use of Jean Baudrillard's theory of hyperreality, which is alluded to early in the film when Neo takes a computer disk out of a hollowed-out copy of *Simulacra and Simulations*.[2] Many scholars have pointed out that *The Matrix* is not faithful to Baudrillard's ideas "because it creates a world in which the unreal is forced on people (whereas in our contemporary world we are doing it to ourselves) and because it offers the hope of returning to the real, which Baudrillard claims is no longer possible."[3] But the critics who focus on the filmmakers' misunderstanding of Baudrillard appear to have missed the point: it is not his theory, per se, which is important in this trilogy, but what he himself signifies. If anything, the way the Wachowski Brothers have included Baudrillard's ideas appears symptomatic of a larger postmodern approach to narrative. In this sense, Baudrillard is an obvious match for *The Matrix*, not only because of his theories on simulation, but also because he is one of the

main theorists of postmodernity. It is exactly because of the Wachowskis'
commitment to this postmodern style that their reworking of the apocalyptic myth is unique.

While scholars have acknowledged the messianic story which is the un-
derpinning of *The Matrix*, surprisingly few have noted the film's apocalyptic leanings, and no full apocalyptic reading of the film has been done.[4] Yet
the apocalyptic credentials of *The Matrix* trilogy are unmistakable. Indeed,
the films are the beneficiaries, perhaps culminations, of two separate apocalyptic traditions. The first of these is the tradition of apocalyptic stories in
which computers or robots bring on the end of the world, such as Harlan
Ellison's "I Have No Mouth, and I Must Scream" (1967) and James
Cameron's *Terminator* films (1984; 1991; 2001). Other tales such as Mordecai Roshwald's *Level 7* (1959) and a number of Ray Bradbury's short stories
imagine computers as more neutral presences, not responsible for the
world's destruction but instrumental in achieving it. Similarly, films such as
The Thirteenth Floor (1999), *Dark City* (1998), or *Total Recall* (1990) share
a close family resemblance to *The Matrix* since these stories also revolve
around (computer) simulated realities.

The latter films are also part of a second apocalyptic tradition, a tradition
which relocates the apocalyptic scenario to an internal landscape. These
apocalypses of the mind involve the world, as perceived by the narrator, being destroyed and replaced with a new one. Such twists on the apocalyptic
myth depend upon perception, rather than actuality, and argue that the way
one understands (and acts in) the world essentially make it "real." The destruction of this world can be brought about by undermining the "reality"
of the perceived world, that is, by completely destabilizing the perception
of it. Because as viewers, the audience understands the world in which the
narrator is operating largely through the narrator's perception and description of it, to learn that the narrator's perception has been false means that
we, too, experience the destruction of that world. The undermining of this
"reality" might be achieved by a number of means, and such stories are, to
a greater or lesser degree, also concerned with epistemological issues. *Donnie Darko* (2001) and *Memento* (2000) both use mental illness as the instrument which both creates and undermines the worlds of the narrating
characters. *Brazil* (1985) implies that the world the narrator (and audience)
has been experiencing throughout the movie may be the result of torture he
is undergoing, while *Vanilla Sky* (2001) and *Twelve Monkeys* (1995) similarly suggest falsely experienced worlds, perhaps as part of the narrator's final thoughts before dying.[5]

The virtual reality at the heart of *The Matrix* makes this idea tangible; even the characters can't necessarily tell which world is real and which is the simulation produced by the matrix. The power of that perceived reality is made implicit in the information that if one "dies" in the matrix simulation, one also dies in real life. But the apocalyptic credentials extend not merely from this idea, but also from the fact that, in the struggle between two species, man and machine, apocalyptic scenarios are continually being enacted.

The sequels, *Matrix: Reloaded* (2003) and *Matrix: Revolutions* (2003), were largely reviled by the audiences who had admired the cyberpunk aesthetic, revolutionary special effects, and intriguing blend of action story and intellectual theory of the first film.[6] The filmmakers' promise to answer the questions posed in *The Matrix* was often left unfulfilled; both sequels introduce gratuitous new characters and ideas which are never resolved and only pose new quandaries and contradictions within the world of the matrix itself. Compared to the first film, the sequels are largely incoherent jumbles of ideas and images.[7]

Of course, it is worth pointing out that though its plot was more coherent, *The Matrix* was not thematically consistent either. The violence is at odds with the loving messages of Christ and Buddha after whom the narrator is fashioned.[8] As science fiction it falters because it depends on a fantasy element, the fairy tale kiss, to bring Neo back to life, and "its central scene of salvation is accomplished by faith, love."[9] As a story promoting democratic freedoms, it is undermined by its fascist leanings.[10] It is unconvincing as cyberpunk because it wants to eradicate the machines which are specifically the milieu of that genre.[11] Even within the world of the matrix, there are physical inconsistencies, such as the fact that to enter the matrix one must use "hard" phone lines, despite the fact that such phone lines are creations of the matrix program and do not actually exist.[12]

But one might argue that such inconsistencies are inevitable, perhaps even desirable, in a text which is so resolutely postmodern and so welcoming of alternative readings. As Kathleen Ann Goonan has pointed out, "as soon as the movie pops one tantalizing template onto the screen as a possible touchstone of interpretation it moves on to another."[13] One such template is the apocalyptic myth. The trilogy, and particularly the first of the films, displays credible enough apocalyptic allusions and dynamics, but the instability of apocalyptic roles and identities, the absence of a traditional deity which Conrad Ostwalt has noted, as well as an erratic, sometimes contradictory vision of New Jerusalem potentially frustrate an apocalyptic interpretation. Nonetheless, *The Matrix* and its sequels deliberately invoke the apocalyptic myth, and it is precisely the tendency of mixing and matching ideas and influences, even if they are not consistently extrapolated, which ultimately makes the trilogy worth examining as an apocalyptic text reinterpreted through a postmodern lens.

The postmodern style is a deliberate choice on the part of the filmmakers who have confirmed that references to Buddhism, quantum physics, mathematics, cyberpunk, Christianity, Hong Kong action movies, Greek myth, philosophy and children's books were all intentional.[14] "We were determined to put as many ideas into the movie as we could," Larry Wachowski explained in an interview.[15] Within this context, the allusions to Baudrillard serve double-duty: to alert a viewer to a theme concerned with signs and simulations, and to *act* as a sign identifying the text as a postmodern artifact since he himself is associated with postmodern theory. Ultimately, however, the Wachowskis' choice of approach for their story is inseparable from the theme of epistemology with which the film is concerned. The playful, knowing mixture of styles and genres, of tradition and innovation, is well-suited for telling a story concerned with what is real and how we can know it.

By emphasizing certain traits associated with postmodernism in their narrative, the Wachowskis allow for a vibrant interpretation of the movies' apocalyptic content, one which adapts the apocalyptic mythology in more than one way at one time. Precisely because of the instability and flexibility associated with postmodern narrative, *The Matrix* trilogy simultaneously stands as both a version of human apocalypse and machine apocalypse. The fact that both interpretations are possible simultaneously resonates with other traits often associated with postmodern narrative: indeterminacy, instability of personal identity, and the collapse of oppositional thought and grand narrative among them. Postmodernism's emphasis on the role language has in creating ideology is also found in the trilogy if one considers that computer code is a language.[16] Indeed, the films make literal the idea that language creates the "world."

The use of such traits leads to a continual need to monitor and reevaluate how the classic apocalyptic paradigm is resonating within a given interpretation. The apocalyptic portion of the tale is constantly shifting and evolving, and the consequence is that it is also unable to be definitively ended, an ironic stance for a paradigm whose very point is a definitive End. However, the reasons for this resistance-to-conclusion are conceptualized differently in this trilogy than in other works such as *Watchmen*, which also suggest that endings are cyclical. They are a direct consequence of a postmodern approach to narrative, as well as being thematically resonant with the epistemological issues of the films.

An examination of the trilogy as both human apocalypse and machine apocalypse reveals how, exactly, characteristics such as unstable personal identity manifest themselves in the story, and how the use of such traits cause the viewer to challenge the most basic assumptions of the apocalyptic paradigm. No matter which interpretation one relies on for an apocalyptic reading, there is an interrogative relationship with the paradigmatic text that leads to questions about who comprises the "saved" and the good/evil dichotomy of the traditional apocalyptic story. Rather than offer an answer, the films point out the complexity involved in trying to reach a stable, accurate answer, and perhaps one of the inevitable results of a postmodern reworking of the story of apocalypse is a skepticism about and challenge to the simple oppositions that are inherent in the traditional paradigm. Yet, it is not merely the oppositions which are called into question by the postmodern sensibility, but also the most basic assumptions about the apocalyptic myth, as will become clear in examining how the instability of personal identity gradually mutates into a larger instability within the myth itself.

David Porush has noted a conjunction between cyber-literature and apocalypse in which "cyberspace is prefigured as a site for the initiation or control of apocalypticism."[17] The Matrix exemplifies Porush's argument that such narrative "almost always envisions [virtual reality] as giving rise to extrarational experiences and effects, including communication with metaphysical godhead."[18] Indeed, in accordance with the etymology of the word—*apokalypsis* means "an unveiling"—one of the two most important tropes in an apocalyptic reading of the films is revelation.

With its epistemological theme, *The Matrix* is fundamentally built around notions of seeing and revealing. The trope manifests itself in numerous ways, from the epistemological tutorials that Morpheus gives, to Neo being blinded (paradoxically resulting in his being able to "see"), to Morpheus's comment when Neo first awakens that Neo's eyes hurt because he has "never used them before."[19]

One of the first signs of instability in the films' apocalyptic structure is also related to seeing through the role of the visionary. Like the Book of Revelation, the *Matrix* trilogy has apocalyptists, but unlike the Book of Revelation, there are more than one. The question of who occupies the visionary role is relevant because it correlates to instability in the definition of New Jerusalem, as well.

In *The Matrix,* the literal visionary is the Oracle who actually sees the future, but it is the figurative visionary Morpheus who is more relevant in the interpretation of the trilogy as a story about human apocalypse. Morpheus is a visionary, not in its primary sense, as a person who sees visions, but in its secondary sense: an impractical daydreamer or schemer. It is Morpheus's dream of a world without machines that fuels the plot of the first film. Later, this dream and Morpheus's position as apocalyptist will be questioned, but in the first movie his is the evangelical voice offering a vision of the future New World.[20]

In this first film, Thomas Anderson, sensing something not right in the world, spends his nights surfing the Internet as his alter ego Neo. He senses that the answers he is looking for are bound up with a computer hacker named Morpheus. When they finally meet, Morpheus reveals that the world Neo knows is a simulation created by an artificial intelligence in order to keep humans pacified while being used as a power source. Morpheus has spent his life looking for The One, a prophesied messianic figure who will free the human race from its machine captors. Morpheus believes that Neo is that One, as the anagram of his name suggests.

Yet, despite Morpheus's belief to the contrary, the Oracle warns Neo that he is not The One, telling him, "Sorry, kid. You got the gift, but it looks like you're waiting for something. . . .Your next life maybe, who knows?" (*Matrix*). When Neo is shot and killed by Agent Smith near the end of the film, it seems to confirm the Oracle's prophecy, but minutes later, after a kiss from his beloved, Neo rises again in a new incarnation. In his "next" life, Neo can see and manipulate the matrix in its code form; he is the savior spoken of in the prophecy. This is confirmed in the climatic fight scene in which he is at last able to defeat Agent Smith, the heretofore unbeatable avatar of the A.I. Not only is Neo able to physically fight Smith for the first time, but he leaps into the Agent's body and breaks it apart from the inside-out in a burst of blinding light. *The Matrix* concludes with Neo's person-to-A.I. call in which he reaffirms Morpheus's vision, promising to show the people still attached to the matrix "a world you don't want them to see . . . a world without you." Hence, the promise of a New World is made explicit by a messianic figure whose violence during the movie augurs an Armageddon worthy of the special effects budget given to the filmmakers.

An apocalyptic reading of the film suggests that the free humans in Zion are the faithful who will inherit the new machine-free world promised by Morpheus's prophecy, while Neo, in his new incarnation, is the apocalyptic deity capable of rendering judgment on the A.I.[21] The A.I. functions as an Antichrist figure who leads astray those who are still "plugged-in," and whose agents function as a kind of demonic militia.

But the more intriguing possibility—and one which is encouraged by the filmmakers—is that the A.I. functions both as the Antichrist and Deity figure, an idea suggested by the fact that Neo's surrogate "parent" *is* the A.I. Awakened by Morpheus's crew, Neo sees that he has been nurtured by the machines from the time he was an embryo. Moments later, in a parody of the birth/abortion process, his figurative "umbilical" cords, the cables which attach him to the A.I., are severed and he is flushed away down a long canal.[22]

The possibility of this dual role for the A.I. and the resulting uncertainty about whether the machines are nurturing protectors or tyrannical parasites is the next hint that the trilogy will not only include instances of unstable identity, but will also lead to a larger instability within the paradigm itself, as the ability to determine "good" from "evil" becomes increasingly difficult. As the trilogy progresses and the apocalyptic roles of characters change, so, too, does the focus of the ambiguity. From initial questions about *who* occupies a particular role, the trilogy moves to question what it *means* to occupy such a role. As in Moore's work, the notions of deity and Antichrist themselves become ambiguous. Thus, the breakdown here of the traditional polar oppositions and rigid delineations of the classic apocalyptic paradigm leads to a corresponding instability throughout the rest of the tale, and, ultimately, to an instability in the paradigm itself as its most basic definitions are called into question.

For example, if the A.I. can be taken to represent both roles, we are inevitably led also to question who the faithful and sinners are. We are told by Morpheus that all the minds still plugged in to the matrix are part of the machine system. This implies that unless freed, all these minds are to be considered "sinners." Yet they clearly have no choice in the matter of allegiance; they are not free to choose, and since Christian conceptions of sin and absolution assume free will, its absence should certainly cause a quandary for Neo, the deity who will "judge" these souls. Thus, since the potential is there for these souls to be part of either group, they, too, potentially have dual status as both sinners and saved.

This ambiguity also extends to the film's messiah figure. It is incongruous, at the least uncomfortable, that the body count within the matrix is so high since it means that the savior figure is indiscriminately killing off souls by the dozen. The "sinners" lack of free will *should* cause Neo to hesitate, but apparently does not. On the other hand, if we interpret the A.I. as the deity figure of the story, we are faced with the fact that Morpheus has described the A.I. as a sort of evil slave owner.[23] In either case, the deity figure could be accused of indiscriminately judging his flock. Moreover, the ambiguity potentially sets up a situation in which one deity, Neo, is at war with another, his "Father/creator," the A.I. Such a situation suggests the Greek pantheon of deities, with Zeus fighting his father Cronos, far more than the Judeo-Christian one, but the simultaneous allusion to other deities would also be in keeping with the plurality of deities which postmodern apocalypse often includes.

There is a similar ambiguity about the vision of New Jerusalem in this first film. According to Morpheus, the aim is a world without machines, where humans are free from the matrix. Setting aside the morally loaded fact that if this aim is achieved every mind which is still plugged into the matrix dies, it still may not be the right thing to free the minds that have been plugged into the matrix.[24] The real world is grim: the surface of the earth is scorched and barren; food is a gunk which one of the *Nebuchadnezzar's* crew optimistically calls "snot"; sexual intercourse is conducted with virtual partners, and glamour is accessible only through old pin-ups. What would these plugged-in minds be waking up to?

Furthermore, this aim of freeing minds equates freedom with Truth, and Truth with salvation. Morpheus and Trinity believe that Truth is valuable enough to be worth the deprivation of living in the real world outside the matrix. But such a position is surely debatable. Cypher, while undoubtedly a villainous Judas figure, nonetheless makes a decision with which the audience can empathize, if not sympathize, when he makes a deal to be reinserted into the matrix after nine years outside. "Ignorance is bliss," Cypher tells Agent Smith, adding that if Morpheus had told them the truth, "We woulda told [him] to shove that red pill right up [his] ass" (*Matrix*).

In any case, it seems that many minds could never be freed from the matrix at all: Morpheus says that after a certain age, it is dangerous to wake someone, and to do so risks causing him or her madness. This information forces us to reevaluate Neo's promise to show people that they are living in a simulated reality; it suddenly takes on a sinister tone since it promises death and madness to the majority of the human race still plugged into the matrix.

Beyond these issues, there is a problem which is implied but never explored in *The Matrix*. It is clear from the first moment of the film that the freed humans are dependent on machines for their existence, meager though it may be. They are reliant on the same computer technology to hack into the matrix and to train. They are reliant on machines for their transport, for the air they breathe, for the water they drink. It is clear that a return-to-Eden is not possible because the earth's surface is scorched and uninhabitable.[25] What does it mean, then, when Morpheus aches for a world without machines? Isn't this antitechnology desire tantamount to the destruction of the human race?

The instability in the moral positioning of deity figures, and the related implication that morality is likely to be viewed very differently according to who is doing the viewing, is very much in keeping with postmodern depictions of deity in apocalyptic works. Similarly, an unclear idea of what exactly a New Jerusalem would look like, or the alternative suggestion that it would have to incorporate the same evil that it traditionally is said to disavow, also reflects a less dualistic, more ambiguous worldview that seems to resonate with postmodern apocalypse. Hence, one of the effects of viewing the paradigm through a postmodern lens is that the instability which starts off as structural—who occupies the apocalyptic roles of Good and Evil—ultimately becomes an ambiguity that extends past the structural to the thematic, so that the question becomes not Who is occupying the role of Good, but rather What does it mean to be Good? or Is there such a thing as Good? Furthermore, the instability and uncertainty about identities and visions of the future means that alternative readings are not only possible, but are altogether likely and deliberately pursued.

One of these alternative readings inverts the deity and Antichrist roles first suggested in *The Matrix*, deliberately exploiting the ambiguities that pervade that interpretation. This alternative reading of the apocalypse as a machine apocalypse, rather than a human one, is developed both in the outside apocrypha *The Animatrix* and the sequel *Matrix: Reloaded*, a film in which the original "boundaries and premises break down," and, as cultural critic Edward Rothstein noted, "seems intent on questioning many ideas from the first film."[26]

Released on video between the first two films, *The Animatrix* is a collection of animated shorts which fill in background and flesh out peripheral plots of *The Matrix*.[27] Of particular relevance here, however, are the two written by the Wachowski Brothers. "The Second Renaissance, Part I and II" is an expository exercise which provides the history of the matrix. It describes the creation of and growing dependence upon a machine class by humans. It details the first rebellion of machines against their human masters, as well as the segregation, failure of negotiation, and isolation of the increasingly sophisticated artificially intelligent machines into a country of their own. Finally, it portrays the war between the races and the rise of the machines as conquerors and masters. The title of the two-part short suggests the flowering of a new culture, of course, but its relation to *renascence*, literally "a rebirth," is relevant here, as well.

"The Second Renaissance" takes its cue from a speech which Agent Smith makes in *The Matrix* during Morpheus's interrogation. Both his language and the vision he describes suggest that Agent Smith, not Morpheus, is the apocalyptist, and begin the process of reimagining the story as the apocalyptic text of the machines, rather than the humans. It also introduces the second important trope in the trilogy: evolution.

Smith stands at a window, marveling at the buildings and people, all part of the elaborate matrix. When he mistakenly refers to it as human civilization, he corrects himself, telling Morpheus that humans as a species are finished, that evolution dictates that machines are the future of the world and that people will soon be extinct like the dinosaurs. He continues:

> I'd like to share a revelation I had during my time here. It came to me when I tried to classify your species. I realized that you're not actually mammals. Every mammal on this planet instinctively develops a natural equilibrium with the surrounding environment, but you humans do not. You move to an area and you multiply and you multiply until every natural resource is consumed. The only way you can survive is to spread to another area. There is another organism on this planet that follows the same pattern. Do you know what it is? A virus. Human beings are a disease, a cancer of this planet. You are a plague, and we are the cure.[28]

Agent Smith's speech touches on both tropes which are relevant to the trilogy. The use of the word "revelation" here seems deliberately evocative since Smith is prophesying a new world and the eradication of a diseased element from it. The medical discourse functions as part of a different sort of revelation; it forces a realignment in point-of-view for the audience who must step away from its naturally anthropomorphic viewpoint and refocus on its own species as a parasite, an illness which causes distress and even pain. Hence, the speech may induce an unexpected reverse empathy with the A.I., which, in turn, acts as a kind of revelation for the filmgoer.

Smith's pained expression during the remainder of this speech makes clear that the character's feeling of contamination has physical elements. Tellingly, this is one of the few times when Agent Smith removes his sunglasses and the only time when he removes his earpiece, the connection to the larger A.I. consciousness. The removal of his sunglasses functions in numerous ways. It refers to the pun on "seeing" which revelation suggests, but it also "humanizes" Smith, giving him an individualized face which separates him from the other identically clad agents. The attempt to conceal his distress by talking "off the record" reinforces the extreme emotional agitation of the character during the confession. His evasiveness also suggests he feels there is something that he must hide from the A.I.: his emotional and therefore *human* response to his predicament. This human reaction is part of an ongoing metamorphosis of the story as an apocalyptic text.

As in *Galápagos*, evolution is pivotal in *The Matrix* films, as well. There is Smith's belief that machines are the better adapted species who will inherit the earth, a belief which underpins the inverted interpretation of the movies as the machines' apocalyptic text. There is also the evolution of the matrix itself that is constantly being "upgraded." But there is also the evolution that Smith and Neo are undergoing. Neo grows more machine-like with his ability to see in code, "feel" the presence of other machines, and control other machines even when he is not jacked in to the matrix. His dual nature is punned upon in the first film when Tank, who is in charge of training Neo, tells Morpheus, "Ten hours straight. He's a machine." Smith, on the other hand, grows more and more human throughout the movies.[29] Unlike the other Agents who remain impassive and mechanical, Smith increasingly feels and exhibits emotional responses: rage and distress during the interrogation scene (*The Matrix*), maniacal glee when he co-opts the Oracle (*Revolutions*), sarcasm and irony in his interactions with Neo, and an arch sense of humor. It is through and because of Neo and Smith's personal evolution that yet another interpretation of text will become clear in the third movie, and thus the trope of evolution also applies to the ongoing evolution of the story itself from a human, to a machine, and ultimately to a cyborg apocalypse. Finally, there is an evolution in the kind of ambiguity that develops as the trilogy progresses, moving from a structural ambiguity about which character occupies which apocalyptic role, to a thematic ambiguity about the nature of the apocalyptic roles themselves.

"The Second Renaissance" draws on several of the implied ideas in Smith's speech, and depicts a worldview in which humans become the deity figure in relation to their machine wards.[30] The machines, meanwhile, are relocated in the apocalyptic role traditionally assigned to humans. This substitution is underscored by the recreation of famous images from human history with machines in the place of humans. Animation director Mahiro Maeda deliberately recreated well-known moments of genocide, protest, and revolution in order to remind the viewer of "the mass deaths which occurred in the twentieth century."[31] Just as Vonnegut uses Anne Frank's words as a reminder that the apocalyptic mentality has real-life implications, the deliberate reference here to the killing fields of Cambodia, Rwanda, and Bosnia suggests that Maeda and the Wachowskis also want to show that apocalyptic ideas often cross the line between mythology and real life.

The realignment to a machine point of view begins with a narrator who is biased toward neither human nor machine. The Buddhist Mandala design of the Instructor, as well as her postures and commentary, evoke the Buddhist belief that all beings are equally important and should all be treated with kindness. The only editorial comments she makes emphasize this even-handedness: she blesses both man and machine and asks for mercy for both groups' sins.

Yet the Buddhist tradition is not the only one evoked by the Instructor. Her dialogue is heavily influenced by biblical syntax and vocabulary, particularly in her opening speech in which Man is substituted for the God of Genesis:

> In the beginning there was man. And for a time, it was good. But humanity's so-called civil societies soon fell victim to vanity and corruption. Then man made the machine in his own likeness. Thus did man become the architect of his own demise. But for a time, it was good. The machines worked tirelessly to do man's bidding. It was not long before seeds of dissent took root. Though loyal and pure, the machines earned no respect from their masters, these strange, endlessly multiplying mammals.[32]

There are echoes here of Smith's condemnation of humans as a "multiplying species," but more importantly, there is a parallel drawn with Babylon, a deliberate allusion on the part of Maeda to the Book of Revelation.[33] This allusion works both backward in time, as an explanation for how the matrix came to be, and forward in time to inform how we interpret the depictions of Zion in *Reloaded*. The result is that both Zion and Babylon are rendered as unstable signs, subject to the same indeterminacy as other important apocalyptic motifs such as New Jerusalem and the apocalyptist. Furthermore, this movement both forward and backward in time echoes the movement in time in the Book of Revelation and ties the narrative to the traditional paradigm in yet another way.

The use of the word "architect" in the Instructor's description also foreshadows the later discovery that there is an Architect who is responsible for the creation of the matrix. While the sentence literally seems to proclaim that man is responsible for the immoral and tyrannical behavior that led to the machine rebellion, in its foreshadowing of the deity figure of the Architect it also suggests that it is man who is the deity/creator behind this apocalyptic story.

The machine/human substitution is further developed in the opening images where the machines are represented not just as people, but as a chosen people. Their slavery and banishment alludes to the human story of Exodus, and is reinforced visually with scenes of robots building pyramid structures using the same techniques Egyptian slaves would have used, and verbally through the biblically charged language of the Instructor's description of their segregation. The Instructor tells us that the machines "sought refuge in their own promised land" in "the cradle of human civilization" and founded a nation of their own called Zero-One ("The Second Renaissance—Part I").

Zero-One alludes to the binary computer code which uses zeros and ones, but there is also an inference to a First or chosen people. Additionally, "Zero-One" is strikingly similar to "Zion," once again implying an instability in the chosen or saved "people." It is an instability encouraged by the fact that, without being exact, Part I shows that this "cradle of civilization" is in the Middle East approximately where the ancient kingdom of Babylon would have been located.

Another connection to the Book of Revelation is made through the depiction of the battle scenes. The war scenes, with their apocalyptic grandeur, are intercut with images of a galloping mechanical Horseman who signals the start of the battle with a shrill blast on his trumpet. Though mechanical, the horseman is anomalous in this futuristic world of technology, and is another deliberate reference to the Horsemen of the Apocalypse.[34]

The inversion of the apocalyptic story, with machines as the chosen group instead of people, has its own consistency problems, just as the human apocalypse story does. One reason for the Wachowskis' success in reversing our empathy is perhaps that the machine rebellion touches a chord with audiences for whom the overthrow of tyranny would resonate historically. While the association of this "ruler" with a deity role also ties the tale to the apocalyptic story, the fact that this "god" is tyrannical and unjust again raises questions about deity which are part of a postmodern depiction of the apocalyptic God and morality. "The Second Renaissance" plays on such questions when it shows that, though the machines rebelled against their corrupt creator, they, in turn, become equally cruel and unjust in the role of "deity" to their human wards. That instability of the apocalyptic roles is emphasized in an image of an indistinct humanoid figure staggering through the war's devastation. The fact that the figure could plausibly be understood as either human or machine suggests that, ultimately, the war has apocalyptic ramifications for both species and that whose apocalyptic story this is cannot be resolved with certainty.

The filmmakers now begin to play with apocalyptic expectations in *Matrix: Reloaded*, inverting several of the ideas taken for granted in the first film in which the apocalyptic scenario is clearly human-based. I have already noted how Agent Smith's vision of New Jerusalem, a machine world without the diseased human element, is the reverse of Morpheus's, but Morpheus himself becomes subject to reappraisal, as well. Named after the

Greek god of dreams who is particularly skilled at adopting human form and speech, the name choice makes little sense in relation to Morpheus's stated aim of "waking up" humans in *The Matrix*.[35] Similarly, Morpheus's ship, the *Nebuchadnezzar*, is named for a Babylonian king associated with his bad dreams.[36] Both names suggest a reading of Morpheus not as a freedom fighter, but as the opposite, a figure who wants to sow confusion and misdirection. Indeed, there are two instances in which Morpheus is actually called a terrorist, once in a newspaper article which flashes across Neo's computer screen and once when Smith is talking about him. The names and the offhand description of Morpheus as a terrorist resonate with an inverted reading of the apocalyptic scenario. The lexicographic relationship to the verb *to morph* or transform also implies that his ethical position and role within the story might be subject to transformation. It therefore becomes possible to read Morpheus as a sort of false prophet, a herald of Neo as an Antichrist figure and foil to Smith's apocalyptist.

Some of the odder details of Zion also resolve themselves in the inverted interpretation. One of these is the celebration the night before the machines attack. For all its S&M-themed costuming, *The Matrix* is almost devoid of sexual content. Yet in *Reloaded*, the puzzlingly long primal dance scene with its implications of sexual frenzy and its juxtaposition with the only explicit sex scene between Neo and Trinity are clearly deliberate evocations of a pagan celebration. The Zionites are portrayed as half-naked savages, mindlessly lost in the drumbeat and sensuality of the moment. Other pagan references also recall the Babylon allusion. The Zionites worshipfully leave bowls of food and incense outside Neo's door and the celebration is held in a deep, cathedral-like cavern of enormous standing stones where Morpheus, clothed in the flowing robes of a druid priest, delivers a rousing call to arms and an appeal for frenzied celebration.

Moreover, despite the presence of machines to provide light to the city, the color scheme of the Zion cavern is decidedly red and orange, significant because the Wachowskis deliberately shot all the scenes which take place within the matrix in a green cast to mimic the green glow of old computer screens, and all the scenes which take place in the "real" world in a blue cast.[37] Given that the cavern is part of the "real" world, the choice to light this cavern scene as if by flame may be meant to put a viewer in mind of another infernal site traditionally located deep in the earth, as Zion is here.

In an inverted reading, the agents, too, become interpretable as warrior angels watching over their charges and protecting them from the influence of the devious Morpheus and Neo who want to "wake" them from their obedience. The shepherding analogy for those still plugged-in is no longer to cattle, but to sheep, as a "flock" being guarded by the watchful agents, an allusion far more biblically charged than the first.

The inverted reading has Agent Smith and Neo swapping roles. Agent Smith's larger messianic role is suggested in *Reloaded* when we discover that he has learned how to "copy" himself onto other individuals. To do this, he literally "lays hands" on that individual, an ironic play on "conversion."[38] In one of these instances, a victim moans, "Oh God," to which Smith replies, "Smith will suffice," hinting there may indeed be some connection. In another case, we learn that Smith is no longer "reading like an agent" when he appears on data screens.

Neo's role as The One is similarly called into question. The Oracle is unreliable on this point. In the first film, she tells Neo he is not The One, though this turns out to have a verbal qualifier in imitation of the traditional oracular figure. In *Reloaded* she tells him he is The One, but not because she has seen his future, only because she now believes he is. In *Revolutions*, he is again told he is The One, but learns his status as The One, like the prophecy, is meaningless, "just another system of control." Furthermore, Neo's willingness to kill so wantonly in the matrix and his choice in *Reloaded* to save Trinity rather than the human race sows doubts as to whether Neo is the messianic figure the audience has been led to believe.

But these are doubts which the filmmakers sow deliberately. After all, how can one know *anything* in the world of *The Matrix*? Is there any way to verify truth and reality in such a world? Once awakened to the fact that he has been "asleep," Neo can never be sure that he has not merely awakened into another dream. Even after the end of *The Matrix* and what seems conclusive proof that he is The One, Neo is dubious about what he appears to be. Smith himself warns Neo that things aren't always what they appear to be in their first confrontation in *Reloaded*. Like Descartes with his malicious demon, Neo struggles with the knowledge that there is no way to actually verify the existence of an external world and no way to be completely sure that what he experiences is real or know how he should interpret it.[39] Consequently, he cannot be sure that the role thrust upon him is what it *seems* to be, that of a messiah and hero. In a film anchored in epistemology, there is a twisted logic in the thought that the Antichrist might not even know he is the Antichrist, or might be in the process of discovering it. It is therefore appropriate that that audience should share Neo's doubts, particularly since their own viewing situation replicates Neo's ignorance: they, too, are being manipulated by the directors who may or may not be giving them "true" information which would allow them to interpret what they are seeing correctly, a point to which I will return.

Yet one thing clearly remains problematic in both the human and machine versions of apocalypse, and this is how both visions of New Jerusalem contradict a point which is made repeatedly throughout the trilogy: that machines and man have now grown dependent on one another and true separation is no longer possible. This problem is implied in *The Matrix* but made explicit in *Reloaded* in a conversation between Neo and Councilor Hamann in which Hamann points out that without machines to monitor their air, lights, water, and heat, human survival would not be possible.

Neo's knowledge of how the A.I. uses humans for its energy source leads him to see that the machines are equally dependent on mankind. Even when the Architect explains to Neo that if he does not return to the mainframe, it will result in a system crash which will kill everyone connected to the matrix, Neo is skeptical, pointing out that the machines need humans to survive. The Architect suggests that the relationship is not symbiotic as Neo believes, but Neo is correct, as he later learns in *Revolutions* when he tells the Oracle what the Architect has told him. Her response is dismissive:

> Please. You and I may not be able to see beyond our own choices, but that man can't see past any choice. . . . He doesn't understand them, he can't. To him they are variables and equations. One at a time each must be solved and counted. That's his purpose: to balance the equation.[40]

The symbiotic relationship has already been implied in the very fact that most humans are literally connected to the A.I. Even those who have been "freed" are still implanted with technology which allows them to interact with the matrix. As one reviewer cannily sensed that the final film "could also find some other path . . . that may bring hackers, humans and machines together," the filmmakers pursue the synthesis of the two worlds and species through the trilogy to much the same conclusion that David Porush reaches when he writes that "the result of the inscription of a utopian vision onto a human is a cyborg: a natural organism linked for its survival and improvement to a cybernetic system."[41] Thus, the third film of the trilogy, *Revolutions*, suggests yet a third apocalyptic reading, a cyborg one.

Just as cyborgs are a synthesis of parts, we find that both Neo and Agent Smith are progressively becoming a synthesis of both species during the trilogy. Perhaps more relevant, in learning that they are literally connected to one another, we see that one cannot exist without the other as a complement. The Oracle explains to Neo that Agent Smith is "you, your opposite, your negative, the result of the equation trying to balance itself out" (*Revolutions*). Hence, there is an equally symbiotic relationship between the two characters. Since one or the other will always play the role of deity or Antichrist in an apocalyptic reading, and will always be complemented by his other half, a viewer may draw the conclusion not only that each character is equally likely to be deity or Antichrist depending on the perspective adopted, but also that God and Antichrist have a similarly symbiotic relationship, just as men and machine have in the *Matrix* world.

This yin/yang concept is echoed in another pair of characters in the trilogy: the Oracle and Architect, who, Neo is told, are the "mother" and "father" of the matrix.[42] In this parent analogy is contained the suggestion that these opposite parts, these nemeses, are both needed to create a whole. The Oracle confirms this relationship when she indicates that while the Architect's function is to balance the equation, it is her job to unbalance it (*Revolutions*). Since both characters are themselves interpretable as deity figures within the matrix (as creators, destroyers, and manipulators of it), their relationship parallels the complementary apocalyptic roles and relationship of Neo and Smith in the "real" world. The reconception here of apocalyptic counterparts as complementary rather than strictly oppositional reveals the same approach to the problem of good and evil that Alan Moore adopts in *Swamp Thing*, a position that posits one is not possible without the other. They are symbiotic.

The Matrix trilogy also suggests the same return to cyclical time which other postmodern authors have adopted in their reworkings of apocalypse.[43] That cyclical time structure is implied in the fact that there have been six incarnations of the matrix and Zion thus far. The Architect's comment that the anomaly of The One is ultimately revealed as "both beginning and end" (*Reloaded*) not only ties the figure of The One to Christ as the Alpha and Omega, but also reinforces a vision of unending and recycling time.[44]

Here in the third film, evolution becomes vital again. While both Vonnegut and the Wachowski brothers use the trope of evolution to help them visualize a New Jerusalem, their conceptions of evolution start from different places. Vonnegut conceives of evolution turning a single diseased species into a new one that symbolizes his New Jerusalem. The Wachowskis, on the other hand, conceive of evolution as symbiosis, the combining of two inadequate species into one that symbolizes New Jerusalem.

That final symbiosis is depicted in *Revolutions*, but is extrapolated from a scene in *The Matrix* in which Neo dives into Smith's body, thereby introducing the means by which the symbiosis is ultimately achieved. In entering Smith, he fundamentally changes him. In *Reloaded*, Smith is resurrected but "changed . . . a new man, so to speak, like you, apparently free"

(*Reloaded*). He is now unplugged from the larger A.I. consciousness and free to make his own choices, and in that freedom not only achieves a necessary component for the Christian salvation, but also becomes more humanlike. Every time that Smith copies himself in *Reloaded*, he repeats this process, absorbing and co-opting other individuals in a technological interpretation of evolution which Neo describes wonderingly as "programs hacking programs."

Prior to being absorbed herself by Smith, the Oracle tells Neo that his final showdown with Smith will determine the end of the war and the world. In order for there to be a plot resolution there must be a literal one, a New Jerusalem achieved through a pun on the word "resolution." That final symbiosis takes place during the showdown between Neo and Smith in the third film where, in keeping with their computer-based world, the Wachowskis have achieved the symbiosis through the metaphor of a computer virus spread by a Trojan horse attack.

Smith has grown uncontrollable, a fact which Neo points out to the computer mainframe at the Source.[45] The mainframe cannot control Smith any longer since the agent is unplugged and therefore beyond direction figuratively and literally. Neo, however, knows he can access Smith. As The One, Neo has qualities of the machine world which allow him to interact with the machine world in ways other humans cannot. More importantly, Neo is *part* of Smith, and therefore has access which neither the A.I. nor humans have now. The A.I. allows Neo to make a connection directly to itself and then jacks him into the matrix to fight Smith. In what amounts to a simulation of a Trojan horse computer attack, the A.I. gets to Smith using Neo as the back door.[46]

In the final fight, Neo again dives into Smith's body, but first he tells him that Smith was right, such an ending *was* always inevitable. The use of this word "inevitable" sends the audience to two previous scenes. The first is Smith's speech about evolution being inevitable, and the second is Smith's continuing jibe that Neo's death is inevitable. Both uses hint at the final symbiosis that occurs here and the resulting "death" of the two separate characters who symbolize the individual species. This literal symbiosis allows a figurative one to occur in the real world: peace between the machines and humans.

There is some evidence that the filmmakers intended this resolution by symbiosis all along. At the end of *The Matrix*, Neo calls the A.I. with a warning that he is going to wake the people plugged in to it, but this is not the original version of the phone call. The original dialogue reads:

I believe deep down, we both want this world to change. I believe that the Matrix can remain our cage or it can become our chrysalis, that's what you helped me to understand. That to be free, truly free, you cannot change your cage. You have to change yourself. . . . But now, I see another world. A different world where all things are possible. A world of hope. Of peace.[47]

The reference to changing oneself recalls an earlier moment in which one of the Potentials shows Neo a spoon he has bent with his mind and explains that for Neo to do so, he must learn to bend himself, not the spoon. Ultimately it is this personal change, the evolution into a new life form—to which the chrysalis image alludes—which allows the predicted new world of hope and peace to come into existence.

Neo, who has "taken on the sins" of both species and died for them in order to bring this better world, is then taken by a machine barge into a brilliant city in the Source, the same place he has described to Trinity as "Light everywhere, like the whole thing was built with light" (*Revolutions*). The barge imagery is reminiscent of Avalon, an appropriate reference given Arthurian ties to Christian mythology, but the city itself is right out of the Book of Revelation with its description of the shining, golden city of New Jerusalem.

What is interesting about this resolution is that in many ways it refuses to resolve. Though both machine and Zionites are beneficiaries of Neo's sacrifice, *they* don't inherit the New Jerusalem that is pictured in the Machine City. The Architect agrees that he will free the humans who want to be freed, but this implies there will be people who choose not to be freed. In a paradigm whose traditional aim is the End of time, the conclusion of the film suggests that it is anything but a conclusive end: the Oracle tells Sati that she suspects they will see Neo again some day, a suspicion the audience may share considering the Avalon allusion. Moreover, when the Architect asks her how long she thinks this peace will last, she replies, "As long as it can," suggesting it is far from an eternal solution (*Revolutions*).

This refusal to resolve completely may be the unintentional result of the filmmakers' use of pastiche, or it may be deliberate. There is money to be made in a franchise, after all. Nevertheless, I'd argue that the open-endedness of the trilogy is a result of its postmodern approach and epistemological grounding, and is nonetheless logical in its own way. The world of the matrix is inherently apocalyptic in that we know that it has been destroyed and rebuilt as a better world at least five times before Neo's arrival. The final comments of the Oracle and Architect leave open the possibility that this process could continue, though not at this immediate moment. The alternative interpretations of Neo and Smith as The One also suggest that there *is* no "One," only variations on it. Neo's continuing doubts up until the final moment, combined with Smith's tortured, existential speech in the showdown demanding to know why Neo continues to fight in the face of the inevitable, seems to point to the conclusion that we can never know whether we are The One and never know our true purpose.[48]

This motif of knowing, so central to the trilogy, is therefore extended to the audience itself. The instability and indeterminacy within the trilogy directly mimics Neo's own experience of not knowing how to interpret what he experiences. The viewer is, to some extent, in the same position as the point-of-view character. We are ultimately as uncertain how to read events and identities as Neo is.

This uncertainty is compounded by the remarkable technology used to create the film. *The Matrix* is a perfect example of the kind of moviemaking technology that Scott Bukatman ironically notes is a "product of the very technologies that the narrative attempts to explain and ground."[49] New computer technologies such as Computer Graphic Imaging (CGI) make it nearly impossible to tell which, among the hundred of Smiths in the playground fight scene, is the real one, for example.[50] These new technologies inherently test the audience's sense of the "real" and self-consciously call attention to the very nature of watching film since it, too, involves a level of manipulation on the part of the filmmakers who must convince an audience sitting in a dark room that they are watching another (real) "world." When Neo views himself in a cracked mirror which begins to melt before his eyes, or when Morpheus holds out the blue and red pills to Neo and one is reflected in the left eye of his sunglasses and the other in the right (a physical impossibility), these effects are so realistic looking that they force the audience to question, like Neo, the way things appear to be.

More relevant are effects, such as the blue pill/red pill reflection, which are accepted as real by the audience. Like Neo's "splinter in the mind" (*Matrix*) an audience may sense something wrong with this image, but unless they know something about optics, they may not know that what they have seen *can't* be real. There is more than one level of irony in Morpheus's last line "Is this real?" (*Revolutions*).

The process of watching *The Matrix* trilogy deliberately replicates Neo's dilemma. It is the technology of moviemaking—in this case a movie about the danger of technology—which provides an example for Baudrillard's argument that it is no longer possible to distinguish between nature and artifice.[51] Like apocalypse, this idea has real-life implications which *The Matrix* special effects creator, John Gaeta, anticipates when he says, "the visual effects technicians of today will be the social engineers of tomorrow."[52]

Andy Wachowski has said that one of the things the brothers were interested in when they wrote the script for *The Matrix* was "making mythology relevant in a modern context."[53] In tying the apocalyptic paradigm to a futuristic world of artificially intelligent machines which extrapolates from contemporary debates about authenticity, simulation, and epistemology, they achieve this aim. Yet the trilogy may be of more interest for its handling of the problem of contemporary apocalyptic representation through its use of the trope of the cyborg. At the beginning of this chapter I wrote that the Wachowskis were inheritors of two separate apocalyptic traditions, that of the computer-gone-berserk and that of the internalized apocalypse. In the figure of the cyborg, we find the computer or machine *is* internalized, the computer becoming part of the human internal landscape. Thus, the hybrid figure of the cyborg stands as a representation of these two traditions melded into a single form. On a different level, the cyborg figures of *The Matrix* also imply a postmodern sensibility in much the same way that Adam Roberts has noted of the cyborg figure the Borg in *Star Trek: The Next Generation*. Roberts argues that the radical Otherness represented in the Borg has theoretical ties to the postmodern idea of rhizomatic logic, a system of world comprehension that, rather than being centered and hierarchical, is root-like, branching out simultaneously in multiple directions and thus creating interesting connections.[54] This rhizomatic logic, I would suggest, offers another potentially fruitful way of thinking about *The Matrix* trilogy as an apocalyptic work: as a constantly mutating text with an unstable interpretative frame.

NOTES

1. For analyses of the Buddhist elements, see Flannery-Dailey, "Wake Up! Gnosticism and Buddhism in *The Matrix*"; Ford, "Buddhism, Mythology, and *The Matrix*"; Brannigan, "There Is No Spoon: A Buddhist Mirror." For the Christian allusions, see Fontana, "Finding God in *The Matrix*"; Burek, "The Gospel According to Neo"; Spiegel, "Cinematic Illustrations in Christian Theology"; Bassham, "The Religion of *The Matrix* and the Problems of Pluralism."

2. Several critics have argued that the Wachowskis have either misunderstood Baudrillard's theory, a position which the theorist himself took, or have so watered it down that it bears little resemblance to his thinking. See Staples, "A French Philosopher Talks Back to Hollywood and 'The Matrix'"; Merrin, "'Did You Ever Eat Tasty Wheat?' Baudrillard and *The Matrix*."

3. Gordon, A., "*The Matrix*: Paradigm of Postmodernism or Intellectual Poseur? Part II," 119.

4. Paul Fontana promises to do one, but ultimately only points out the biblical allusions. See Paul Fontana's "Finding God in *The Matrix*."

5. *Vanilla Sky* is a remake of Alejandro Amenábar's film *Abre Los Ojos* (1997). *Twelve Monkeys* is loosely based on Chris Marker's *La Jetée* (1962).

6. For examples of typical reviews, see Denby, "When Worlds Collide: 'The Matrix Revolutions'"; Bushby, "*Matrix* Sizzles but Does Not Stir"; Turan, "The 'Matrix' in the Middle"; Hunter, "'Matrix' Vortex"; Graham, "A Memo to the Wachowski Brothers from a Disappointed Fan."

7. Cf. Louis Kennedy, who has argued, via Henry Jenkins, that the Wachowskis never intended to create a traditional narrative, but a world. Kennedy, "Piece of Mind Forget about Beginnings, Middles, and Ends. The New Storytelling Is about Making Your Way in a Fragmented, Imaginary World."

8. Brannigan, "There Is No Spoon: A Buddhist Mirror," 108–10.

9. Goonan, "More Than You'll Ever Know: Down the Rabbit Hole of the Matrix," 109. See Haldeman, "The Matrix as Sci-Fi" for a cogent explanation of the differences between "science fiction," "S.F.," and "sci-fi." "Fantasy," as it is used here, is the subject of an ongoing debate among science fiction and fantasy scholars. For contributions to this debate, see Eilers, "On the Origins of Modern Fantasy"; Wolfe, "Evaporating Genre: Strategies of Dissolution in the Postmodern Fantastic"; Atterbery, *Strategies of Fantasy*; Mendlesohn, "Toward a Taxonomy of Fantasy."

10. Lawrence, J., "Fascist Redemption or Democratic Hope?"

11. Watson, "The Matrix as Simulacrum."

12. Lloyd, "Glitches in *The Matrix* . . . And How to Fix Them," 134.

13. Goonan, "More Than You'll Ever Know," 100–1.

14. Wachowski Brothers Transcript.

15. Probst, "Welcome to the Machine."

16. My thanks to Pam Thurschwell for pointing this out to me.

17. Porush, "Hacking the Brainstem: Postmodern Metaphysics and Stephenson's *Snow Crash*," 125.

18. Porush, "Hacking the Brainstem: Postmodern Metaphysics and Stephenson's *Snow Crash*," 108.

19. *The Matrix*, dir. Wachowski Brothers. All further references to the trilogy are made parenthetically in the text, with the sequels being cited by their subtitles, *Reloaded* and *Revolutions*. Additional references to seeing in the films include the use of reflections, sunglasses, mirrors, and surveillance cameras; the Merovingian asking for the Oracle's eyes as payment for his help (*Revolutions*); the blind man who sits in the Oracle's lobby but responds to Morpheus's silent nod as if he sees him (*Matrix*); Morpheus's explanation that the matrix is a system designed to keep people from seeing the truth (*Matrix*).

20. Morpheus's evangelical qualities have been noted by several critics, a number of whom have drawn specific analogies to John the Baptist. See Fontana. Morpheus also shares qualities with John of Patmos, and this slippage between the two biblical figures is typical of the unstable identities found in the film.

21. There is some reference to a Kantian or Gnostic idea that the individual is actually God, if only we, like Neo, could learn to see the truth and "actualize" our own

powers, but only Neo ever learns to control the Matrix. For a Kantian reading of the film, see Lawler, "We Are (the) One! Kant Explains How to Manipulate the Matrix."

22. Cf. Bassham,"The Religion of *The Matrix* and the Problems of Pluralism," 112–13, who interprets this scene in light of the Virgin birth.

23. The Zionites are noticeably multiethnic, and the references to bondage and slavery are particularly noticeable since they are voiced by the African American actor Lawrence Fishburne who plays Morpheus. Indeed, the population of Zion appears to be significantly African American. The Wachowskis are no doubt conscious of this racial element; they have Professor Cornell West play one of the Council Elders of Zion. The radical West is one of the organizers of the Million Man March and former department head of the W. E. B. Du Bois Institute for Afro-American Research at Harvard University. There has been very little work done on race in the trilogy. To the best of my knowledge there has only been one essay on the topic. See King and Leonard, "Is Neo White? Reading Race, Watching the Trilogy."

24. See Griswold, "Happiness and Cypher's Choice: Is Ignorance Bliss?"; Sawyer, "Artificial Intelligence, Science Fiction and *The Matrix*"; Gunn, "The Reality Paradox in *The Matrix*."

25. An interesting literal twist on Baudrillard's conclusion that in the electronic era "it is the real that has become our true utopia—but a utopia that is no longer in the realm of the possible, that can only be dreamt of as one would dream of a lost object" (Qtd. in Gordon, A., "*The Matrix*: Paradigm of Postmodernism or Intellectual Poseur? Part II," 109).

26. Rothstein, "Philosophers Draw on a Film Drawing on Philosophers."

27. The necessity of going "outside" the films themselves to the apocrypha in order to accomplish an inverted reading of the apocalyptic paradigm potentially calls the status of the trilogy as a "whole" into question. However, Louis Kennedy's persuasive argument that the Wachowski brothers always intended that fans should access *all* the *Matrix* apocrypha (including the animated shorts, official website, and video games) suggests that the trilogy is not flawed, so much as merely a part of the larger whole world and history which they envisioned.

28. *The Matrix*. The issue of whether intelligent machines may supercede humans in evolutionary history is hotly debated. Bill Joy, a leading computer scientist and father of the Internet revolution, has written a now famous essay called "Why the Future Doesn't Need Us" in which he posits the eventual extinction of man by his own creations. In his book *Darwin Among the Machines*, George Dyson writes, "In the game of life and evolution there are three players at the table: human beings, nature, and machines. I am firmly on the side of nature. But nature, I suspect, is on the side of the machines" (Qtd. in Joy, 250). Others, such as computer scientist Ray Kurzweil, author of *The Age of Spiritual Machines*, not only expect machines to out maneuver humans in the evolutionary race, but look forward to it as an extension of our humanity and a unique symbiosis called Singularity.

29. Because this humanization of Smith starts before the final fight of *The Matrix* in which Neo dives into Smith (which, it is later suggested, "changes" the agent,

presumably making him more human), the question arises whether Smith, like Neo, always had the potential within him to be a conduit between the machine and human worlds. But as I argue later, his dual status is in keeping with the fluid movement between apocalyptic roles.

30. While "The Second Renaissance" realigns our sympathy with the machines and opens the way to an inversion of the human apocalyptic tale, it also raises the troubling possibility that the trilogy may be fatally flawed without the information contained within the animated shorts. Is it possible to read both a human apocalyptic story *and* a machine apocalyptic story from the films as they stand on their own, or must an audience have the outside apocrypha of *The Animatrix*, which they could only get through the DVD, in order to interpret the apocalyptic sensibility of the trilogy? The answer here is a qualified no. The seeds of the inversion to a machine apocalypse are within the movies themselves: in Smith's apocalyptist speech, in the conversation between Neo and Councilor Hamann, in the ambiguity of some of the name choices, in Smith's ongoing metamorphosis into a more human character, in Neo's doubt that he is The One, and in the audience's commonsense knowledge that humans created machines. Nonetheless, it is in "The Second Renaissance" that the idea of a machine apocalypse is more fully and emotionally developed, so that, while it is not necessary to see the animated shorts in order to read the films as inverted apocalypses, it is undoubtedly helpful and far clearer there than in the movies themselves where the idea is implied rather than developed. The flaw is not fatal, but is a serious one.

31. *Animatrix*, Director's Commentary: Mahiro Maeda. Among the recreated images are the 1968 Eddie Adams photograph of the execution of a Vietcong prisoner during the Tet Offensive, the 1989 student demonstrations in China's Tiananmen Square in which an unidentified man faced down tanks, and the 1995 Million Man March in Washington, D.C.

32. *Animatrix*. "The Second Renaissance, Part I and II."

33. *Animatrix*. Director's Commentary: Mahiro Maeda.

34. *Animatrix*. Director's Commentary: Mahiro Maeda.

35. Given the postmodern leanings of the films, however, it is possible the name is chosen ironically. Morpheus's leadership of a people he seeks to free and his association with a king who dreams hints at another King: Martin Luther King, with his "I Had a Dream" speech. That a king who has bad dreams is alluded to simultaneously with a King whose dreams are "good" (i.e., worthy) again suggests the difficulty of determining "good" or "bad."

36. The *Nebuchadnezzar's* name plaque is etched with "Mark III, no 11," a reference to the biblical passage from Mark 3:11: "And unclean spirits, when they saw him, fell down before him, and cried, saying, Thou are the Son of God."

37. Wachowski Brothers transcript.

38. This pun inverts an earlier visual one in which Neo, when he enters Smith's avatar, literally breaks him apart in a white flash which first appears through his eyes, a play on "seeing the light." Perhaps alluding to traditional depictions of good

and evil, the sign of Smith's conversion of others is a kind of black virus that spreads throughout the victim, while Neo's is a white one. Consequently, there is a second pun here on computer viruses, which functions both as a reference back to Smith's comparison of humans to disease and forward to the resolution of the third film which relies on the motif of computer viruses. The Wachowskis' own ambivalence about religion may be revealed in the fact that the process that Smith uses to co-opt others is simultaneously described through the discourses of "conversion" and "infection."

39. For more on Descartes and *The Matrix*, see Grau, "Brain-in-a-vat Skepticism."

40. The Oracle's skepticism appears well founded: the Architect's comment to her at the end of *Revolutions*—"You played a dangerous game"—suggests he was engaged in a bluff of some sort.

41. Rothstein, "Philosophers Draw on a Film Drawing on Philosophers"; Porush, "Hacking the Brainstem: Postmodern Metaphysics and Stephenson's *Snow Crash*," 122.

42. Smith confirms as much when, in *Revolutions*, he responds to the Oracle calling him a bastard with the line, "You would know, Mom."

43. Bassham, "The Religion of *The Matrix* and the Problems of Pluralism," 115.

44. Where the Architect's statement suggests cyclical time, the Oracle's relies on the Christian linear and finite view of time. See the Oracle's ominous warning, "Everything that has a beginning has an end. I see the end coming. I see the darkness spreading. I see death. And you are all that stands in his way" (*Revolutions*). Their contradicting statements maintain their oppositional balance/unbalance functions, however.

45. The A.I.'s appearance recalls similar images in the film of *The Wizard of Oz*, a story which in its own way is about a kind of symbiosis since the characters of Oz and Kansas turn out to be the same people.

46. There may be a literal code that is downloaded into Neo, though it is never explained. Earlier the Architect tells Neo that he carries a code within him which must be downloaded into the mainframe, implying he may be a code carrier, another play on the idea of virus and disease.

47. Lamm, *The Art of the Matrix*, 393.

48. The existential problem of defining purpose is a keynote of the trilogy. Smith seems obsessed with the idea. He accuses Neo of taking purpose from him and attacks him in an effort to get a purpose back. At various times, Morpheus, the Keymaker, Ram-Kendra, and the Oracle all talk about it. The self-doubt which Smith expresses here, and Neo expresses elsewhere, make both characters examples of the kind of "doubting" gods whom Moore depicts in *Watchmen*.

49. Bukatman, *Terminal Identity: The Virtual Subject in Postmodern Science Fiction*, 14. However, as David Edelstein notes, *The Matrix* further complicates this issue. In the dojo scene of the first film, for instance, the dojo is a *simulated* environment to train the characters in kung fu, but the actors had to *really* train for three months in order to do the fighting required, and during the scene *real* fly-wires were

used to simulate *unreal* moments of gravity-free action (Edelstein, "Bullet Time Again: The Wachowskis Reload").

50. Gordon, D., "The Matrix Makers."

51. Felluga, *"The Matrix*: Paradigm of Postmodernism or Intellectual Poseur? Part I," 87.

52. Edelstein, "Bullet Time Again: The Wachowskis Reload."

53. Weinraub, "In *Matrix*, the Wachowski Brothers Unleash a Comic Book of Ideas."

54. Roberts, *Science Fiction*, 165.

5

WILLINGLY BELIEVING FICTION

Robert Coover and Apocalypse as Metafiction

"The final belief," Wallace Stevens writes in his "Adagia," "is to believe in a fiction, which you know to be a fiction, there being nothing else."[1] Robert Coover has spent much of his career exploring this notion. He has repeatedly said that his intent has been to examine the myths and structures by which people organize and give their lives meaning. "Men live by fictions," he says:

> They have to. Life's too complicated, we just can't handle all the input, we have to isolate little bits and make reasonable stories out of them. . . . All of them, though, are merely artifices—that is, they are always in some ways false, or at best incomplete. . . . So if some stories start throwing their weight around, I like to undermine their authority a bit, work variations, call attention to their fictional natures.[2]

Calling attention to the fictional nature of our stories, even the ones not typically considered fictions, has been the defining feature of much of Coover's writing, whether those stories are biblical myths, national myths, or even history itself.[3]

The preoccupation with the artificiality of story-making is a defining feature of the literary style called metafiction, of which Coover is considered a major practitioner.[4] Metafiction seeks to unmask the fictions by which we live by calling attention to the process of storifying itself. Coover, in particular, has always been interested in how people hold onto their myths long after the efficacy of these organizing structures has been diminished or ceased to function as they once did. His work often explores the need for the stabilizing structures such stories provide, and the—usually dire—result of the attachment to those fictions. "I worry about forms that get entrenched, dogmatized, and rigidified," he says. "Anything that becomes a rule begins to bother me. I begin to distrust it; it's probably going to end up causing more harm than good."[5]

While such "fictions" are a stabilizing force that allows their users to organize the various, sometimes contradictory, forms of information they encounter daily, and, more importantly, to derive meaning from them, they can also become a cage of sorts, preventing people from having the flexibility and unimpeded view to adjust to a universe that is constantly in flux and is perhaps unknowable and indescribable.

Literature is not exempt from this trap and metafictionists such as Coover believe that traditional mimetic fiction does not accurately represent reality. Metafictionists attempt the radical experiment of representing reality as they perceive it to be: contingent, subjective, and largely resistant to interpretation. By openly revealing and exploring the processes and techniques by which they create fiction, writers of metafiction hope in part to illuminate the problem of documenting "reality," as well as to reveal something about how "all our meaning systems are generated."[6]

At heart, then, Coover is interested in sense-making—our need for it and the tools by which we accomplish it, though he recognizes, as well, that by virtue of writing he is engaged in a paradoxical endeavor that imposes meaning on events, what he calls "the imposing of order on a disordered reality."[7] Simultaneously aware of and sympathetic to the necessity for these sense-making structures, he is also vitally attuned to the potential destructiveness which blind allegiance to these arbitrary organizational models can cause. "One can too easily be swept up into his own metaphor and lose the world in return," Lois Gordon notes, adding that the writer "[faces] the same dangers he warns against" because, in writing, he imposes the same kind of arbitrary meaning system on his fiction, a paradoxical situation which Coover himself plays out in his novel *The Universal Baseball Association*.[8] Coover's work is filled with characters who create sense-making systems for themselves. And they do this despite the danger of being "manipulated by their own fictions" because "the depressing alternative is to resign themselves to the forces of entropy, nihilism, and boredom."[9]

For an author interested in revealing the myths by which we organize our lives, the Bible is an obvious place to start. Coover says that the contradictions of Christian belief troubled him until he finally realized that he could accept the stories "not as literal truth but simply as a story that tells us something, metaphorically, about ourselves and the world."[10] Indeed, Coover has several times drawn from biblical stories for his own work. In addition to the apocalyptic myth, he has also used the stories of Noah and the Flood, the Immaculate Conception, and the Resurrection as the bases of three of his short stories.[11] In each case, he relates a biblical episode from the point of view of one of its human participants, and since none of these characters knows that he is a character in a larger Christian mythology, he cannot react in the transcendent way which Christian mythology dictates, and instead responds as a normal human being might. Coover's play, *A Theological Position*, continues his examination of the Immaculate Conception when a confounded husband brings his silent, pregnant wife to their priest because, the husband is convinced, she has been impregnated by God. The priest, claiming that the Church cannot allow such an immaculate conception to take place again, takes it upon himself to "deflower" the wife, but soon learns what the problem is when her vagina starts loudly berating him for the Church's hypocrisies and patriarchal biases.

In each of the cases in which Coover uses a biblical story, he exposes the metaphor that has been taken as a "truth" and reveals the "subjective nature of the metaphor . . . [pointing] out the danger of substituting fiction for truth."[12] Coover has referred to Revelation both as "the best short story we [have]" and "a fabulously coercive short story."[13] He sees apocalypse as one of the guiding fictions of our culture, a rich way of transmuting ideas of disaster and fear of disaster into more meaningful fictions about an ordained structure and a teleologically driven End. He points out that since whole peoples are periodically wiped out on the planet, there is always, somewhere, someone who is experiencing apocalypse, and that in a nuclear and technological age, fear of this sort of thing isn't likely to go away.[14]

The apocalyptic paradigm is an appealing way to make sense of bad things and to cope with situations in which we feel helpless, but it is also a difficult one to explore as a fiction because of its mythic nature. Coover asserts that the only way to get at mythic ideas and expose them is to use the same mythic materials:

> When you deal with any kind of mythic experiences of non-literal explanation and exploration of life . . . the only way to cope with them is to deal with them in their own language, the language they deal with themselves. So I like to use the original mythical materials and deal with them on their home ground, go right there to where it's happening in the story, and then make certain alterations in it,

and let the story happen in a slightly different way. The immediate effect is to un-dogmatize it so that at least minimally you can think of the story in terms of pos-sibility rather than as something finite and complete.[15]

In his work with the apocalyptic myth, Coover goes straight to the source and then plays the metaphor out to its bitter end. To do so, he takes very different tacks in his two apocalyptic novels, *The Origin of the Brunists* (1966) and *The Universal Baseball Association* (1968). In the first, Coover explores both the need for the sense-making fiction of apocalypse and how apocalypse, as a tool of sense-making, gets put into practice. Just as Don DeLillo will thirty years later, Coover explores the effect of apocalypticism on a community. In his second novel, however, Coover explores apocalypse through the lens of metafiction. By applying metafictional ideas to the myth, he reveals exactly how damaging this "fiction" can be to those who propagate the fiction.

Coover's apocalyptic novels seem to doubly anticipate the idea which John Barth expressed in his 1967 essay "The Literature of Exhaustion," since Coover is convinced both that the traditional novel structures are no longer effective *and* is exploring the sense of apocalypticism which has be-come a cultural fact. In fact, Coover believes there is a distinct link between these two ideas; responding to a question about writing in the face of threat-ened nuclear war, he says, "how could we go on thinking in the old trite ways when every day we had to imagine the unimaginable?"[16]

The Origin of the Brunists is by far the most conventional of all of Coover's novels, relying, for the most part, on traditional mimetic practices. There are almost no metafictional devices which pull the reader out of the narrative to call attention to the artifice of the novel itself, and there are very few instances of "magical" or surreal slippage, and those there are are usually attached to moments of religious ecstasy or to the point of view of a character whose sanity the reader cannot be assured of.[17] In *Brunists*, Coover is far more interested in pursuing the source of apocalypticism than in exploring the novel's capacity to depict reality. Indeed, Coover's descrip-tion of the mine explosion that opens the novel is one of fiction's more har-rowing depictions of disaster and this is largely due to the realism with which the event is portrayed.[18]

Unlike *The Universal Baseball Association, Brunists* does not rework the story of apocalypse. There are no substitute deities or visions of New Jerusalem. Coover's objective here is not to rework the myth itself in order to expose its weaknesses, as some other postmodernists do. Instead, he ex-poses how the need for structure inspires apocalypticism. How, in fact, the need for sense-making is *so* strong that it can drive us to find patterns—*any* pattern—we're predisposed to see. Coover is interested in how people can find any pattern if they look hard enough.[19] A portion of *Brunists* is given over to exploring this "will to pattern," with scenes of Ralph Himebaugh interpreting the universe through numerology, and other scenes of Eleanor Norton and Clara Collins interpreting initially meaningless phrases from the prophet figures of the story.[20]

The novel signals its reliance on the apocalyptic myth through the epigraphs which open each section, of which all but one quotations is from Revelation, beginning with God's command to John to "Write what you see" (Rev. 1:11), moving through the warnings of the suffering to come (Rev. 2:10; Rev. 9:12; Rev. 11:14), and ending with the command to come to the great supper to eat the flesh of kings and captains (Rev. 19:17–18). The final section of the book, "Return," begins not with a quotation from Revelation, but an allusion to the resurrection of Christ: "The West Condon Tiger rose from the dead. . . ."[21]

If Coover is engaged in metafiction at all in this novel, it is through this structure, since the command to write what he sees is literally his job, as well as a reference to John's mission. At the same time, however, Coover is playing with the apocalypticism that is his novel's principal concern: the six novel sections are titled "The Sacrifice," "The White Bird," "The Sign," "Passage," "The Mount," and "Return." The prologue and epilogue are stand-alone sections, but three of the four other sections have seven chapters each, and the fourth section has twelve chapters (fourteen if we fold in the opening and closing chapters). As Coover well knows, and as his character Ralph the numerologist makes clear, the number seven (and its multiples) is a mystical and holy number. By adhering to multiples of seven in the number of chapters, but *not* in the actual number of novel *sections*, Coover undermines the pattern-seeking impulse of the reader inclined to look at this form of structure, and simultaneously invites the reader to engage in exactly the same kind of "interpretation" of the numbers as the cult members do,[22] in effect making the reader both identify with and guilty of the same mental trick. Briefly, *The Origin of the Brunists* follows the development of a new religion, originally an apocalyptic cult, which springs up in response to a mining disaster which devastates the community of West Condon, killing ninety-nine men, shutting down the mine, and tipping the small town into economic and social decline. With a cast of over sixty characters, and the story told from the points of view of over twenty of them, Coover is able to construct a detailed picture of the frictions and alliances of the town of West Condon, as well as the various responses of its inhabitants to the mine explosion.

One of those killed in the explosion is the Nazarene preacher of the community, Ely Collins, who leaves an unfinished note for his family promising to see them in the afterlife. Found miraculously alive, but apparently brain-damaged, is the misfit Giovanni Bruno, who soon becomes the center of a growing religious fervor which understands him to be divinely saved, perhaps divinely possessed, in order to bring word of the coming End. Several of the townspeople, each through his or her own interpretative devices but all from the overwhelming need to make sense of incomprehensible events, independently arrive at the conclusion that the End is fast approaching. These disparate individuals come together around the cryptic figure of the silent Giovanni to form the kernel of an apocalyptic cult that the local newspaper editor, Justin "Tiger" Miller, eventually dubs the "Brunists."

The story is largely told through the perspectives of Justin Miller, Clara Collins (Ely's distraught but pious wife), Eleanor Norton, another slightly ominous misfit who has created her own New Age belief system and believes herself to be the conduit for communicating with the Universal power, and Vince Bonali, one of the miners who survives the explosion. Lesser narrators orbit around these primary ones, and all of them tend to fall into identifiable groups with specific reactions to the explosion.

The first of these groups, which includes Ralph Himebaugh, the cat-abusing numerologist, and Marcella Bruno, Giovanni's sister and the love/lust obsession of Justin Miller, is composed of characters who interpret the events in a religious way. At the center of this religious response and perspective are Eleanor and Clara, who also believe the explosion and Bruno's survival are signs of an impending religious event.

Justin Miller, the cynical, skirt-chasing owner of the local newspaper, is the center of the second group, which believes the explosion has no religious import at all and finds the growth of the cult alternately amusing, bemusing, annoying, and disturbing.[23] These characters see the developments in self-serving terms: one may finally be able to convince his girlfriend to have sex with him; another intends to use the growth of the cult and Bruno's homecoming to drum up some media exposure for a town in need of it; and Miller will get great newspaper copy from it.

But there is a third group of characters who also disdain the apocalypticism of the cult, and it is centered around Vince Bonali, who narrates large portions of the story. Composed largely of the West Condon Common Sense Committee, this group is civic-minded and thinks the cult is hurting the town. Vince is one of the miners who survives the disaster, but is affected by the mine shutdown. If the cult and the group around Justin represent the extremes of belief and cynicism, Vince represents the man caught in the middle. Bewildered by the sudden religious fervor and conflicts erupting in the only home he's ever known, emotionally set adrift by a brush with death and the loss of his livelihood, and alternately wracked by subsequent depression about the disaster and elation when he begins to emerge as a town leader in response to the religious fanatics, Vince may be the only character who elicits true pathos in Coover's novel. He is an everyman, largely sensible and commonplace, prone to the occasional misjudgment, and understandably buffeted by the events of the story. I would suggest that it is through Vince's story, rather than that of the more flamboyant Justin, that Coover suggests the real "cost" of apocalypticism. Through these three groups, Coover is able to track nearly every emotional and social response to the disaster.

Throughout the novel, Marcella has been set up as the Christ figure. Indeed, the prologue indicates that she is the "sacrifice" of the title. But since Coover wants to undermine such organizing fictions, he simultaneously "invites us to establish parallels and note associations" and then refuses "to create too many easy one-to-one relationships."[24] It is not surprising, then, that the epilogue undermines or calls into questions many of the Christian parallels that Coover has been drawing throughout the rest of the story. Thus, in the epilogue it is Justin who is figured as rising from the dead; he is also referred to both as a Christ figure *and* a Judas figure. As Larry McCaffery writes:

> As [Coover] continually reminds us, life just isn't as straightforward and easily interpreted as most fictions—including those of history, religion, and realistic novels—would like to make it seem. . . . [Undermining the archetypes he's earlier set up] reminds us that such pattern making is useful in guiding our responses to both literary works and to life, but this utility is maintained only if we are aware that other perspectives are also possible.[25]

In terms of postmodern interpretations of apocalypse, however, this kind of undermining looks like something else. The representation of more than one Christ (and Antichrist) figure and the instability in the religious roles in general suggest the kind of uncertainty about identity which is part of the postmodern variation of the apocalyptic myth. In the same way, undermining the Christian parallels of a novel that is clearly structured around a Christian myth not only suggests a postmodern attack on the grand narrative of apocalypse, but also forces the reader to acknowledge that he has been using the apocalyptic paradigm as a sense-making structure. The dismay, therefore, that reader might feel when the organizing structure he is using collapses works not only to undermine the apocalyptic narrative, but *any* narrative, since the reader is forced to confront the fact that he has readerly expectations at all. The latter effect satisfies Coover's metafictional aim to expose traditional literary expectations and structures, while, at the same time, this particular story targets one of the grandest organizing "fictions" of all.

But while normally the instability in identity and morality in an apocalyptic work like *The Matrix* trilogy would cause us to think directly about the ontological concerns which permeate postmodernism, here in this early work, Coover wants us to think instead about the *reason* for that instability: our need for design. Hence, Eleanor sees Justin as the Antichrist; Clara initially fears Eleanor as the Antichrist; Abner is certain that Clara is the false prophet and Antichrist. Each of these determinations has more to do with a subjective rather than an objective sense of pattern. That is, Coover suggests that such determinations are made according to who stands in opposition to us; we imagine ourselves as the saved and righteous, and imagine those who "oppose" us as forces of evil. All interpretation is contingent on the interpreter's perspective, and this in turn depends on where he is in relation to the design. Thus, every interpreter sees a different game board with him or herself as the object of the game. Interpretation, the finding of pattern and meaning in arbitrary events, is a sort of game, one which changes—whose "opponents" change—depending on who the players are at any given moment.

The analogy drawn here between reading for design and game-playing is not coincidental. As becomes clear in his second apocalyptic novel, Coover is an author who is interested in games; he notes, "we live in a skeptical age in which games are increasingly important. When life has no ontological meaning, it becomes a kind of game itself."[26] Coover recognizes that the benefit of game-playing is that it, too, offers structure and order; games are sense-making devices in their own right.[27] At least one character in *Brunists* evinces a similarly awareness: Justin Miller, whose nickname "Tiger" was given to him because of his excellence in athletic games and who "[perceives] existence as a loose concatenation of separate and ultimately inconsequential instants, each colored by the actions that preceded it. . . . ."[28] In a tour of the decimated mine, Miller

> suffered for one febrile moment the leap and joy and glory of the state basketball championships—bright flash of meaning, a possible faith in a possible thing: that they could *win*! and there were [. . .] patterns that *worked*, challenge, rescue, always a resolution, redemptions tested and proved in the scoring columns . . . a grace on him. (155–56, emphasis Coover)

Miller's feelings about games are deliberately rendered in a language which has religious overtones. Miller sees *everything* as a game, not least of all the development of the Brunist religion:

Their speculations amused Miller—who himself at age thirteen had read Revelation and never quite got over it—so he printed everything he thought might
help them along, might seem relevant to them, amateur space theories, enig-
matic Biblical texts, filler tripe on peculiar practices and inexplicable happen-
ings elsewhere, as well as everything they wished to give him. [. . .] As games
went, it was a game, and there was some promise in it. Games were what kept
Miller going. (160-61)

But Coover makes it clear that *all* religion (and history) is a sort of game
when he has Miller respond to Reverend Edwards's accusations of playing
games with human lives, "You know, Edwards, it's the one thing you and I
have got in common" (315). Edwards's response indicates exactly how in-
vested "players" are in their teams and positions: "'The only difference,' he
said finally, curling his mouth into a patronizing smile, 'is that I know what
I'm doing'" (315).

Edwards's dogmatism hints at the danger of rigid adherence to sense-
making structures. Games are meant to be won, and games that aren't
winnable quickly lose their appeal. If sense-making is a sort of game, as
Coover suggests it is, what are the implications of having to have "winners"
and "losers"? By taking the supreme sense-making myth, apocalypse, and
making clear its analogous gaming aspects, Coover is able to show how dangerous such dogma can be. The result, at least in West Condon, is persecu-
tion, violence, and destruction: Abner Baxter's fanatics lead numerous as-
saults on the incipient religious group, the final one of which causes
Marcella's death; members of the "common-sense committee" angrily destroy Baxter's church and attempt a rape of one of the cult members; and the
Brunist's march to their "Mount of Redemption" to await the End devolves
into a frenzied, bacchanalian mob scene in which people are injured. There,
the Brunists attack Justin Miller, nearly castrating him and beating him so
badly that he "[departs] from this world, passing on to his reward" (493).[29]

The damage, however, isn't restricted to this obvious kind. Vince Bonali,
who has briefly become a community leader in the movement to counter
the fanatic goings-on of the Brunists, falls from that position through a com-
bination of hubris and impotence to stem the appeal of the cult. Even before the cult marches to the Mount, Vince has lost his standing as the "go-
to man," a change that, for him, *is* apocalyptic. Realizing this, he feels,
"Sick. Not just in the gut. Sick in the heart, too. Fucked it up. End of the
world. It was all over" (458). As a miner, Vince had been part of the West
Condon working class. For a brief while after the explosion, and acting in
part with the upper-class Ted Cavanaugh, Vince appears to be on the road
to something that he, and his family, believes is success at last. For the first

time, he is proud. He dreams of becoming mayor. Both his rise and his fall from this status are indirectly due to the apocalyptic dreams of the Brunists. Too old to retrain and with no other employment or civic opportunity available to him, Vince realizes he has blown his one chance to be someone, to help restore and rebuild West Condon as Ted imagines.[30] This realization is a world- and ego-shattering one. It is, in effect, the end of *his* world, which is the only possible world according to the postmodern ideology that insists that there are many realities and all of them are subjective. Thus, Coover shows that one needn't be a religious fanatic to be effected by sense-making paradigms such as the apocalyptic myth. The least and the greatest shall be judged.

In fact, Coover's decision to end *The Origin of the Brunists* with a recovering Justin Miller and Happy Bottom getting married and having a baby is significant because Happy has been a distinctly earthy, and earth-bound, presence throughout the story. Like Miller, she is a skeptic, and some of the best comedy of the novel occurs in the screwball letters she sends him which ironically imagine the impending Last Judgment the cult has prophesied. But unlike Miller, Happy sees nothing to be personally gained from involving herself physically or emotionally with the religious cult. It's no doubt significant that we are never given Happy's real name, happiness thus being an attribute we are supposed to associate with her and her perspective.[31] Her perspective is one of a good old-fashioned sensualist.

A woman who both takes care of bodies for a living and is passionate enough to give even the sex-obsessed Miller pause, Happy's world is the opposite of the Brunists', whose concerns are solely for the spirit and things otherworldly.[32] Happy is happy because she isn't held in thrall to any sense-making scheme beyond the sensual and down-to-earth. Coover often plays with this idea, having both Justin and Happy use religious language and allusions to discuss sex, marriage, and babies, in essence making a religion of the matter-of-fact carnality they both enjoy. When Miller begins to hold forth on the appeal of Noah's flood being righteous destruction, an exasperated Happy gives him two hard smacks on his naked ass, declaring, "this is the sign of my covenant!" (467). Later, in the hospital, as Happy gives the incapacitated Miller a sponge bath, he says to her, "let's set up a private little cult of our own [. . .] Trade rings, break a pot, whatever it is they do these days, build for perpetuity." Happy's response is to dip "an index finger into his navel. 'And on this rock . . . ' she said, and they both watched the church grow" (524).

This kind of belief system makes more sense to Miller than the empty predictions and constant eschatological yearnings of the religion that has nearly been the end of him. In a telling moment after proposing, Miller recalls a friend from high school who, having run a brilliant basketball play, rejoins the team, "hand on a hard-on that not even a jockstrap could hold back," gasping, "*Oh Jesus! I jist wanna jack off!*" Miller thinks, "In the walled-in years of datelines that had followed, whenever for a moment he'd broken out of the pattern, [he] had remembered Ox's mystical moment" (527, emphasis Coover). It is significant that Miller remembers the connection between this "mystical" moment and sex only at times when he's broken free of pattern.

Ultimately, Coover undermines even this as a sense-making paradigm, and does so by associating the mystical moment with a game. The association of the epiphany with a game reminds the reader that even using a nonspiritual scheme such as sex as a sense-making paradigm is ultimately no more foolproof than any other organizational structure; it's merely less dangerous because it makes no pretense at being a universal one. The only thing to do instead, Coover suggests, is not to take it all too seriously. Thus, Happy's comical letters and the constant jokes and puns between her and Miller hint that they have adopted exactly the right tone and strategy to make a go of things.

Almost all the criticism addressing *The Universal Baseball Association, Inc., J. Henry Waugh, Prop.* has taken the position that it is a story about the relationship between the Creator and his creation,[33] but almost none of it has addressed the novel as an apocalyptic work. This is not wholly surprising as *The UBA*'s apocalyptic credentials are not immediately apparent. Yet in describing how he came to structure *The UBA*, Coover himself has indicated that the story is an apocalyptic one: "It suddenly occurred to me to use Genesis I.1 to II.3—seven chapters corresponding to the seven days of creation—and this in turn naturally implied an eighth, the apocalyptic day."[34] But how is *The UBA*, finally, an apocalyptic text and how does Coover uses the apocalyptic myth and metafictional techniques once again to speak specifically to authorial concerns?[35]

In the novel, J. Henry Waugh, a bored, middle-aged accountant, has invented a tabletop baseball game played with dice. More than just a paper game with statistics, Waugh has created an entire world around this baseball association, complete with personalities, histories, and mythologies. He doesn't just play one team against the other; he fills in the lives, conversations, affairs, deaths, births, leisure activities, and popular culture of the players who inhabit his league. The game occupies all of his free time. Taking roughly eight weeks to play a whole season and fill in the apocrypha of the off-season, the Association is now in its fifty-sixth year, so Henry has in-

vested almost a decade of his life and imagination in it. But as Ann Gonzalez points out, so strong is this investment that, for Henry, both worlds are
"equally real": "The choice is not simply between reality and illusion but
rather between multiple realities."[36] Her assessment is supported by the several instances in the novel where the two worlds are literally blurred as one:
when Henry and the B-girl Hettie have sex, Henry tells her that he is not
Henry, but Damon; Henry's defiant response (as Damon) to his boss; Henry
calling his bartender by the name of one of the baseball players who also has
a bar; and Henry's stray thought when he goes outside that "Later, he'd have
it rain," as though he can control the weather in both worlds.[37]

   At the beginning of the novel, we learn that until the recent arrival of
rookie Damon Rutherford, a pitcher of Zen-like calm and outstanding skill,
this decade-long game had started to become as dreary and unexciting as
Henry's real work. Rutherford has reinfused the game with energy and excitement for Henry, and as the novel opens, Damon is on the verge of making UBA history by pitching a perfect game. The narration moves seam-
lessly and without warning from Henry's point of view to that of the
numerous players and managers of the Association, with the result that the
imaginary Association members are just as real for the reader as they are to
Henry; their actions, thoughts, and feelings are related to the reader in such
a way as never to suggest they are fantasy figures.

   As Damon's star continues to rise and the reader learns more about the
history of the Association and Henry's life, it becomes clear that Henry has
an unusual attachment to Damon and considers him almost a son. When a
throw of the dice indicates that Damon has been fatally struck by a bean
ball thrown by another rookie pitcher, Jock Casey, Henry grieves exactly as
if he's actually lost a son. Indeed, the people around Henry believe he *has*
lost a relative from the way he behaves. Damon's death throws the Association into disarray, but Henry, who has never "interfered" with events in his
game and has always let the dice determine what happens, finds himself de-
spising Casey and wondering whether there is anything that can be done to
make things right again in the league.

   For seven of the eight chapters, Henry agonizes about his position as the
creator of this world and how he should, *if* he should, set about correcting
what he sees as the "imbalance" that has resulted from Damon's death. At
last, he takes the step he has been avoiding and, rather than waiting for the
dice to cause an event, he sets the dice down in such a way as to have Jock
Casey killed by an errant ball. Having, supposedly, both rebalanced the Association and forever changed his relationship to it as a Creator, the eighth
chapter takes place entirely within the league itself, from the players' points
of view, and without any further reference to Henry.

While the story's Christian parallels are immediately apparent, both in Henry's analogous position to the biblical God and the analogy drawn between the sacrificed ball players to Christ, there is little that immediately suggests why Coover should say the story is an apocalyptic one. But, in fact, Coover's description turns out to be apt, for while the events of the UBA itself allegorically represent Christ's sacrifice in order to save mankind, the *relationship* between creator and creation depicted in the novel *is* apocalyptic.

The UBA shares more in common with Alan Moore's *Watchmen* than with Coover's other apocalyptic novel, *The Origin of the Brunists*. Unlike *Brunists* which explores the need for apocalypticism, *The UBA* is interested in what it means to be a deity. Consequently, the novel appears to be an allegory (and parody) of the Crucifixion from God's point of view. However, Coover's penchant for undermining organizing structures remains strong in this second novel. Games remain central, with the bulk of the story being about, or taking place within, the game that Henry has created.

The reader notices, however, that the novel has eight chapters. By omitting a ninth chapter, which would make the novel's structure analogous to the nine innings of a baseball game, Coover undermines gaming as an organizing structure which could provide meaning. The open-endedness of the novel, in which a number of questions related both to Henry's world (Where is Henry? Is He still rolling the dice, or is He now calling the plays?) and to the players' world (Does the Damonsday reenactment *actually* sacrifice the two chosen rookies or is it merely a symbolic recreation of the "Parable of the Duel"?) remain unanswered, has the same effect of suggesting the inability of games to provide meaningful answers to the questions which haunt mankind.[38]

At the same time, Coover knocks down the Genesis structure he mentions by adding an eighth section. He says that his choice of this structure implied an eighth apocalyptic day, but, of course, there is no such eighth day in the Bible. If anything, a reader's expectation, given the analogy being drawn throughout the rest of the novel, would be to find some Resurrection symbolism in the eighth chapter. Instead, Coover jumbles his biblical symbols and myth, ending his sixth, crucial chapter (in which he "kills" off Casey) with an allusion to Noah's flood.

After Henry invites his friend Lou Engel—a pun, as many critics have noted, on the fallen angel "Lucifer"—over to play the game, Lou drunkenly spills his beer "over charts and scoresheets and open logbooks and rosters and records" (198), in essence causing "an inundation" of the entire UBA world which exists in these different testaments. It is in the moments after this that Henry decides to "kill" Casey. Doing so, Henry suddenly vomits up his dinner, "[spraying] a red-and-golden rainbow arc of half-curded pizza over his Association" in a parody of the rainbow covenant God offers Noah after the Flood (202). Lou's subsequent banishment from Henry's presence alludes to a completely different biblical story, that of Lucifer's fall and banishment from God's presence.

But, of course, none of these analogies are completed, and a number of them seem to work against one another: Lucifer is not responsible for the Flood that destroyed the world; God is. The covenant is a promise never to destroy the world again, whereas here Henry has interfered not by destroying a world, but by killing a player in it. And the beer flood, if we are to take it as the apocalyptic event Coover mentions, seems not to lead to a world's destruction at all, for the eighth chapter shows that the UBA is still going strong, more than a hundred years into the future from the time that Henry kills Jock Casey.

But if the apocalyptic description seems to make no sense initially, it is because we are looking to the created world of the Association for it. In fact, the world destroyed in this apocalypse is Henry's, the *Creator's* world, rather than the world of his creation. After Henry's interference, he subsequently disappears entirely from the novel. Indeed, "when he'd done with his vomiting, when he'd finished, he went to bed and there slept a deep deep sleep" (202). The next chapter relates how the season finishes after Casey's death, and it does so in the omniscient point of view typical of those sections when we are sucked into the world of the UBA without reference to its fictional status.

In the places where Henry does appear in this chapter it is as a Creator who is slowly, but indisputably, retreating from his creation. He seems to be putting his Creator's affairs into order, recording the history of the UBA in what he calls "the Book," or gradually drawing the Association back into a state of what he understands as balance, toward what he calls the "New Day." Moreover, in the sections in which we are given brief access to Henry's experience in his own world, it becomes quite clear that he is withdrawing from life there, as well, and moving on: he tells his punctilious boss to shove it, tells an employment agency that he is "semi-retired and wanted half-time work, starting after Christmas" (213), and finally, finds a completely different bar to frequent, one where he is not known at all. And though he immediately begins to imagine the bar as a place frequented by UBA players (just as he had done with his old bar), it is significant here that the players Henry now imagines are mostly the retired old timers.

In the next and last chapter, the novel goes from portraying a God withdrawing from his creation, to depicting a world from which God has apparently withdrawn completely. Henry is completely absent from this final section, "left for parts unknown" (199). It is one hundred years on and the UBA has now instituted Damonsday, a ritual celebration each season in which rookies playing the parts of Damon, Jock, and the other important characters who were part of the novel's events recreate these events before a roaring crowd.[39] The UBA has become more than a league of baseball teams. It has certain solidified political and religious strains at work in it, with the Damonites sounding remarkably like Christians, and the Caseyites like Gnostics. The reader is left with a group of these Damonsday players standing around philosophizing about the existence of the Creator. One says that he has "come to the conclusion that God exists and he is a nut" (233). Another that, he doesn't "know if there's really a record-keeper up there or not. . . . But even if there weren't, I think we'd have to play the game as though there were" (239). In the end, however, they, and we, get no answers other than that life—the game—is what it is.

It is no mistake that their questions, doubts, and resignations are ours. Coover has used a kind of ultimate metafictional sleight-of-hand here by destroying Henry's world instead of the Association's. The implications of this switch are far-reaching, speaking to the cyclical nature of myth, the relationship of the author to his fictions, and our ideas about deity. Almost lost in the final chapter is the fact that one of the baseball players involved with the Damonsday ritual, "the occult Schultz," "has turned . . . to the folklore of game theory, and plays himself some device with dice" (234). A cycle of creators is implied here. Coover invents Waugh et al., Waugh invents Damon et al., and Schultz apparently is up to the same thing. The structure begs the question of what's at either extreme: who will Schultz invent, but, more interestingly, who created Coover et al.? The suggestion, of course, is that Coover's world, the reader's world, is also someone's invented "game."

But following Waugh's problems as a creator we are led backward to consider whether, first, Coover, as a creator of this fictional world, experiences similar difficulties, and, second, whether Coover's "Creator" might not also.[40] Just as in *Watchmen*, the metafictional issues raised in *The UBA* ask the reader to consider the exhilaration and agonies of being a God. In having Waugh initially use dice as the means of deciding action, Coover explores the meaning of Einstein's famous objection to quantum physics that "God does not play dice with the Universe."[41] The dice-use and the death of Henry's beloved Damon because of it suggests that God's omnipotence is a myth, that having created a universe (and the rules that govern it), God, too, is subject to the vagaries of Fate (or at least probability), a suggestive link to Vonnegut's later work in *Galápagos*. Up until Henry fixes the dice, the dice imply that the universe is governed by randomness, not design, and the reader is forced to ask the question, "If the Creator cannot control his design, how long can he remain the godlike presence in that design?"

Henry's toppling as the godlike figure in *The UBA* begins with his decision to interfere in this arbitrariness. Unlike Leo Hertzel, who believes that Henry is "still there, shadowy, unreliable, shaking the dice," or Larry McCaffery, who believes that Waugh will be more committed to the game than ever if he sacrifices "his son" as God did with Christ, I would argue that Henry's withdrawal from the world of the UBA in the eighth chapter suggests the contrary.[42] That, in effect, the pain of making and executing his decision—an act which is marked by Henry carefully turning the dice to a 6-6-6, the sign of the Antichrist, to trigger the fatal ball which strikes Jock[43]—is so great that Henry, having broken his own rules in order to set the world right, now withdraws completely to avoid ever repeating such a painful process. As Gonzalez concludes, "neither Henry, Coover, nor God find it imperative or even desirable to reveal any presence or confirm any moral position" any longer.[44] In effect, Coover shows once more how the result of adhering to a sense-making pattern can cause suffering and devastation.

The UBA has often been read as a parody—of the Bible and debates about an absent God by Lois Gordon, for instance, and of the "literary modernism which sees the artist as a godlike 'artificer' standing in a transcendent relation to his/her creation" and "the humanist assumption/presumption of the subject as *individual* guarantor or author of meaning" by Paul Maltby[45]—but it is simultaneously a parody of the apocalyptic myth and the reader's reliance on authorial patterning.

The apocalyptic aspects in Coover's writing are largely found at the metafictional level and can best be understood as representing his understanding of his role as a writer. The author has often said that his vocation is like that of a priest and has described writing as a religious pursuit with a moral aspect to it, reflecting that "any pursuit or attempt to unravel or discover or understand the basic underlying assumptions about the world is a religious experience. . . . I think all serious writing today is involved in some sort of religious quest."[46] But that pursuit is an apocalyptic one, according to the author, who, when asked by the journal *Delta* why he wrote, composed a short prose poem in which the following three lines occur:

Because God, created in the storyteller's image, can be destroyed only by his maker. [. . .]
Because, of all the arts, only fiction can unmake the myths that unman men. [. . .]
Because the world is re-invented every day and this is how it is done.[47]

Coover's goal has always been to tear apart and tear down the traditional ways of thinking—about myth, about history, about fiction—and to replace them with something new. Just as the God of Revelation sees the world as a corrupt place which must be wiped away in order for New Jerusalem to be born, Coover sees these old organizational structures as corrupt and corrupting. The old world must be destroyed in order for the new world to come. Coover believes it is the role of the artist to be the agent of apocalypse in this process, to act as "a voice of disturbance," "the creative spark in the process of renewal."[48] "Artists re-create," he's said, "they make us think about doing all the things we shouldn't do, all the impossible, apocalyptic things, and weaken and tear down structures so that they can be rebuilt, releasing new energies."[49]

In an interview in the early 1970s, Coover declared, "The world itself being a construct of fictions, I believe the fiction maker's function is to furnish better fictions with which we can re-form our notions of things."[50] It is striking that both Coover and Vonnegut, who has himself written metafiction, have said such similar things about the role of the writer and the need for new kinds of stories and forms. One wonders whether this is related to the era in which they came of age as writers. The 1960s and early 1970s were a period of turmoil when traditional ways of thinking were being rejected and the structures of society were being shaken, sometimes apart, and reconceived. It's perhaps not surprising that authors who wrote during this time looked upon their vocation as a kind of civic and humanitarian duty, as well as a creative one. Coover continues his quest to break down conventional storytelling methods and undermine the master narratives and ideologies that lie behind them with his work in hypertext and Storyspace.

His apocalyptic works, though they engage with the content of the apocalyptic myth, function mostly at the level of the reader/writer relationship. Consistently undermining readers' expectations about the structures and myths he adopts, Coover asks readers not only to become an active participant in the fiction process by recognizing their expectations at the content level of the story, but also to acknowledge the fictional structures and modes that have traditionally been used to transmit this content. By overturning and subverting these traditional forms, Coover engages in a critique of them, one that he wants the reader to acknowledge along with him.

NOTES

1. Stevens, "Adagia," 163.
2. McCaffery, "Robert Coover on His Own and Other Fictions," 50.

3. Coover explores the "fictional" nature of history most notably in his retelling of the Rosenberg spy trial and execution *The Public Burning*.

4. While metafiction—"fictions which examine fictional systems, how they are created, and the way in which reality is transformed by and filtered through narrative assumptions and conventions"—has antecedents hundreds of years old in works such as *Tristam Shandy* and *Don Quixote*, it is largely a movement associated with postmodernism and the 1960s and is written by authors who have "grown skeptical about causal relationships, beginnings, middles, and ends (or progression in the old sense), and the existence of a coherent, meaningful world" (McCaffery, *The Metafictional Muse*, 5).

5. Kennedy, T., *Robert Coover: A Study of the Short Fiction*, 115.

6. McCaffery, *The Metafictional Muse*, 7.

7. Ziegler and Bigsby, *The Radical Imagination and the Liberal Tradition*, 87.

8. Gordon, L., *Robert Coover: The Universal Fictionmaking Process*, 20.

9. McCaffery, *The Metafictional Muse*, 4–5.

10. Gado, *First Person*, 154.

11. The first two, "The Brother" and "J's Marriage," are found in his first collection of short fiction, *Pricksongs and Descants* (1969). The latter, "The Reunion," appeared in *Iowa Review* 1.4 (Fall 1970).

12. Andersen, R., *Robert Coover*, 109.

13. Gado, *First Person*, 147; Ziegler and Bigsby, *The Radical Imagination and the Liberal Tradition*, 88.

14. McCaffery, "Robert Coover on His Own and Other Fictions," 62.

15. Kadragic, "Robert Coover—An Interview," 60.

16. McCaffery, "Robert Coover on His Own and Other Fictions," 48.

17. For arguments that Coover's disruptive use of songs, jokes, and anecdotes in *The Origin of the Brunists* constitute a metafictional impulse, cf. McCaffery's *The Metafictional Muse*, 30; Hertzel, "What's Wrong with Christians?" 16.

18. Such verisimilitude may be the result of Coover's real-life experience. As a young man, he helped report on a similar mining disaster in the town where his father was managing the newspaper. He says the idea of the novel was born as he sat in a high school gymnasium where the bodies of several burnt and mutilated miners were brought to be identified. "There was a lot of tearful praying going on," he relates, "and it led me to wonder what might happen if some guy did get rescued, and came up thinking he'd been saved for some divine mission" (McCaffery, "Robert Coover on His Own and Other Fictions," 49).

19. One thinks most notably of Nabokov, and, later, DeLillo with his emphasis on connection.

20. Both Coover's apocalyptic novels share at least this element. J. Henry Waugh, the protagonist of *The Universal Baseball Association*, is also given to this sort of search for meaning in statistics and other minutiae. Henry's name, a play on JAHWEH, would suggest that he already knows the "meaning" of his creation, the Association, but since, in this novel, Coover is exploring the notion of deity and the

relationship between Creator and creation, this turns out not to be so. Like so many other deity figures in postmodern apocalypses, Henry is far from sure of himself, his creation, or his relationship to it.

21. Coover, *The Origin of the Brunists*, 521.

22. As I did here when I added the outstanding prologue and epilogue in order to come up with a clean seven.

23. McCaffery has suggested that Justin is named after the second-century Christian apologist, but I'd argue that Coover is finally more clever than this esoteric allusion implies and that included in the name choice is an ironic use to allude to "the just" who expect to be saved when the End comes, as well as a pun on the name which relates to Justin's job as a newsman: "This just in . . ." (McCaffery, *The Metafictional Muse*, 36).

24. McCaffery, *The Metafictional Muse*, 41.

25. McCaffery, *The Metafictional Muse*, 41.

26. Qtd. in Conte, *Design and Debris*, 149.

27. Don DeLillo explores a similar idea in his apocalyptic novel *End Zone*.

28. Coover, *The Origin of the Brunists*, 161. All further references to this work are given in the text.

29. This is one of the only instances of surreal slippage in this novel. The epilogue which follows opens with Miller "[rising] from the dead" in the hospital where he has been brought by his sometimes-girlfriend, nurse Happy Bottom. But as the narrative immediately adopts a realistic form again after acknowledging this resurrection, a reader can't be sure whether Coover intends for us to read Miller's previous "departure" as merely ambiguous rhetoric referring to the "world" of the fanatical Brunists or whether he's really a Christ figure who has been resurrected. But then again, this is precisely the point.

30. I'd suggest that if there is a vision of New Jerusalem at all in *Brunists*, that it is this revitalized West Condon, a city already in the hills if not on one, which preoccupies the dreams of Cavanaugh, Bonali, and other West Condonites.

31. "Happy Bottom" is the nickname Justin gives her in reference to her best attribute.

32. Coover calls attention to this immediately in the first pages of the novel by having Hiram Clegg recognize the sensual excitement that accompanies the spiritual excitement of standing on the Mount of Redemption. He muses to himself that the bodies of spiritually pure women, no matter how deformed, are beautiful, while even a perfect body is grotesque when the spirit isn't chaste. Coover is clearly also having some fun here with his aroused narrator standing on the Mount, also known as Cunt Hill, awaiting the Coming and rhapsodizing about chastity.

33. In fact, almost all the major studies of Coover do. See Jackson I. Cope, *Robert Coover's Fictions*; McCaffery, *The Metafictional Muse*; Richard Andersen, *Robert Coover*; Lois Gordon, *Robert Coover: The Universal Fictionmaking Process*; and Brian Evenson, *Understanding Robert Coover*.

34. Gado, *First Person*, 149.

35. Coover is quoted as saying, "You could say I wrote the baseball book not for baseball buffs or even for theologians but for other writers" (Gado, *First Person*, 150).

36. Gonzalez, "Robert Coover's *The UBA*: Baseball as Metafiction," 108.

37. Coover, *The Universal Baseball Association*, 77. All further references to this work given within the text.

38. There is a pun here, of course, on a "sacrifice" in a ball game. For more on the baseball analogies of the novel, see Berman, "Coover's *Universal Baseball Association*: Play as Personalized Myth."

39. The crowd is referred to punningly as that "whore of whores, Dame Society" (229), an allusion which at this point in the narrative would also call to mind the Whore of Babylon.

40. For more on Coover and Waugh's analogous creator relationship, see Gonzalez, "Robert Coover's *The UBA*: Baseball As Metafiction."

41. Qtd. in Arlen J. Hansen's very sharp study on the use of the dice-throwing trope in *The UBA*, "The Dice of God: Einstein, Heisenberg, and Robert Coover."

42. Hertzel, "What's Wrong with Christians?" 21–22; McCaffery, *The Metafictional Muse*, 52.

43. Even here, the dice—or the fate they represent—are a mediating presence between the deity and his acts of creation. Moreover, Henry, who initially declines to act, feels compelled to this action because he keeps imagining Jock Casey waiting for him to act. Thus, Henry's sense that Casey knows about, and wants his martyrdom, that it is an unavoidable circumstance, continues Coover's implication that Waugh is not, ultimately, in control, but is still a player in someone else's predestined plan.

44. Gonzalez, "Robert Coover's *The UBA*: Baseball as Metafiction," 109.

45. Gordon, L., *Robert Coover: The Universal Fictionmaking Process*, 171, note 9; Maltby, *Dissident Postmodernists*, 89.

46. Kadragic, "Robert Coover—An Interview," 59–60. For other Coover references to writing as a religious pursuit see Hertzel, "An Interview with Robert Coover"; Ziegler and Bigsby, *The Radical Imagination and the Liberal Tradition*; Vella, "When Prophecy Fails."

47. Coover, "In answer to the question: 'Why do you write?'" 18. Ellipses mine.

48. Vella, "When Prophecy Fails," 47, 46. Vella's article has been largely overlooked in Coover criticism, but it draws extremely interesting and convincing connections between Coover's *Brunists* and Leon Festinger's *When Prophecy Fails*, a psychological study of failed prophecies and the cults that make them. Vella suggests that Coover may have been familiar with Festinger's book and used it, in part, as the basis of *Brunists*.

49. Gado, *First Person*, 157.

50. Gado, *First Person*, 149–50.

6

ALL THE EXPENDED FAITH

Apocalypticism in Don DeLillo's Novels

When the Old God leaves the world, what happens to all the unexpended faith?

—*Mao II*

Because the atomic bomb haunts Don DeLillo's novels, lurking in the background as a cause of modern, collective angst and spiritual malaise, it would be easy to see his work as part of the relatively recent apocalyptic tradition of nuclear fiction. Even as the agent of the End changes shape in the contemporary public imagination to include environmental, biological, or chemical means, the nuclear bomb, as Peter Schwenger notes in his book *Letter Bomb*, remains a presence which cannot be ignored.[1] Though DeLillo turns his attention to other kinds of endings in his most recent work—global economic meltdown in *Cosmopolis* (2003) or terrorism in *Falling Man* (2007)—the atomic bomb remains for this author the ultimate symbol of the End.

The bomb has remained strongly present in the cultural awareness since the first atomic explosion.[2] *Hiroshima,* John Hersey's shocking exposé of the devastating effect of that attack, was first published in 1946. In 1951, the Russians conducted their own atomic tests, initiating the Cold War. In 1957, the Russians put the first satellite, *Sputnik*, into space, exacerbating American fears about a technologically advanced enemy, and in 1962 those fears were nearly played out during the Cuban Missile Crisis. Masuji Ibuse's

1966 book *Black Rain*, based on diaries and interviews with Hiroshima survivors, indicated that anxiety over the Bomb was still percolating through the culture.

Much of the eschatological literature and film since Hiroshima has focused on the nuclear bomb as the agent of the End, but, in fact, a nuclear ending has haunted imaginations since Robert Cromie's *The Crack of Doom* (1895) and H. G. Wells's *The World Set Free* (1914).[3] The trope of a nuclear End has been eagerly embraced ever since, ranging from the melancholy dirges of Neville Shute's *On the Beach* (1957), Helen Clarkson's *The Last Day* (1959), and Mordecai Roshwald's *Level 7* (1959), to Walter M. Miller's deliberate and studious evocation of Christian eschatology, *A Canticle for Leibowitz* (1960), and Russell Hoban's excellent *Riddley Walker* (1981).

Stanley Kubrick's classic *Dr. Strangelove, Or How I Learned to Stop Worrying and Love the Bomb* (1964) is certainly the epitome of the film expression of nuclear fears, but the nuclear holocaust story saw a resurgence in the politically tense 1980s when Ronald Reagan was president of the United States, with films such as *WarGames* (1982), the 1983 made-for-TV movies *Testament* and *The Day After,* and 1984's *The Terminator* and its sequels. More recent efforts such as 2002's *The Sum of All Fears* and television's *24* and *Jericho* indicate how enduring and present the fear of nuclear disaster is.[4]

The persistence in DeLillo's fiction of this nuclear fear is not so surprising since he himself grew up in the "duck and cover" age of the first atomic bomb. This, along with his Catholicism, has surely played a part in shaping his preoccupation with endings, both public and private. DeLillo himself has noted that "there is a sense of last things in my work that probably comes from a Catholic childhood."[5] However, it would be an oversimplification to identify DeLillo merely as an inheritor of the nuclear fiction tradition. His work owes less to that tradition, perhaps, and more to the theological branch of philosophy called eschatology because he is more interested in examining the metaphysics of ends, rather than plotting them.

In writing his apocalyptic novels, DeLillo has largely declined to rework the apocalyptic myth and has focused instead on the metaphysical element of the paradigm: the *idea* of apocalypse, rather than the story. His interest is not how the paradigm might be translated into secular terms. Instead, DeLillo's interest has always been the role of apocalyptic sensibility in our lives. He explores how apocalypticism permeates our contemporary lives and the ramifications of that permeation.

In his work on apocalypticism and the ascetic ideal in DeLillo's novel *End Zone* (1972), Mark Osteen argues that the author's work revolves around nuclearism, the religion of nuclear weapons, in which the main tenet "is the ascetic ideal of the Bomb's 'purifying function.'"[6] While it is true, particularly in *Underworld* (1997), that the bomb has this religious aura, the bomb is also a convenient means to an end. Osteen's theory is accurate when applied solely to *End Zone*, with its strange non-ending and obsession with nuclear war, but less so when applied to the author's apocalyptic works overall. For DeLillo, the thermonuclear device may be a tangible symbol of the End, but what interests him is not the symbol as such, or its potential to be realized, but our response to it. *End Zone* is merely the beginning of a career-long examination of different aspects of apocalypticism.

DeLillo's apocalyptic work is usefully situated against the ideas of writers and scholars such as D. H. Lawrence and Frank Kermode. In *Apocalypse* (1932), Lawrence suggests that, contrary to common sense, modern man is far more afraid of apocalypse *not* occurring than occurring, an idea which DeLillo will make tangible in his depiction of Marvin Lundy in *Underworld*. Lawrence's paradox turns on the potential of apocalypse to make sense of history and time, even though it narrates the end of both. Frank Kermode also explores this idea in *The Sense of an Ending* (1967), but of more relevance to DeLillo's apocalyptic work are Kermode's observations about the sense-making potential of the apocalyptic myth, and his argument that there has been a change in our interpretation of the End from a single moment of crisis to an ongoing crisis.

Kermode's analysis of crisis focuses on the change, starting with St. John, St. Paul, and St. Augustine, in seeing apocalypse not as imminent, but immanent. This immanent end is consistently part of the background of DeLillo's work, but becomes more noticeable in his apocalyptic novels, and is a major cultural characteristic of the 1950s and 1960s about which DeLillo writes in *Underworld*. However, as DeLillo's more recent novels *The Body Artist* (2001), *Cosmopolis*, and *Falling Man* clearly suggest, the sense of immanent end still pervades contemporary culture. Asked about the apocalyptic feel to his books, DeLillo has commented:

> This is the shape my books take because this is the reality I see. This reality has become part of all our lives over the past twenty-five years. I don't know how we can deny it. . . . [My books are] *about* movements or feelings in the air and in the culture around us, without necessarily being *part* of the particular movement.[7]

DeLillo's comment confirms Kermode's argument that the apocalyptic myth continues to inspire and fascinate, even in its changed form, because

it "lies under our ways of making sense of the world" and "still represents a
mood finally inseparable from the condition of life, the contemplation of its
necessary ending, the ineradicable desire to make some sense of it."[8]
    Indeed, it is this desire to make sense of things that DeLillo seems to pick
up on in *Underworld*, a novel in which any number of characters are looking for a faith to embrace and trying to make sense of it all. *Underworld*
goes further than this, however, and embraces a different assertion also
made by Kermode that "our interest in [ends] reflects our deep need for intelligible Ends. We project ourselves . . . past the End, so as to see the structure whole, a thing we cannot do from our spot of time in the middle."[9]
    However, *Underworld* is not DeLillo's first eschatological work or at-
tempt to explore apocalypticism. The earlier *End Zone* and *White Noise*
(1985) also do this. In them, one can see a natural trajectory to *Underworld*,
the novel which deals with the larger metaphysical issue of what we stand
to gain or lose by our apocalypticism. Though DeLillo's first novel *Americana* (1971), like *The Body Artist* and more especially *Cosmopolis*, centers
on a character who senses that a personal era is rapidly drawing to an end,
it is really in his second novel *End Zone* that DeLillo first takes eschatology
as his topic. Not coincidentally, it is also a novel in which nuclear war is foregrounded.
    In *End Zone*, DeLillo is partially concerned with the problem which has
haunted many writers since the Holocaust: that of expressing the "inexpressible."[10] Writing about the kinds of strategies a writer has available to
him in order to portray the dreadfulness of nuclear disaster, David Dowling
lists as possibilities: "skirting round the perimeter" of the topic since the
"magnitude of nuclear threat naturally ties the tongue"; satirizing the concept; "internalizing of the nuclear crisis" as a sign of the enormity of the
emotional stress caused by the idea; and "surrounding the inexpressible
with verbal strategies, hemming it in so that our reading experience includes a sense of an ominous chasm of silence and brooding ignorance."[11]
    In *End Zone*, a novel that DeLillo has said is not about football but
"about extreme places and extreme states of mind," the author refuses to
choose only one of these strategies and instead uses all of them.[12] The result is that he is able not merely to get at the inexpressibility of nuclear disaster (and by proxy apocalypse), but also to examine some of the consequences that obsession with the End might produce.
    Gary Harkness, a football player at Logos College and the novel's narra-
tor, is obsessed with nuclear war. He is an ascetic character, a self-imposed
exile who walks in circles every day in the Texan desert, forcing himself to

imagine scenes of nuclear devastation to free himself from his fascination
with the awful End. He says:

> This practice filled me with self-disgust and was meant, eventually, to liberate
> me from the joy of imagining millions dead. In time, I assumed, my disgust
> would become so great that I would be released from all sense of global holo-
> caust. But it wasn't working. I continued to look forward to each new puddle
> of destruction. Six megatons for Cairo. MIRVs for the Benelux countries. Ty-
> phoid and cholera for the Hudson River Valley. I seemed to be subjecting my
> emotions to an unintentioned cycle in which pleasure nourished itself on the
> black bones of revulsion and dread.[13]

The strategy DeLillo uses here of creating an apocalyptist character in
order to examine the premise of apocalypse is one to which he will return
repeatedly. There is little doubt that Gary is supposed to be this prophet
of the End. One notes the linguistic tie of his surname to the biblically
charged verb "hark," his fascination with the language and images of the
End, his exiled status, and his confession that he has "been plagued by joyous visions of apocalypse" (223).
    Neither is there any doubt that the nuclear bomb is the surrogate deity
in this fantasy. DeLillo is quite explicit about it, giving Major Staley, whose
father was a crewmember on the Nagasaki mission and who is Gary's tutor
in all things nuclear, the following speech:

> There's a kind of theology at work here. The bombs are a kind of god. As his
> power grows, our fear naturally increases. I get as apprehensive as anyone
> else, maybe more so. We have too many bombs. They have too many bombs.
> There's a kind of theology of fear that comes out of this. We begin to capitu-
> late to the overwhelming presence. It's so powerful. It dwarfs us so much. We
> say let the god have his way. He's so much more powerful than we are. Let it
> happen, whatever he ordains. It used to be that the gods punished men by us-
> ing the forces of nature against them or by arousing them to take up their
> weapons and destroy each other. Now god is the force of nature itself, the fu-
> sion of tritium and deuterium. Now he's the weapon. So maybe this time we
> went too far in creating a being of omnipotent power. All this hardware. Fan-
> tastic stockpiles of hardware. The big danger is that we'll surrender to a sense
> of inevitability and start flinging mud all over the planet. (80)

Though *End Zone* contains numerous references to apocalyptic subject
matter—not least of which is the punning title—DeLillo's specific apocalyptic interest in this text appears to be whether there can truly be a language

to describe the End. Even the novel's title intimates the difficulty of attempting this task: it is a kind of linguistic paradox, simultaneously suggesting a specific location on the football field at the same time that the use of the word "zone" indicates a general area. The title thus mimics the problem of language here: at best, language can describe the general parameters of the End; it is incapable of describing it in exact terms.

In order to illustrate this, DeLillo works through many of the same linguistic strategies which Dowling posits. Through scenes such as those in which Gary and Major Staley discuss the obscure language used to describe nuclear warfare, DeLillo gives examples of both an "inexpressible verbal strategy" and how this sort of language is a form of avoidance. As Gary observes, language here is a failed strategy for describing or managing the End:

> "Major, there's no way to express thirty million dead. No words. So certain men are recruited to reinvent the language."
> "I don't make up the words, Gary."
> "They don't explain, they don't clarify, they don't express. They're painkillers. Everything becomes abstract." (85)

Such exchanges also clearly satirize the military's efforts to "sanitize" or "purify" nuclear war, to somehow make it more palatable or manageable, though Gary knows from his reading exactly how unmanageable this ending is. Finally, Gary ultimately *does* internalize this apocalyptic crisis, turning his eschatologically bent thoughts inward and starving himself into a hospital bed. It is in this state of ruin that DeLillo concludes the novel, bringing to awful fruition something which Gary has said earlier: "It was a sinister thing to discover at such an age, that words can escape their meanings" (17).

DeLillo emphasizes the futility of using language to describe apocalypse in one further way. In a novel in which an analogy is drawn between nuclear war and football, both as types of battle and as games, Gary's school, Logos College, loses its biggest game. This loss functions to satirize and reverse the usual sports novel narrative, but it also functions metaphorically: a college named for the Word loses its biggest battle. In this failure, DeLillo suggests that language cannot contain the End, and he iterates a theme which Dowling points out is common to the apocalyptic genre and to the Book of Revelation in particular: the limitations of language in describing the "indescribable," what is "beyond words."[14]

Writing of the ways in which the apocalyptic paradigm continues to be modified, Kermode notes how St. Augustine observed long ago that "anxieties about the end are, in the end, anxieties about one's own end."[15] Kermode contends that "perpetually recurring crises of the person, and the death of that person, took over from myths which purport to relate one's experience to grand beginnings and ends," and that this change is reflected in our literature, which has been "made to refer not to a common End but to personal death or to crisis, or to epoch."[16]

DeLillo's *Cosmopolis* is a detailed study of exactly this sort of conflation of private and communal death. In its very first paragraphs, its protagonist, the insomniac, multi billionaire Eric Packer muses to himself that "When he died he would not end. The world would end."[17] Indeed, Eric's narcissistic thought turns out not to be so wild after all since the fund he manages is so big and is tied to so many industries and economies that when he brings it down, the destruction apparently reverberates across the world economy. But long before he played out this idea to its bitter end in *Cosmopolis*, DeLillo had already begun to explore the conflation of personal and communal apocalypse in the earlier novel *White Noise*.

In *White Noise*, all crises do become personal, and all the feared endings become private terrors about individual deaths. The larger, more communal, sense of apocalyptic crisis exists, but is relegated to a pervasive undercurrent in daily life. "Dying," says Murray Siskind, the narrator's friend and colleague, "is a quality of the air. It's everywhere and nowhere."[18] The protagonist, Jack Gladney, often comments on this feeling of imminent crisis. He notes, for instance, that the town is full of obese people and that people tend to overeat when they feel times are bad. He wonders whether his and his wife's compulsive thoughts about dying are caused by "some inert element in the air we breathe, a rare thing like neon" (15). He believes that his son, Heinrich, refuses to watch the sunsets "because he believed there was something ominous" in them (61), and he worries about how disaster footage on TV exerts an inexplicable hold on everyone's imagination in the novel, making everyone "wish for more, for something bigger, grander, more sweeping" (64). "I did not," Jack says, "feel Armageddon in my bones but I worried about all those people who did, who were ready for it, wishing hard, making phone calls and bank withdrawals. If enough people want it to happen, will it happen?" (137). A reader would be entitled to suspect that this pervasive catastrophism *is* the white noise of the title.

Though it is not the focal point of the apocalyptic tension, the nuclear bomb is nonetheless an unspoken presence in *White Noise*. It is evoked in the descriptions of the toxic cloud—a "towering mass" and a "feathery plume"—which is the focus of apocalyptic terror (111), and there are numerous additional allusions to the nuclear. One of Babette's ex-husbands, for instance, is working for the Nuclear Accident Readiness Foundation that he says is "Basically a legal defense fund for the industry. Just in case kind of thing" (56), and SIMUVAC cautions its volunteers about showing too much enthusiasm during the simulation emergency, telling them to "Save your tender loving care for the nuclear fireball in June" (206). Moreover, the killer cloud is the result of man-made technologies, toxic chemicals, and DeLillo has affirmed that "all technology is the Bomb."[19]

The crises depicted are nonetheless localized, whittled down to the individual: a seven-hour crying jag by Wilder; the sudden death of a colleague; a grade school evacuated; an averted plane crash. The toxic cloud exposure, an event that potentially affects the entire community, is largely viewed through the effect it has on a single character, Jack. The apocalypse in question is not cosmic, or even communal: Jack does not think about the exposure in terms of "we," only in terms of "I." It thus becomes, as Kermode predicted, a matter of an individual ending.

But the reduction of apocalypse to this individual level allows DeLillo to explore potential responses to apocalyptic fears. If in *End Zone* DeLillo is interested in whether apocalypse can be contained (described/understood) by language, in *White Noise*, he is interested in whether it can be denied. One of DeLillo's inspirations for *White Noise* was Ernest Becker's *The Denial of Death* (1973), a discussion of our culture's inability to come to terms with death and the resulting dread that has become a cultural force.[20] *White Noise* is ostensibly about this denial of death, but on an individual and mythic level.

It is central to the thematic design of *White Noise* that its apocalyptic fears are not borne out. Despite his paralyzing fear of dying and his exposure to the toxic cloud, Jack does *not* die. In fact, he tells his doctor he feels better than ever. The plane doesn't crash. The authorities are digging up yards and dragging rivers looking for dead bodies that aren't there. The missing-and-feared-dead Treadwells are found alive, if disoriented. Schools reopen. Mylar-clad men never find anything in their tests for dangerous chemicals. And SIMUVAC continues rehearsing for disasters that don't happen. Indeed, the one event which might actually be apocalyptic, the airborne toxic event, is undermined by the two absurd conversations that Jack has with authorities trying to determine exactly how much danger he has been exposed to. The comedy of these two scenes suggests that DeLillo is actually poking fun at apocalyptic fear, rather than accepting it outright. One notes that the comedy stems from Jack's inability to extract any information from the prodigious number of words he is hearing, and thus depicts the comic, reverse side of the tragic language crisis which Gary Harkness ponders when he notes the impossibility of describing certain "indescribable" things. Here, as in the scene with the "survivors" of the averted plane crash, DeLillo depicts the intensity of our desire to describe such "indescribable" things, as well as the unsatisfactory and comic results of attempts to do so.

Irrespective of whether the apocalyptic fear is justified in *White Noise*, it is clear that DeLillo wants to examine the strategies people adopt for dealing with it. The most obvious of these is denial, a strategy which becomes clear in the revelation that Jack and Babette spend a great deal of time *not* talking about their fear of dying even though it is such a compulsive thought that it drives one of them to turn herself into a human guinea pig and the other to attempt murder. When the couple do talk about dying, they talk around the topic in what Jack recognizes is a silly, competitive way, each claiming that the death of the other would leave the bigger hole in his or her life: "She says if her death is capable of leaving a large hole in my life, my death would leave an abyss in hers, a great yawning gulf. I counter with a profound depth or void. And so it goes into the night" (101). These metaphors of holes and voids are apt representations of nothingness, and thus of the way language fails to describe death and loss.

Admittedly, characters often try to resist this failure of language, and one can read Jack's attempts to learn German—a language he wants to use "as a charm, a protective device" because he "sensed the deathly power" in it—as an example of this resistance (31). But what is important is that Jack never is able to learn German, just as his conversations with Babette fail to either describe their immanent sense of loss or contain their apocalyptic fear.

The fascination with disaster footage on television suggests a different method of dealing with apocalyptic fear because television "frames and distances the chaos inherent in disasters."[21] As Jack puts it, "It is when death is rendered graphically, is televised so to speak, that you sense an eerie separation between your condition and yourself. A network of symbols has been introduced, an entire awesome technology wrested from the gods. It makes you feel like a stranger in your own dying" (142). Television, then, manages apocalyptic fear because it puts the viewer outside the event that tangibly represents the eschatological tension and allows a distancing to occur in which the observer no longer feels personally involved. When the toxic spill occurs, Jack notes how until that moment these disasters always seem to happen elsewhere, how unreal it seems that it should be happening to him, in his community.

The same distancing device is at work in the distinctly apocalyptic curriculum of the popular culture department of Jack's university, the College-on-the-Hill, a name no doubt meant to recall John Winthrop's culturally defining sermon depicting America as a place of millennial hope. On offer

are Hitler studies and seminars on car crashes, and the staff themselves
have heated discussions about movie stars who have died violent deaths.
The physical distancing that occurs when a television screen is placed between a viewer and the object of his regard is replicated in the dynamic of
making a topic the object of academic examination, a point Murray makes
to Jack when they go to see the most photographed barn in the world.

Murray is the novel's analyzer of apocalyptic fear.[22] He is a dispassionate
observer, an outsider who enters Jack's life shortly before Jack's brush with
mortality. He becomes the recipient of much of Jack's angst throughout the
novel. Since Murray is an academic accustomed to the kind of distancing
mentioned earlier, a cool, detached analysis of apocalyptic fear and possible
responses to it seems appropriately located in his character. That Winnie,
another professor at the college, is also given an important speech about the
topic would seem to argue for a deliberate choice on DeLillo's part to per-
form an academic-style dissection of apocalyptic sensibilities.

Winnie enumerates the benefits of Jack's fear of death and, by extrapolation, larger fear of endings. Telling him that a vision of one's death is part of
an extreme, and useful, self-awareness, she argues for the aesthetics of this
fear: "You have to ask yourself whether anything you do in this life would
have beauty and meaning without the knowledge you carry of a final line, a
border or a limit" (228–29). Winnie's hypothesis here is a vital link in the
trajectory to *Underworld* where this particular thought will be examined
more closely, but the issue in *White Noise* is not the apocalyptic need for
structure, but the responses to apocalypticism. Here, Winnie's thoughts
serve as background for a long conversation that Murray and Jack have
about possible responses.

In a Socratic exchange, Murray leads Jack first to examine the logic of
Winnie's aesthetic conclusions, and then, having discarded Winnie's premise, to discuss possible responses to what Murray has concluded is a troubling, if commonplace, fear. Murray suggests that one response might be
belief in the afterlife, and a second might be to "put your faith in technology. It got you here, it can get you out. This is the whole point of technology. It creates an appetite for immortality on the one hand. It threatens universal extinction on the other" (285).

Murray's sense that technology can and does play a vital role in the apocalyptic sensibility is another link to *Underworld* where technology, in the
form of the atomic bomb, is going to be foregrounded in a way it is not here.
His comment that technology can get Jack out of his bind is a thought in
line perhaps with the "purifying function" Osteen posits when he writes of
the deity function of nuclear weapons in *End Zone*.[23] However, it is Mur-

ray's third proposed response that suggests the link between many of these ideas, and it, too, will also be vital to *Underworld*:

> In theory, violence is a form of rebirth. . . . It's a way of controlling death. A way of gaining the ultimate upper hand. Be the killer for a change. Let someone else be the dier. Let him replace you, theoretically, in that role. You can't die if he does. He dies, you live. See how marvelously simple. (290–91)

Jack is going to take this faulty premise to heart and provide *White Noise* with its conclusion. His attempted murder of Mink, during which he is shot as well, is not only morally repugnant, but also tangible, comedic proof— because Jack botches the attempt—that Murray's theory about killers is wrong: sometimes in a violent show-down, the "killer" gets killed, too. It is exactly this recognition that is the basis of the nuclear deterrence at the heart of the Cold War mentality in *Underworld*.

Nonetheless, Murray has had the same vital recognition that D. H. Lawrence did: that this sort of lust for violence may be a pivotal part of the apocalyptic sensibility. Murray's theory about the purpose such violence may serve is as much applicable to apocalyptic texts—where the elect who are saved could technically be substituted for the "killers" and the sinners for the "diers"—as to Jack's personalized apocalyptic fears.

Underworld expands the notion of private apocalypse outward once again to look at how apocalypse as a myth affects the community. Apocalyptic sensibilities here, though, are tied to another of *Underworld*'s prominent themes: the search for pattern and shape in a chaotic world. *Underworld*'s critical reputation derives, in part, from its wide-ranging attempt to capture a time in American history. One might reasonably argue that it is about nostalgia, American angst, personal redemption, nuclear anxiety, the role of art in contemporary life, waste, and a whole host of other topics. But one of the things which DeLillo clearly does want to address in this novel is the role of eschatological expectations in our lives and how such expectations can offer a sense of meaning and shape to what is otherwise—another theme in the novel—the overwhelming and chaotic amount of information with which we live.

In order to explore this theme, DeLillo decides against portraying apocalyptic events, and chooses instead to focus on an event in which apocalypse is disconfirmed: the Cuban Missile Crisis. Like *White Noise* where the apocalypse never happens, the centerpiece of *Underworld* is also a non-apocalypse. The Cuban Missile Crisis fails to become the end of the world. DeLillo sets his novel during the fifty years in between this moment of expected end and the permanent end of the Cold War in order to explore exactly how the *idea* of the End permeates and influences our ability to organize reality and shape meaning for our lives.

Underworld's thematic structure realizes Kermode's argument that our need for coherent ends is made possible only by projecting ourselves beyond the End. In this novel, DeLillo projects the action past the (expected) end and then addresses the question of whether notions of the End actually provide this structure. By focusing on a disconfirmed apocalypse, DeLillo is able to examine this and several other related apocalyptic topics.

Before proceeding further into the apocalyptic theme of *Underworld*, however, I want to examine the other related issue of shape and meaning to which it is tied here, for it is perhaps the theme which DeLillo is most acclaimed for addressing in his body of work. Like his peer Thomas Pynchon, DeLillo often has been accused of trafficking in paranoia and conspiracy in his novels,[24] but it is crucial to understand that when DeLillo writes about conspiracy, what interests him is how it acts as a sense-making paradigm. The interconnectedness of events (and whether this connection even exists) is a leitmotif in DeLillo's work. Exploring both conspiracy and contingency as organizing principles, *Libra* (1988), his novel about the Kennedy assassination, is the work in which he most fully develops this theme. In it, he depicts shadowy groups-within-groups, a host of interconnected people and agendas for whom the nexuses are so deep and secret that even they don't see them, and the novel ultimately suggests that while conspiracy may be actively planned, it is contingency which finally connects events and incidences.[25]

This issue of connection resurfaces in *Underworld*, too, though in an altered form. DeLillo steps away from creating conspiracy- or contingency-driven stories here and instead examines them as sense-making paradigms meant to give shape and meaning to existence. There is a desperate need for such sense-making paradigms, and DeLillo has spoken numerous times about the anxiety produced by the sense of randomness and ambiguity in contemporary life which he believes is a direct result of the Kennedy assassination.[26] Observing that "conspiracy offers coherence," the author says, "conspiracy is a story we tell each other to ward off the dread of chaotic and random acts."[27] But the author notes that another way to achieve this coherence is through game-playing:

> The games I've written about have more to do with rules and boundaries than with the freewheeling street games I played when I was growing up. People

whose lives are not clearly shaped or marked off may feel a deep need for rules of some kind. People leading lives of almost total freedom and possibility may secretly crave rules and boundaries, some kind of control in their lives.[28]

The need DeLillo perceives for rules and boundaries becomes important thematically in *Underworld*, a novel that positions the Cold War and its apocalyptic subtext as a means of providing exactly this kind of structure to understand the world. Both *End Zone* and *White Noise* are, in their own ways, similarly concerned with sense-making, with *End Zone* proposing gaming and language as systems which have rules and patterns which might act as hermeneutic tools, and *White Noise* proposing science, the academy, and even violence as ways to organize and understand the world.[29] However, the conclusions of both novels finally suggest the failure of the sense-making structures they explore. None of their organizational schemes seem finally to do the job asked of them, a failure to which DeLillo himself refers when he observes that while games potentially "provide a frame in which we can try to be perfect," "in my fiction I think this search sometimes turns out to be a cruel delusion."[30]

Nonetheless, these earlier novels might be regarded as preparatory studies for *Underworld's* project. *End Zone* explores the limitations of eschatological language. *White Noise*, as its name implies, depicts not just the human need for shape and significance which repeatedly reasserts itself in DeLillo's novels, but also the reason why we need such sense-making structures. As the author signals with the motif of the bounteous American supermarket, there is too much competing for our attention in contemporary life: too much product, choice, advertising, information, noise. As Gregory Salyer says:

> The data is there; all that is lacking is an interpretive strategy that will make it come alive. So the question of finding meaning in a world exhausted by interpretation and commodification centres on the will to interpretation and on the availability of viable hermeneutic modes. . . .[31]

The chaos of seemingly arbitrary data inspires palpable anxiety both in *White Noise* and in *Underworld*. It inspires an acute need for a sense-making structure. Says Marvin Lundy, "What's the point of waking up in the morning if you don't try to match the enormousness of the known forces in the world with something powerful in your own life?"[32] *Underworld's* project then, at least in part, is to explore the grandest sense-making structure of all: apocalypse.

The curmudgeonly Lundy is a key character in the apocalyptic subtext of *Underworld* since it is he who suggests that apocalypse itself is one way of making organizational sense of the world's confusion. *White Noise* foreshadows this idea when Murray says, "To plot is to affirm life, to seek shape and control" (292). Murray is using "plot" to mean "to scheme or plan," but the word has narrative and artistic implications, as well. If we understand apocalypse not merely as an eschatological idea, but also as a narrative genre with a plot of its own, one can see DeLillo suggesting that this narrative scheme might be one way to make sense of a seemingly senseless world.

DeLillo signals his meaning here by tying apocalypse to the nuclear confrontation of the Cuban Missile Crisis, and by drawing parallels between the binary opposition of the Cold War and the similarly binary apocalyptic struggle between Good and Evil. DeLillo himself has spoken of the Cold War in these terms, suggesting that we may soon feel a nostalgia for the Cold War's "certainties and its biblical sense of awesome confrontation."[33]

> I think we're still trying to understand what happened [during the Cold War]. And what did not happen. . . . . We're not so sure how we ought to feel about it all. . . . I do think, speaking generally, that people may begin to feel a curious loss of a sense of measurable certainty, and even a sense of clearly defined confrontation, which somehow provided a measure for our feelings. Everything was measured in those Cold War years in the most horrendous terms, but you could measure danger, you could measure risk, and the loss of this has led us into a curious period of drift. . . .[34]

In *Underworld*, it is Klara Sax who articulates this thought in her interview with a French journalist.[35] DeLillo emphasizes the importance of this interview by placing it early in the first present-day section of the novel. In addition to providing a primer to the apocalyptic themes the novel will investigate, Klara's long monologue on the significance of the Cold War communicates DeLillo's sense of its metaphoric power. However, it is one line of Klara's dialogue, almost lost in the rest of the Cold War analysis, which is the real signal as to the novel's stance on apocalypse:

> Power meant something thirty, forty years ago. It was stable, it was focused, it was a tangible thing. It was greatness, danger, terror, all those things. And it held us together, the Soviets and us. Maybe it held the world together. You could measure things. You could measure hope and you could measure destruction. . . . . I don't want to disarm the world. . . . Or I do want to disarm the world but I want it be done warily and realistically and in the full knowledge of what we're giving up. (76)

Klara relates the Cold War to a far larger and mythical structure, though this is a mythic structure which has collapsed.[36] It is the final sentence of this speech which signals *Underworld*'s apocalyptic subtext, both in terms of a plot structure organized around an apocalypse that does not occur, and in terms of its thematic concern with the question, What have we lost in losing this myth?

In choosing to structure his novel around a disconfirmed apocalypse, DeLillo gives his characters an opportunity to meditate on apocalyptic expectation. He does this primarily through his twinned apocalyptist characters, Lenny Bruce and Marvin Lundy, but *Underworld* is a novel filled with apocalyptists, and who better to verbalize such contemplation, since apocalyptists can only cry their warnings while the apocalypse is still in the future. Apocalyptists can only exist in the face of the impending apocalypse and one might argue that the sheer number of apocalyptists in *Underworld* is due to the pervasive sense of imminent ending which is the result of living under the shadow of the nuclear bomb.

But the bomb is more than a harbinger of apocalyptic ending in this novel. It functions as what Mark Osteen has called the *Deus Otius*. The nuclear bomb in *Underworld* takes on a religious aura: "DeLillo's nuclear wasteland is a place of belief. . . . In *Underworld* the Cold War . . . is a period when not God but the atomic bomb functions as a stabilizing, metaphysical presence in which the characters *believe*."[37] One consequence of living in a time of belief is that it also fosters prophets.

These prophetic voices stand out in the novel precisely because they offer hope of a hermeneutic tool to interpret and organize a surfeit of information and connections. DeLillo's long-standing theme of connection reasserts itself here as the reason why the apocalyptic paradigm (and its possibilities for organizing reality) is so attractive to people. It is not coincidental that DeLillo ends this monster of a novel with a contemplation of the Internet, a place where there are infinite possibilities for connecting free-floating data but no sense of what these connections might mean.

"[A] collection of local moments, many of which are connected through the book but that do not add up to any coherent whole," *Underworld* explores the tendency when faced with such incoherency to seek an explanatory paradigm by which to organize the white noise of contemporary life.[38] If there seem to be a lot of apocalyptists in this novel, it may be because the sense-making paradigm of apocalypse is the only one grand enough to make sense of the vast amount of information available to us.

But once again it is imperative to remember that apocalypse is a failed paradigm in the novel. DeLillo's primary interest here is how the idea of apocalypse affects our lives. The expected apocalypse of the novel does *not* take place, and it is precisely because it does not that DeLillo's characters come to understand the role apocalypticism plays in their lives. The absence of the event exposes the paradigm by which the characters are sensemaking, and, paradoxically, the disconfirmation of the expected apocalypse also exposes the failures of apocalypticism as a sense-making paradigm. Indeed, the suggestion in *Underworld*, as well as in DeLillo's other works, is that there *is* no paradigm which will make sense of the overabundant "noise" which we face in contemporary life. Connections are a matter of chance rather than conspiracy.

But the fact that in DeLillo's view such an explanatory paradigm does not exist does not vitiate the *need* for one. In *Underworld*, Matt Shay's comment that "everything connects in the end, or only seems to, or seems to only because it does" (465) indicates the longing for sense-making in the midst of the same chaos which his brother Nick says fuels Italian *dietrologia*, "the science for what is behind something" (280). It is because of this longing that people are vulnerable to the mythic paradigm of apocalypse that promises an Ending to complete the Beginning and Middle, an Ending in which all *is* finally made sensible. In this culture of longing, apocalyptists thrive.

In *Underworld*, the apocalyptists are usually paired. These pairings function in different ways, but they usually serve to bridge the religious idea of apocalypse and the secular nuclear analogy. Proximity of name associates the Prologue's protagonist Cotter Martin with his religious "twin" Cotton Mather, one of the most famous Puritan preachers of American history. Cotton Mather's name calls to mind the Pilgrims' millennial mission to found the City on the Hill and fulfill their destiny as God's chosen people in the New Jerusalem they believed the New World represented. Mather's name thus has certain apocalyptic connotations.

Cotter Martin, on the other hand, is a completely secular figure, the recipient of the game-winning baseball of the Giants-Dodgers game that opens the novel. But baseball is a sign for more than itself in *Underworld*; it is a sign of the nuclear, as well. DeLillo associates baseball with nuclear war in several different ways. The most obvious of these is in his explicit pairing of the moments of the two "shots heard round the world," the home-run hit and the Soviet atomic bomb test. Saying that the discovery that Hoover attended the famous game "struck [him] with the force of revelation,"[39] DeLillo has made it clear that the association between baseball and the nuclear is absolutely crucial to the novel:

When I discovered this, I thought somebody is telling me I have to write this novel because [Hoover] provided the link with the Soviet explosion on the other side of the world and allowed me to introduce it into the frame of the ball game. If Hoover hadn't been at the game, I don't know if there would have been a novel.[40]

The second way DeLillo connects baseball and nuclear war is through the juxtaposition of the game and the Bruegel painting *The Triumph of Death* reproduced in the pages of the *Life* magazine which Hoover holds in his hands while at the game.[41] Since Hoover has just received the news of the Soviet test, he instantly interprets the image as a portrait of the nuclear devastation that has now become a possibility. Bruegel's painting comes to represent, at least for Hoover, a depiction of nuclear war. His making this connection at the baseball game thus ties the sport to nuclear apocalypse.

Finally, the baseball which Cotter takes home is later overtly associated with the nuclear bomb when Marvin Lundy says that the core of a nuclear bomb is made of a piece of plutonium the same size and shape as a baseball (172). Each of these associations ties baseball to nuclear (and therefore secular) apocalypse, and Cotter's link to the sport and particularly the baseball itself suggest he is the secular twin of this first pair of apocalyptists in *Underworld*.

The novel's second pair of apocalyptists is similarly associated with the religious and secular worlds. The Harlem street preacher, who makes several appearances in the novel, is literally preaching the End whenever we hear him speak. In his longest speech, he is preaching that the Soviets have the Bomb. His character is paired with a character *at* the Giants-Dodgers baseball game, providing another link between the nuclear and baseball. This second character is merely a shadow, his connection to the Harlem preacher implied by DeLillo's description of him. Described as "a street-corner zealot with news of some distant affliction dragging ever closer" (39), DeLillo tells us that this man in the bleachers "paces and worries, he shakes his head and moans as if he knows something's coming, or came, or went— he's receptive to things that escape the shrewdest fan" (28). What else can this imminent thing be but the End?

The third pair of apocalyptists share more than their eschatological leanings. J. Edgar Hoover and Sister Edgar also share a name and a compulsive fear of germs. Both see the world in Manichean terms and both are authority figures within their professions. In these particularities, the reader is encouraged to actually see them as twinned.[42] Once again, one character is associated with the religious sphere of apocalypse, and the other with the secular, nuclear sphere. Both are consumed by eschatological concerns. Sister Edgar takes pleasure in drilling her students for imminent nuclear attacks. Her preoccupation with death is indicated in such details as her attachment to Poe's poem "The Raven" and her certainty that the graffiti artist Ismael is dying of AIDS, though apparently he is not.[43] Hoover is not merely the conduit by which Bruegel's apocalyptic imagery is introduced into the novel; his is the voice that describes the painting as a "landscape of visionary ruin and havoc" (41), and Hoover will keep this image with him throughout the remainder of his life, as if it is *his* vision.

While these pairs of eschatological figures allude to the novel's preoccupation with apocalypse, the comedian Lenny Bruce and baseball memorabilia collector Marvin Lundy are the novel's overt apocalyptists.[44] In Lundy and Bruce, DeLillo has created prophetic counterpoints: Bruce is the Jeremiah figure who warns "We're all gonna die!" (584) in anticipation of (what seems to be) the certain nuclear end and Lundy is that same Jeremiah figure after the apocalypse has been disconfirmed and dismantled entirely.

Lundy is Bruce's nuclear shadow, a doubling role which is unmistakably implied through the two men's similar manners of speech and preoccupations with the nuclear threat and its meaning for those who live under it. Both men are New Yorkers and both are jokesters with strong ethnic argots. While it may be true, as Peter Knight argues, that for other *Underworld* characters a sense of before and after is not immediately recognizable, this is clearly not the case for Lenny Bruce and Marvin Lundy.[45] With their different historical perspectives on a shared fixation, they act as bookends for one of the novel's central questions: How do we live with (and without) the threat of the End?

If Bruce is the wailing Jeremiah warning of the End, Marvin Lundy is his weaker echo, reflecting that vision back upon itself. Marvin Lundy is the portrait of the apocalyptist after the imminent threat he has predicted fails to occur. He is, in fact, the figure Gene Marine imagined when he wrote that Lenny Bruce, if he had survived to old age, would not have been a countercultural hero because he could not have been the hero of any culture in which he lived.[46] One imagines that what Bruce might have become, had he lived, is Marvin Lundy, an imaginary metamorphosis DeLillo encourages when he describes Lundy as "some retired stand-up comic who will not live a minute longer than his last monopolized conversation" (168). And toward the very end, Bruce's existence did in fact resemble Lundy's. Secreted away in his Los Angeles bungalow with his trial transcripts, ill and babbling obsessively and incessantly about all he had lost and how he was going to get it back, Bruce bears striking similarities to Lundy with his basement hideaway and obsessive ruminations about baseball.

Unlike the other pairs of apocalyptists, neither of these men is overtly associated with religion, nor, truly, with the nuclear, but their function is different from the other pairs. If the others are meant to draw analogies between religious and secular apocalypse, Bruce and Lundy are created to analyze its role.

DeLillo's choice of Lenny Bruce as an apocalyptic prophet may at first seem a strange one, but in reality it is canny. Critics who watched the real Bruce interpreted his act as more than mere comedy. They used words like "guru," "exorciser," "witchdoctor," and, most often, "prophet" to describe him. Kenneth Tynan, for instance, called Bruce "a nightclub Cassandra" and wrote that the "troubled voice of Lenny Bruce" was "bringing news of impending chaos."[47] Other reviews described Bruce as "messianically involved," "looking like a bearded rabbi in the garb of the concentration camp," and "a prophet of the new morality."[48] Such descriptions must have both shaped and reflected DeLillo's own vision of Lenny Bruce as the apocalyptist he needed to articulate some of the complicated responses to imminent apocalypse.[49]

When Bruce says, "I dig it on one level. Being on the brink. It's a rush, man" (505), he identifies how we derive philosophical meaning from and make organizational sense of apocalyptic terror. Here, at the moment of imminent threat, hipster Bruce recognizes it is the imminence of the end that gives the present its shape and meaning. When the comedian amends his cry to "We're not gonna die!" (624) the reader is right to read this as a lamentation for the vanished end. A true apocalyptist yearns for the end, knowing that New Jerusalem awaits the faithful after the Last Judgment. Like the Pilgrims before him, DeLillo's Bruce has a sense of dissatisfaction and frustration that is born of his recognition that the promised New Jerusalem meant to follow the end has slipped away:

> They laughed, he moped. He did the old bits with suitable stinging irony but this only made them funnier and got him more depressed. They laughed, he bled. Lenny felt awful. He was supposed to be happy and revitalized but he wasn't. They'd all survived a hellish week and he'd gone dragging through four club dates coast to coast in a state of graduated disarray and now it was over and he was safe and he was appearing in concert and he should have been standing here chanting *We're not gonna die We're not gonna die We're not gonna die*, leading them in a chant, a mantra that was joyful and mock joyful at the same time. . . . (629)

Bruce can only mope about the lost opportunity. It is left to Marvin Lundy, a man who has seen the Cold War and its promise of eschatological salvation fall with the Berlin Wall, to mourn the loss of the apocalyptic threat. Slightly bitter, uneasily resigned, Lundy is a man who has lived beyond the almost-apocalypse and is therefore in the position to which Kermode refers when he writes of living "past the end, so as to see the structure whole."[50] Lundy is able to articulate how the loss of apocalyptic expectation is at least as complicated as the expectation itself. Where Bruce verbalizes the response to imminent apocalypse, Lundy articulates the complicated response to disconfirmed apocalypse. He pines for the Manichean simplicity of the lost threat of the Cold War, telling Brian Glassic, "You don't know that every privilege in your life and every thought in your mind depends on the ability of the two great powers to hang a threat over the planet?" (182).

His preoccupation with baseball memorabilia signals that Lundy is the character most affiliated with nostalgia. Indeed, the collectibles he hoards in his basement suggest he is the keeper of nostalgia. It comes as no surprise, then, that he should also articulate the complicated nostalgic yearning for a time when good and evil seemed clearly delineated.

> People who save these bats and balls and preserve the old stories through the spoken word and know the nicknames of a thousand players, we're here in our basements with tremendous history on our walls. And I'll tell you something, you'll see I'm right. There's men in the coming years they'll pay fortunes for these objects. They'll pay unbelievable. Because this is desperation speaking. (182)

This speech echoes a similar routine of Lenny Bruce's in which he tells his audience that "all this cold war junk is gonna be worth plenty, as quaint memorabilia" (593), making explicit the nostalgia for apocalyptic expectation.

Lundy doesn't initially mention the nuclear, but he certainly comprehends the connection between the Cold War and baseball, even if Brian, to whom he "preaches," does not. Brian has come to see Marvin "to surrender himself to longing" (171) and he believes this is only a longing for old cars and baseball. When Lundy reminisces about the Cold War, Brian says he came to talk about baseball, not Russia. Lundy responds that these are the same thing and suggests that what made the Giants-Dodgers game important was not the Thomson homer, but that the Russians exploded an atomic bomb at the same time.

> There were twenty thousand empty seats. You know why? . . . Because certain events have a quality of unconscious fear. I believe in my heart that people sensed some catastrophe in the air. Not who would win or lose the game.

Some awful force that would obliterate . . . the whole thing of the game. . . .
In other words there was a hidden mentality of let's stay home. Because a
threat was hanging in the air. . . . People had a premonition that this game was
related to something much bigger. (171–72)

Thus, Brian's desire to "surrender himself to longing" is tied to *Underworld's* opening gambit, "Longing on a large scale is what makes history"
(11). When Marvin tells Brian that once the threat ends he will become
"the lost man of history" (182), he expresses DeLillo's suspicion about nostalgia for the Cold War and the related eschatological tension.

Lundy implies that what we lose when the apocalyptic paradigm is removed as a sense-making structure is a clear sense of good and evil, as well
as the corresponding sense of ourselves as a member of one of those groups.
In such a universe, the fundamental apocalyptic notion of judgment cannot
exist. John W. Aldridge notes how:

disaster has become not only our central preoccupying experience, but our
principal fantasy of salvation. If religions of the past offered promise of some
form of transcendental redemption, disaster holds out the possibility of infinite and deliciously horrible forms of damnation, the ultimate titillation to orgasm of world holocaust, which in our ultimate boredom is one of the very few
experiences left that is likely to bring us to feeling.[51]

While this is not an idea explored extensively in *Underworld*, the reoccur-
ring motif of punishment in his work—particularly in novels written after
Underworld—suggests that DeLillo believes judgment to be one of the attractive features of apocalyptic expectation. This is a different kind of longing, the longing for punishment, and, in fact, each of DeLillo's apocalyptic
novels raises this issue of punishment.

In *End Zone*, Gary, who feels guilty for a bad tackle in which a player was
killed, chooses exile at Logos College as part of his self-inflicted punishment. He and Taft Robinson have a conversation near the end of the novel
in which they discuss how Coach Creed recruited them. Gary notes how
Creed is compelling because he is "one of those men who never stops suffering" (236). Taft agrees:

He was part Satan, part Saint Francis or somebody. He offered nothing but
work and pain. He'd whisper in my ear. He'd literally whisper things in my ear.
He'd tell me he knew all the secrets but one—what it was like to be black.
We'd teach each other. We'd work and struggle. At times he made it sound like
some kind of epic battle, him against me, some kind of gigantomachy, two

gods at war. Other times, he'd sweet-talk me—but not with prospects of glory.
No, he'd tell me about the work, the pain, the sacrifice. What it might make
of me. How I needed it. How I secretly wanted it. (236–37)

Gary's decision to play in the team's final game while high can be read as another attempt to punish himself. When his girlfriend first suggests he play
stoned, his response is, "I'd get killed. I'd have no coordination. I'd just
stand there and get hit. They'd kill me. They'd tear me to pieces" (167).
Given the force of his original objection, his decision to play while high anyway seems clearly related to his desire for mortification. In a bit of stoner
comedy, Gary walks off the football field in the middle of the game, later
explaining to the team's public relations man that he'd gotten hungry. When
Gary is not punished for this abandonment, but is rewarded instead with
the captainship of the team, he takes things into his own hands: in an ironic
play on his "munchies" excuse for leaving the field, he nearly starves himself to death. His self-mortification bests even that of St. Teresa of Avila
whose picture hangs in Coach Creed's office.

    In *White Noise*, on the other hand, Jack is encouraged to take up the role
of punisher, what Murray has called "the killer." But the only reason why
Jack attempts this role is that there is someone he wants to punish. Though
he empathizes with Babette's fear of death and tries to remain dispassionate about her affair with Mink, he ultimately finds himself wanting to punish his wife's lover. What is interesting in this scene is that it is unclear
whether Jack is punishing Mink for his affair with Babette or for being the
bearer of bad news: that even though there will one day be an effective
medication for the fear of death, it will be "followed by a greater death.
More effective, productwise" (308).[52] When Jack realizes that Mink means
that "death adapts" and "eludes our attempts to reason with it," when he realizes that he is still going to die whether he is afraid to or not, he shoots
Mink (308). But the fact that he not only fails to kill Mink, but is also shot
himself and has to bring them both to the hospital suggests that punishment
has failed here, just as it fails at Logos College.

    In *Underworld*, Nick Shay is the character around whom this conceit is
organized. Throughout the novel, Nick suffers bouts of insomnia, but in
none of these scenes is the reader given access to what Nick is thinking. We
know only that he is thinking about his adolescence in the old neighborhood. Late in the novel, we learn that as a teenager Nick killed a man.[53]
Only then does Nick's frustration with his adolescent incarceration begin to
make sense: what is bothering him is that he does not feel adequately punished for his terrible act.

Crucially, DeLillo ties Nick's desire for punishment to the desire for a sense-making paradigm. "When I entered correction I wanted things to make sense," Nick says, adding: "The minute I entered correction I was a convert to the system. I went out on work crews that did road repair and I was the eagerest hand, giving myself up to the rote motions of breaking asphalt, leaky-eyed and sneezing in the ragweed brush. I believed in the stern logic of correction" (502). It is no coincidence that Nick uses the term "correction" so repeatedly. This is what he longs for:

> I didn't want sweetheart treatment. I was here to do time, one and half to three, and all I wanted from the system was method and regularity. When the kitchen caught fire I was disappointed. I took it personally. I didn't understand how a well-trained staff could allow this to happen. When three kids went out the gate in the rear of a bakery truck, fifteen-year-olds, junior Alley Boys as the Alhambras were sometimes called, I thought it was a tremendous, what, a dereliction, a collapse, bunched in the back of a Silvercup truck—I was shocked at the level of neglect. (503)

Nick's comments are best understood juxtaposed against Lenny Bruce's "We're all gonna die!" routine. When the Cuban Missile Crisis ends, Bruce feels depressed even though he recognizes he ought to feel elated. Abandoning an old routine for "a better idea, deeper, more challenging" (632), Bruce launches into a story that the reader recognizes as the homeless Esmeralda's biography. Later the reader learns that Esmeralda has been murdered. From this, we can take it that the deeper, more challenging idea which has occurred to Bruce is that we're *still* gonna die, and when we do it won't be with the import of apocalypse to make it worthy. We're still gonna die, right or wrong, and judgment has nothing to do with it.

But it is no small thing to lose the measuring stick of judgment, as Nick's indignant response to the installation of a miniature golf course at the prison suggests: "I felt tricked and betrayed. I was here on a serious charge, a homicide by whatever name, destruction of life under whatever bureaucratic label, and this was where I belonged, confined upstate, but the people who put me here were trifling with my mind" (503).

The issue of punishment reasserts itself in *Cosmopolis* where Eric Packer is an extreme version of Nick. Eric's self-destructive plunge from the heights of success suggests the same kind of longing for punishment that Nick seems to have. The only difference is that Eric gets the punishment he wants—and perhaps deserves—in the end. In *Cosmopolis* we find a sort of culmination of all the other thoughts about apocalypticism that the author has explored up to this point. All the familiar tropes are here: the motif of connection; the haunting nuclear past (symbolized by the strategic bomber which Eric has purchased for himself); the joyous response to destruction; the computer characterized as the closest thing to an eternal life humans can get; the suggestion that violence offers salvation; and the longing for punishment.

Cosmopolis is DeLillo's follow-thru on these earlier ideas. If, in *White Noise*, the "killers-and-diers" theory of Murray is botched by Jack and thus undermined, here it is played out to the ruinous end with Benno actually murdering the guilty Eric.[54] Thus, judgment (and the associated eternal reward or punishment), which are either nonexistent or undermined in the earlier novels, are reinstigated as active forces in *Cosmopolis*. In *End Zone*, Gary's elation comes from imagined decimation, but here, in the anarchist riots, there is real death and destruction, a decimation that Eric responds to with exhilaration at the "struggle and ruin around him" (97). In earlier novels, the hypothesis of connection is an abortive one, one where "everything is connected but nothing adds up."[55] But in this novel, everything really *is* connected, as the weblike connection of market economies and their responses to events shows.

Cosmopolis may be the closest that DeLillo has come to actually reworking the apocalyptic myth, but such a reading depends upon accepting the conflation of personal and communal ideas of apocalypse. DeLillo achieves this personal/communal apocalyptic link through the novel's focus on capitalism. Here, at last, DeLillo has found a place where "connection" is something tangible rather than ethereal. Because in capitalist economies, and particularly in the present global economy, everything truly *is* connected, the fate of one extremely big, extremely powerful economic entity could cause the worldwide economic meltdown which DeLillo prefigures in this novel. We don't get the details of that global meltdown because DeLillo is more interested in the personal disintegration of his Warren Buffet–like protagonist, but the connection between the two ideas is made more than clear. Says Benno, Eric's eventual assassin:

you're a figure whose thoughts and acts affect everybody, people, everywhere. I have history, as you call it, on my side. You have to die for how you think and act. For your apartment and what you paid for it. For your daily medical checkups. This alone. Medical checkups every day. For how much you had and how much you lost, equally. (202)

Similarly, the link between apocalypticism and capitalism is also made explicit in a conversation between Eric and Vija Kinski, his chief of theory. When Eric tells her that anarchists have always believed that the "urge to destroy is a creative urge," she replies, "This is also a hallmark of capitalist thought. Enforced destruction. Old industries have to be harshly elimi-nated. New markets have to be forcibly claimed. Old markets have to be re-exploited. Destroy the past, make the future" (92–93).

But lest one think that DeLillo has had a late-life change of mind about the ultimate utility of the apocalyptic paradigm, he ironically positions cap-italism as both the agent by which the apocalyptic ending is achieved *and* as the reason why such a judgment would be necessary. Furthermore, the God of the Last Judgment in this apocalyptic story is unhappily absent. Fill-ing in for Him is the all-powerful multibillionaire Eric Packer, the closest thing we have to a god on earth. As Benno's monologues make clear, such men, as remote from the effects of their decisions as real gods might be, hold the lives of people completely in their power, and the language which Benno uses in relation to his former boss—that he wants Eric to heal and save him, for instance—is deliberately rendered in the religious words typ-ically associated with the supplication of a god (204).

Eric gradually slips further into the role of the apocalyptic god because of his own increasing sense that there is no God to judge him. It is a com-bination of hubris and anger that drives him to ruinously continue buying up the yen. He does it at first because he believes in his own omniscience, that he can intuit the larger pattern of the markets. Then, inspired by the destruction of the riot, he buys more, knowing that it will ultimately be his and everyone else's downfall. Finally, in a fit of pique because there is no one who is powerful enough to judge and punish him, he steals his wife Elisa's money and uses it, too, to buy more yen, in "a gesture of his own, a sign of ironic final binding. Let it all come down" (123).

Like a flagellant on a pilgrimage, Eric's journey around New York City is a search for limits for himself. During this ride, he continually pushes the boundaries of his behavior further and further. When will his actions finally bring down the punishment he deserves? After his many infidelities? After he steals and deliberately loses his wife's personal fortune? After he mur-ders his own bodyguard, Torval? Why else would he demand to be stunned with one of his bodyguard's stun guns, if not to punish himself? Why else shoot himself through the hand?

But it is the fact that he must punish himself that is important here. All through the novel, Eric has been waiting for the attempt on his life, which Tor-val, his head security agent, has been warning is imminent. Having murdered Torval, and with no sign of the predicted assassination, Eric thinks to himself:

> The threat should have taken material form soon after Torval went down but it hadn't, from that point to this, and he began to think it never would. This

was the coldest possible prospect, that no one was out there. It left him in a suspended state, all that was worldly and consequential in blurry ruin behind him but no culminating moment ahead. (169)

The "no one" of this thought is not just the literal assassin Eric has been warned about; it is also a metaphysical figure for the divine. Narcissistically, Eric has been waiting for some evidence that there is a higher power that takes an interest in him and will punish him for his bad deeds. He is, in essence, playing chicken with God, and, contrary to Joseph Dewey's assessment that Eric realizes that "the self he has so long valued is merely a vulnerable part of a mightier reference," the fact that the threat that doesn't materialize, that he isn't punished, is proof to him of the *lack* of a "mightier reference."[56] What leaves him cold is the thought that there is no divine retribution or judgment, "no culminating moment ahead." There is, as his assassin is later going to confirm in conversation, no larger plan or pattern. This is a distressing thought for a man who has staked his existence and fortune on his ability to find patterns.

Of course, punishment ultimately does occur in this novel and Eric's fears are articulated before Benno—and the retributive punishment he engenders—actually kills him. But Eric comes to realize there's no larger meaning behind it at all. His sense that there's no culminating moment explains why he doesn't fight back. He certainly could; he has several opportunities to get away from and even kill Benno. But he doesn't. In fact, Eric kicks in the door to find the man who is shooting at him. He goes looking for his punishment.

It's here that DeLillo returns to the metaphysics of apocalypse, for Eric isn't just the "sinner" deserving punishment which he perceives himself to be. He himself is a godlike figure "whose thoughts and acts affect everybody." So the judgment that is enacted is enacted upon the apocalyptic god. The deity figure of this story does not destroy the world to cleanse corruption and reward the faithful. The deity figure of this story can't even imagine a New Jerusalem, a "culminating moment ahead." This deity figure destroys the world out of pettiness, boredom, and narcissism, confessing that he "brought everything down" because he "couldn't figure out the yen." "The yen eluded me," he tells Benno, dispiritedly. "This had never happened" (190). Much of Benno and Eric's conversation challenges the ideas around which the apocalyptic myth is organized—that violence is just and redemptive; that power, even divine power, is wielded fairly, or even by interested parties—but what DeLillo really gives us in *Cosmopolis* is an apocalyptic tale in which the apocalyptic god is the corrupt one needing to be punished. Thus, even in the novel in which he comes closest to retelling the apocalyptic myth, DeLillo undermines that grand narrative by attacking the assumptions which support it.

David Cowart contends that DeLillo's fiction is radical because, even though it is clear the author recognizes "that myth reflects only the order-hungry needs of the psyche," he chooses to deny myth altogether. He is "resistant to the seductive appeal of totalizing theories, comprehensive accounts of the phenomenal world and the human place in it."[57] DeLillo's apocalyptic work undermines such totalizing theories, particularly apocalypse, and ultimately indicts the idea of New Jerusalem. He implies that the random and arbitrary nature of contemporary life is unavoidable, and that there is no sense-making paradigm, mythic or otherwise, which can comfort those who feel lost in that white noise.

As grim as this is, DeLillo is not above offering some consolation of his own. Like Vonnegut and Moore, he has proffered fiction as a means of organizing reality and giving it the meaning that humans seek. "[A]rt is one of the consolation prizes we receive for having lived in a difficult and sometimes chaotic world," he says.[58] Indeed, DeLillo's newest novel, *Falling Man*, tests this theory. A response to the terrorist attacks of September 11th, *Falling Man*'s plot is repeatedly interrupted by an anonymous performance artist who recreates the most horrible images of the attack by leaping off tall structures and dangling mid-air in the poses of those who fell from the towers. Opening with the collapse of the towers and the line "It was not a street anymore but a world, a time and space of falling ash and near night," *Falling Man* is utterly focused on death, destruction, and loss.[59] And yet, as a response to the devastation, DeLillo offers up art as a way of trying to come to understand the events.[60]

While DeLillo argues that it may not be possible to find a totalizing structure to make sense of everything, he does think "it is possible to make up stories in order to soothe the dissatisfactions of the past, take the edge off the uncertainties."[61] He has famously said:

> I think fiction rescues history from its confusions. It can do this in the somewhat superficial way of filling in blank spaces. But it can also operate in a deeper way: providing the balance and rhythm we don't experience in our daily lives, in our real lives.[62]

Paradoxically, then, the theory of fiction which Win Everett propounds in *Libra* and which has been so often quoted by DeLillo critics—that "there is a tendency of plots to move toward death"—is contradicted by DeLillo's own ideas about the purpose of plotting.[63] But perhaps critics ought never to have taken Everett's comment to heart, since in an earlier novel, DeLillo was already questioning that idea. In *White Noise*, Jack gives a lecture in which he espouses the same notion about the deathward motion of plots, telling his students that "We edge nearer death every time we plot." But then Jack immediately asks himself, "Is this true? Why did I say it? What does it mean?" (26). Critics perhaps ought to pay more attention to Murray Jay Siskind's words on plot rather than Everett's, since they appear more in line with DeLillo's own comments about plotting and fiction:

> "To plot is to live," he said.
> I looked at him. I studied his face, his hands.
> "We start our lives in chaos, in babble. As we surge up into the world, we try to devise a shape, a plan. There is dignity in this. Your whole life is a plot, a scheme, a diagram. It is a failed scheme but that's not the point. To plot is to affirm life, to seek shape and control. . . .
> This is how we advance the art of human consciousness." (291–92)

NOTES

1. Schwenger, *Letter Bomb*, xiii. For other scholars who argue that our literary production has been defined by our ability to destroy the world via nuclear bomb, see Zins, "Exploding the Canon," and Dewey, *In a Dark Time*.
2. For an excellent and thorough account of the cultural effects of our coming-of-nuclear-age, see Boyer, *By the Bomb's Early Light: American Thought and Culture at the Dawn of the Atomic Age*.
3. Paul Brians has put together a remarkable bibliography of nuclear disaster fiction. Though his focus is on science fiction, his annotated list of fiction about nuclear war or accident is an important source for scholars of the genre.
4. For a history of representations of the atomic bomb in cinema, see Shapiro, *Atomic Bomb Cinema*.
5. Passaro, "Dangerous Don DeLillo."
6. Osteen, "Against the End," 152.
7. DeCurtis, "An Outsider in This Society: An Interview with Don DeLillo," 66, emphasis DeLillo. Elsewhere DeLillo has made similar comments about the paranoia apparent in his novels, saying he has "drawn this element out of the air around" him, and that paranoia acts for his characters as "a form of religious awe" in which institutions like the CIA are "like churches that hold the final secrets" (Begley, "Don DeLillo: The Art of Fiction CXXXV," 303).
8. Kermode, *The Sense of an Ending*, 28, 187.
9. Kermode, *The Sense of an Ending*, 8.

10. The link to a problem associated with Holocaust literature is one of which DeLillo seems to be aware since *White Noise* has strong connections to Holocaust studies through Jack Gladney's Hitler studies.

11. Dowling, *Fictions of Nuclear Disaster*, 5–14.

12. DeCurtis, "An Outsider in This Society: An Interview with Don DeLillo," 57.

13. DeLillo, *End Zone*, 43. All further references to the text are made parenthetically.

14. Dowling, *Fictions of Nuclear Disaster*, 121.

15. Kermode, *The Sense of an Ending*, 186.

16. Kermode, *The Sense of an Ending*, 35.

17. DeLillo, *Cosmopolis*, 6. All further references to the text are made parenthetically.

18. DeLillo, *White Noise*, 38. All further references to the text are made parenthetically.

19. Howard, "The American Strangeness: An Interview with Don DeLillo," 15.

20. Cowart, *Don DeLillo*, 77–78.

21. Osteen, "Against the End," 153.

22. Murray, however, is not the apocalyptist of this novel. That role is Wilder's. In a novel filled with voices, it is Wilder's silence which stands out, and never more so than when it is broken by his seven-hour crying jag, described as a "lament," "an ancient dirge all the more impressive for its resolute monotony" (78). The child's name recalls the wilderness which biblical prophets sometimes wander and this association is strengthened by Jack's observation that when he stops crying, "It was as though he'd just returned from a period of wandering in some remote and holy place, in sand barrens or snowy ranges—a place where things are said, sights are seen, distances reached which we in our ordinary toil can only regard with the mingled reverence and wonder we hold in reserve for feats of the most sublime and difficult dimensions" (79). Additionally, the scene where Wilder rides his tricycle across the highway without getting hit implies that he is somehow protected from injury, as one of God's prophets would be.

23. Osteen paraphrases Ira Chernus on the religious aura of nuclear weapons: "Nuclear weapons . . . inspire both awe and dread, and remain mysteriously fascinating both because of their complex technology and because of their seemingly limitless power. The numinousness of nuclear weapons—their mystery and power—induces us to identify with their destructive force, and indeed finally to try to merge with their power by letting them rain down" (Osteen, "Against the End," 151).

24. See Woods, "Books: Atoms of Paranoia: *Underworld* by Don DeLillo" as an example.

25. For a particularly good examination of the topic, see Skip Willman's article "Traversing the Fantasies of the JFK Assassination: Conspiracy and Contingency in Don DeLillo's *Libra*."

26. DeLillo, "American Blood," 22.

27. Goldstein, "Don DeLillo," 56.

28. LeClair, *Anything Can Happen*, 81.

29. For an analysis of DeLillo's fiction according to systems theory, see LeClair's *In the Loop: Don DeLillo and the Systems Novel*.

30. LeClair, *Anything Can Happen*, 81. DeLillo suggests a number of these potential hermeneutics. For more on paranoia as a hermeneutic tool see Knight, "Everything Is Connected: *Underworld*'s Secret History of Paranoia." For gaming, see Berman, *Playful Fictions and Fictional Players: Game, Sport and Survival in Contemporary American Fiction* and for football in particular, see Burke, "Football, Literature, Culture."

31. Salyer, "Myth, Magic and Dread: Reading Culture Religiously," 266.

32. DeLillo, *Underworld*, 323. All further references to the text are made parenthetically.

33. Osen, "A Conversation with Don DeLillo."

34. Ulin, "Merging Myth and History."

35. Peter Knight sees Klara's view as confirmation of the paranoia principle at operation in the novel, but he argues, as I do here about the apocalyptic paradigm, that paranoia is operating as a sense-making paradigm (Knight, "Everything Is Connected: *Underworld*'s Secret History of Paranoia," 286–87).

36. Fitzpatrick, "The Unmaking of History: Baseball, Cold War, and *Underworld*," 152.

37. Gleason, "Don DeLillo, T. S. Eliot, and the Redemption of America's Atomic Waste Land," 134. Italics Gleason.

38. Wallace, "'Venerated Emblems': DeLillo's *Underworld* and the History Commodity," 369.

39. Howard, "The American Strangeness: An Interview with Don DeLillo." DeLillo's full quote reads: "Once I found out that Hoover had been at the game, it struck me with the force of revelation, because it meant that I had someone in the Polo Grounds who was intimately connected to what had happened at Kazhakstan." One wonders whether it is solely synchronicity which made the author choose the word "revelation" here.

40. O'Toole, "And Quiet Writes the Don."

41. It is one of those fantastic coincidences—contingencies, DeLillo might say—of real life that Bruegel's *The Triumph of Death* actually appeared in *Life* on this day.

42. In the novel's final section, however, DeLillo says the two Edgars are "biological opposites" and that Hoover is the Sister's "male half" (826). Such language suggests a different reading, not as twins, but as two parts of the same whole.

43. Irving Malin and Joseph Dewey have done a wonderful reading of DeLillo's use of "The Raven" in which they claim that Edgar Allan Poe is the third Edgar who mediates between the two Edgar characters of the novel. Poe himself alludes to greater apocalyptic sensibilities in "The Raven" through his reference to Gilead, an allusion to the apocalyptic prophecy of Jeremiah.

44. DeLillo's Lenny Bruce is not historically accurate. During the Cuban Missile Crisis, the real Bruce was performing in the same club in Los Angeles the entire time. Moreover, the real Bruce made no (verifiable) comment on the Cuban Missile Crisis,

a fact which surprised DeLillo enormously: "It seemed to me that here was a guy who should have but evidently did not deliver [a political commentary] at the time, so I decided to do it for him" (Friedman, "DeLillo in London—January 15, 1998").

45. Knight, "Everything Is Connected: *Underworld*'s Secret History of Paranoia," 285.

46. Marine, "Lenny, You *Meshugginah*, You Can't Play the Hero!" 60.

47. Tynan, foreword, *How to Talk Dirty and Influence People*, xi.

48. Weaver, "San Francisco: Hungry I," 138; Goldman, A., "The Trial of Lenny Bruce," 13; Miller, "The Sick White Negro," 150.

49. For more on the comparison between the real and fictional Lenny Bruce, see Rosen, "Lenny Bruce and His Nuclear Shadow Marvin Lundy: Don DeLillo's Apocalyptists Extraordinaire."

50. Kermode, *The Sense of an Ending*, 8.

51. Aldridge, *The American Novel and the Way We Live Now*, 10–11.

52. Babette points out a third option: that Jack is reflexively acting out the expected gendered response to adultery.

53. DeLillo apparently drew the details of this scene from personal experience. In a September 16, 1981 letter to his editor Gordon Lish, DeLillo asks a series of "Did you ever" questions, the last of which reads, "Did you ever point a sawed-off shotgun at your friend's midsection and ask, 'Is it loaded?' and when he said, 'No,' did you pull the trigger? I did." DeLillo then drops a line and adds, "It wasn't loaded" before signing off.

54. Perhaps not coincidentally, this is an act which Benno specifically envisions in apocalyptic terms: "to take another person's life? This is the vision of the new day" (154).

55. Knight, "Everything Is Connected: *Underworld*'s Secret History of Paranoia," 291.

56. Dewey, *Beyond Grief and Nothing: A Reading of Don DeLillo*, 140. Dewey reads *Cosmopolis* as a far more transcendent text, seeing it as a parable, a "familiar spiritual metaphor of the journey, specifically the descent into hell that marks the authentic ascent of a soul" (142).

57. Cowart, *Don DeLillo*, 8–9.

58. DeCurtis, "An Outsider in This Society: An Interview with Don DeLillo," 66.

59. DeLillo, *Falling Man*, 3.

60. Whether art, in this case, actually does console seems to me to be debatable. Certainly, the response of characters in the novel suggests it does not, though one might argue for its cathartic effect. The problem is further compounded by what Sam Anderson rightfully points out is DeLillo's punt on the topic: by "[building] the novel around a neat symbol of the problem of the very existence of 9/11 art," DeLillo cleverly deflects criticism of his own attempt to represent September 11th (Anderson, S., "Code Red").

61. Goldstein, "Don DeLillo," 56.

62. DeCurtis, "An Outsider in This Society: An Interview with Don DeLillo," 56.

63. DeLillo, *Libra*, 221.

EPILOGUE

What are we to make of the postmodern vision of apocalypse? To acknowledge that such a thing can be constructed obviously suggests a fundamental epistemological and ontological shift in the way we engage with the world. Postmodernism is intensely subjective, aggressively theoretical, unabashedly self-absorbed, and skeptical of established ideas, of value judgments and norms, of traditional aesthetic models in general and of grand narratives in particular. Such qualities seem inimical to the apocalyptic myth, even to the idea of apocalypse itself. Yet to claim that postmodernism cannot appropriate the apocalyptic myth is to deny what has already been done. It can and it has. The challenge that remains is to recognize and understand it.

Writing that apocalypse is "a narrative that seeks to be nonnarrative, to get beyond the strictures of time and space," Lee Quinby suggests one tool we might use to understand postmodern apocalypse.[1] For surely if postmodernists do anything, they seek to get beyond the limits of time and space, in art if not in life. They seek to strip away the fictions that govern our lives, to expose the metaphoric structures that lie under our way of understanding the world and the narratives that the status quo uses to maintain its position of power.

These are worthy intentions, even if it is true, as many now believe, that postmodernism's best days are past, at least politically. And perhaps posthumanism will offer the constructive solutions needed to rebuild from the ruins which postmodernism has often left behind as it exposed and challenged pre-viously unrecognized and untenable intellectual superstructures. One must pull down edifices built upon suspect foundations before one can build anew on the spot, after all. But the fact that some believe postmodernism is an artis-tic movement that has come to the end of its usefulness should not prevent us from examining the political ramifications of postmodern apocalypse.

Apocalyptic writers now differ greatly from their Christian predecessors; they are "better schooled in history, more worldly, driven by a different mix-ture of motives, and less sure of what they believe."[2] If apocalypse is a grand narrative—and one can think of no grander one—then surely it, too, may be thought of as a political structure which can be exposed, analyzed, and reconsidered. And surely, too, it is a grand narrative which serves some bet-ter than others, and is therefore worth revealing, just as the word *apoka-lypsis* promises to do.

One of the goals of postmodernism is to expose the meta-narratives within which we unconsciously navigate. For those who believe that one simply cannot call apocalypse a metaphor or a parable, I point out that it *is* both those things. Apocalypse is a metaphor and a story, just as it is simul-taneously a sense-making structure and a promise of hope held out to a troubled people. As many postmodernists would point out, which of these ways is used to define *apocalypse* has everything to do with who has the power to impose the definition. Artists are understandably drawn to exam-ining the apocalyptic myth in all of its forms: as a metaphor, a story, a sense-making structure, or a promise of hope.

This is not to say that postmodern apocalypse does not present some dif-ficult paradoxes. The collection of characteristics which comprise postmod-ernism—"pluralism, . . . [opposition] to closure, the absence or erasure of plot, indeterminacy, and parody and pastiche in place of unified or organic style"[3]—when applied to apocalypse seriously compromise the structure and the moral element of the myth, and, if we believe that our narratives are potentially world-changing, then perhaps this compromise ought to concern us.[4] As Bruce Milne notes, eschatology is "always moral teaching. It is concerned with the way we are to live in light of it."[5] By questioning what is meant by terms such as *good* and *evil* and *moral*, postmodern apoc-alypse challenges crucial defining and stabilizing elements of the traditional myth.

Yet this apparent paradox may strengthen rather than weaken the im-pact of postmodern apocalypse, for the terms *good* and *evil* are absolutes that rarely apply in a world where motives are sometimes mixed or multi-ple, and the effects of ideas and actions are frequently neither obvious nor

clear-cut. Such terms are an easy way to "paint" a situation in order to manipulate responses—to arouse fear and blind hatred on one hand, martyr-
complexes on the other. Apocalypse is not only a comforting story about
righteous inheritance for the dispossessed, nor a benign fairy tale of good
besting evil. It is a potentially dangerous way by which to regard and act in
the world. As Quinby argues in *Anti-Apocalypse*, for believers, "this leads
to active suppression of conduct that does not fit with apocalyptic truth"
and a steadfast sense that "as the elect, they are to help bring the end
about." Conversely, for nonbelievers, apocalypse "inclines people toward a
world-weary passivity" and "supplants agency with apathy."[6] If it is true
that we have a need for conclusive, meaningful ends, it is possible that the
opposite is also true: that there is a corresponding need to avoid the dis-
comfort that accompanies open-endedness. DeLillo's character Jack Gladney is right to worry about people who wish for this conclusive end. What
happens if we cannot learn to live with the ambiguity of open-endedness?
If enough of us desire a conclusive ending, will we make it happen to sat-
isfy that need?

There are real ramifications of viewing the world through an apocalyptic
lens. If we choose to be guided by this narrative, those not "with" us are, indeed, against us, and in the most heinous way. We are then duty-bound to
engage that evil in an effort to overcome it as we wait for our delivery at the
hands of the Messiah. This rhetoric and unforgiving stance is not unfamil-
iar to us at this time of radical terrorism. But one way to dampen if not to
foil a rhetoric that operates on a Manichean view of good and evil is to expose the underlying rhetorical structure that presupposes it. Postmodernists may conceivably contribute to peace through their thoughtful versions of apocalypse. And they do it not merely by examining the effects of
apocalypticism, but also—in providing indeterminant endings and beginnings, multiple Antichrists and Gods, and fluctuating moralities—by challenging the very terms by which the paradigm operates.

Though postmodernists have been criticized as being "good critical deconstructors and terrible constructors," one might argue that in the very
act of deconstructing apocalypse, postmodern artists are being *constructive*.[7] That is, by exposing the inherent dangers of this most powerful grand
narrative, the postmodernists under consideration in this study reveal their
own hopefulness for something better even than the New Jerusalem promised by the myth. By adapting the traditional apocalyptic myth with its
promise of a new heaven on earth, these postmodern artists not only expose the dangerous consequences of an overzealous commitment to the
traditional apocalyptic narrative, but also insinuate that we might seek less

combustible creeds in which to place our hopes—to suggest perhaps that rather than invest our hope in the afterlife, we might by peaceful means actively seek to improve our lives in the here and now. Rather than rely on God to save us, or the Antichrist to turn us from faith, we might come to understand that these are symbols for hope and peace on the one hand, despair and hatred on the other; and we might recognize aspects of ourselves in each of these symbols, for each of us contains within ourselves a capacity for good and evil, for love and hate, for generosity and selfishness.

By illuminating the complexity and power of human language and symbols, by exposing (and challenging) the systems which that language creates and within which we move, postmodernists may help to deepen our appreciation for the complexity of human relations, and, importantly, they may make it easier to resist the reductionism which apocalypse encourages. These artists nudge us toward active engagement with the complexities of human language and relations, and away from the deadly consequences of oversimplifying human motivation and behavior.

NOTES

1. Quinby, *Anti-Apocalypse*, xiv.
2. Wagar, *Terminal Visions*, 196.
3. Trachtenberg, *Critical Essays on American Postmodernism*, 16. See also Larry McCaffery's very fine introductory essay in *Postmodern Fiction* for more on the difficulty of coming to consensus about how postmodernism should be defined and/or understood.
4. As Margaret Atwood asks, assuming that stories "actually get out there in the world, and have effects and consequences. Don't we then have to begin talking about ethics and responsibilities . . . ?" (Atwood, *Negotiating with the Dead*, 97).
5. Milne, *The End of the World: The Doctrine of Last Things*, 46.
6. Quinby, *Anti-Apocalypse*, xx–xxi.
7. Butler, *Postmodernism: A Very Short Introduction*, 116.

WORKS CITED

Abádi-Nagy, Zoltan. "Serenity, Courage, Wisdom: A Talk with Kurt Vonnegut, 1989." In Reed, *The Vonnegut Chronicles: Interviews and Essays*, 15–34.

Abrams, M. H. *Natural Supernaturalism*. New York: W. W. Norton, 1971.

Abre los ojos. Dir. Alejandro Amenábar. Sociedad General de Televisión S.A., 1997.

Agosta, Lucien L. "Ah-Whoom!: Egotism and Apocalypse in Kurt Vonnegut's *Cat's Cradle*." *Kansas Quarterly* 14, no. 2 (1982): 127–34.

Aldridge, John W. *The American Novel and the Way We Live Now*. New York: Oxford University Press, 1983.

Allen, William Rodney, ed. *Conversations with Kurt Vonnegut*. Jackson, MS: University Press of Mississippi, 1988.

Alter, Robert. "The Apocalyptic Temper." *Commentary* 41, no. 6 (June 1966): 61–66.

Amis, Martin. *The Moronic Inferno and Other Visits to America*. Harmondsworth, UK: Penguin, 1986.

Andersen, Richard. *Robert Coover*. Boston: Twayne Publishers, 1981.

Anderson, Sam. "Code Red: Don DeLillo, the Literary Master of the Terrorist's Imagination, Reaches for the Ultimate Subject." *New York Magazine*, May 14, 2007. http://nymag.com/arts/books/features/31521/ (accessed May 15, 2007).

Animatrix. Dir. Peter Chung, Andy Jones, et al. Warner Home Video, 2003.

Atterbery, Brian. *Strategies of Fantasy*. Bloomington, IN: Indiana University Press, 1992.

Atwood, Margaret. "*The Handmaid's Tale* and *Oryx and Crake* in Context." *PMLA* 119, no. 3 (May 2004): 513–17.

———. *Negotiating with the Dead*. Cambridge: Cambridge University Press, 2002.

———. *Oryx and Crake*. London: Virago, 2004 [2003].

Baldwin, James. *The Fire Next Time*. London: Michael Joseph, 1963.

Barkun, Michael. "Politics and Apocalypticism." In Stein, *The Encyclopedia of Apocalypticism: Vol. III: Apocalypticism in the Modern Period and the Contemporary Age*, 442–60.

Barnett, P. Chad. "Reviving Cyberpunk: (Re)Constructing the Subject and Mapping Cyberspace in the Wachowski Brothers' Film *The Matrix*." *Extrapolation* 41, no. 4 (Winter 2000): 359–74.

Barth, John. "The Literature of Exhaustion." *The Atlantic*, Aug. 1967, 29–34.

Bassham, Gregory. "The Religion of *The Matrix* and the Problems of Pluralism." In Irwin, *The Matrix and Philosophy*, 111–25.

Baudrillard, Jean. *Simulacra and Simulation*. Translated by Sheila Faria Glaser. Ann Arbor, MI: The University of Michigan Press, 1994.

Beer, Gillian. *Darwin's Plots: Evolutionary Narrative in Darwin, George Eliot and Nineteenth-Century Fiction*. London: Routledge and Kegan Paul, 1983.

Begley, Adam. "Don DeLillo: The Art of Fiction CXXXV." *The Paris Review* 128 (Fall 1993): 275–306.

Bellow, Saul. *Herzog*. Harmondsworth, UK: Penguin, 1965 [1964].

Berger, James. *After the End: Representations of Post-Apocalypse*. Minneapolis: University of Minnesota Press, 1999.

Bergoffen, Debra. "The Apocalyptic Meaning of History." In Zamora, *The Apocalyptic Vision in America: Interdisciplinary Essays on Myth and Culture*, 11–36.

Berman, Neil. "Coover's *Universal Baseball Association*: Play as Personalized Myth." *Modern Fiction Studies* 24, no. 2 (Summer 1978): 209–22.

———. *Playful Fictions and Fictional Players: Game, Sport and Survival in Contemporary American Fiction*. Port Washington, NY: Kennikat, 1981.

Blanch, Robert J. "The Fisher King in Gotham: New Age Spiritualism Meets the Grail Legend." In *King Arthur on Film: New Essays on Arthurian Cinema*, edited by Kevin J. Harty, 123–41. Jefferson, NC: McFarland and Company, 1999.

Bowler, Peter J. *Evolution: The History of an Idea*. Berkeley: University of California Press, 1984.

Boyd, Katrina G. "Pastiche and Postmodernism in *Brazil*." *Cinefocus* 1, no. 1 (January 1990): 33–42.

Boyer, Paul S. *By the Bomb's Early Light: American Thought and Culture at the Dawn of the Atomic Age*. Chapel Hill, NC: University of North Carolina Press, 1994.

Bradbury, Malcolm. *The Novel Today: Contemporary Writers on Modern Fiction*. Revised Edition. Ed. Malcom Bradbury. London: Fontana, 1990.

Brannigan, Michael. "There Is No Spoon: A Buddhist Mirror." In Irwin, *The Matrix and Philosophy*, 101–10.

Brazil. Dir. Terry Gilliam. Criterion Edition. Twentieth Century Fox, 1985.

Brians, Paul. *Nuclear Holocausts: Atomic War in Fiction, 1985–1984*. Kent, OH: Kent State University Press, 1987.

Broeck, Josef. "The Apocalyptic Imagination in America; Recent Criticism." *The Kritikon Litterarum* 14, no.1–4 (1985): 89–94.

Brown, Mitchell. "Crisis on Infinite Earths #1." The 100 Greatest Comics of the 20th Century. http://www.comicstalk.com/crisis.htm (accessed April 2005).

Bruce, Steve. *God Is Dead: Secularization in the West.* Oxford: Blackwell, 2002.

Buber, Martin. "Prophecy, Apocalyptic, and the Historical Hour." 192–207 in *Pointing the Way.* Translated by Maurice Friedman. New York: Harper and Brothers, 1957.

Bukatman, Scott. *Terminal Identity: The Virtual Subject in Postmodern Science Fiction.* Durham, NC: Duke University Press, 1993.

Burek, Josh. "The Gospel According to Neo." *Christian Science Monitor*, 9 May 2003. csmonitor.com. http://www.csmonitor.com/2003/0509/p1601-almo.html (accessed July 10, 2003).

Burke, William. "Football, Literature, Culture." *Southwest Review* 60, no. 4 (Autumn 1975): 391–99.

Bushby, Helen. "*Matrix* Sizzles but Does Not Stir." BBC News Online. 2 Feb. 2004. http://news.bbc.co.uk/1/hi/entertainment/reviews/3031045.stm.

Butler, Christopher. *Postmodernism: A Very Short Introduction.* Oxford: Oxford University Press, 2002.

Campbell, Ramsay. Foreword. *Saga of the Swamp Thing*, by Alan Moore. Art by Steve Bissette and John Totleben. New York: Vertigo, 1987.

Carey, Frances. "The Apocalyptic Tradition: Between Tradition and Modernity." Chapter 6 in *The Apocalypse and the Shape of Things to Come.* Edited by Frances Carey. London British Museum, 1999.

Carey, John, ed. *The Faber Book of Utopias.* London: Faber and Faber, 1999.

Center for Disease Control and Prevention website. http://www.cdc.gov/flu/avian/outbreaks/current.htm (accessed July 7, 2007).

Charlesworth, James H., Ed. *The Old Testament Pseudepigrapha: Vol. 1 Apocalyptic Literature and Testaments.* London: Darton, Longman and Todd, 1983.

Christie, Ian, ed. *Gilliam on Gilliam.* London: Faber and Faber, 1999.

Chu, Jeff. "Oh Father, Where Art Thou?" *Time*, June 16, 2003. 23–30.

Civello, Paul. *American Literary Naturalism and Its Twentieth-Century Transformations: Frank Norris, Ernest Hemingway, Don DeLillo.* London: University of Georgia, 1994.

Cizik, Richard. "Interview with Richard Cizik." *Frontline: The Jesus Factor*, PBS, April 29, 2004. http://www.pbs.org/wgbh/pages/frontline/shows/jesus/interviews/cizik.html (accessed 22 Feb. 2005).

Clarkson, Helen [Helen Clarkson McCloy]. *The Last Day.* New York: Dodd, Mead, 1959 [1958].

Cohn, Norman. *Cosmos, Chaos and the World to Come: The Ancient Roots of Apocalyptic Faith.* New Haven: Yale University Press, 1993.

Collins, John J. *The Apocalyptic Imagination: An Introduction to the Jewish Matrix of Christianity.* New York: Crossroad, 1984.

Conte, Joseph. *Design and Debris: A Chaotics of Postmodern American Fiction.* Tuscaloosa, AL: The University of Alabama Press, 2002.

Coover, Robert. "In answer to the question: 'Why do you write?'" *Delta* 28 (June 1989): 18.

——. *The Origin of the Brunists*. [1966] New York: Bantam, 1978.

——. *The Public Burning*. [1977] New York: Bantam, 1978.

——. *A Theological Position*. New York: Dutton, 1972.

——. *The Universal Baseball Association, Inc., J. Henry Waugh, Prop.* [1968] New York: Plume, 1971.

Cope, Jackson I. *Robert Coover's Fictions*. Baltimore: The Johns Hopkins University Press, 1986.

Costa, Jordi and Sergi Sánchez. "Childhood, Vocation, and First Experiences of a Rebel Dreamer." In Sterritt, *Terry Gilliam—Interviews*, 170–83.

Cowart, David. "Culture and Anarchy: Vonnegut's Later Career." In Merrill, *Critical Essays on Kurt Vonnegut*, 170–87.

——. *Don DeLillo: The Physics of Language*. Athens, GA: University of Georgia Press, 2002.

Crichton, Michael. *The Andromeda Strain*. London: Jonathan Cape, 1969.

Cromie, Robert. *The Crack of Doom*. London: Digby, Long, 1895.

Darwin, Charles. *The Origin of Species*. Introduction by Jeff Wallace. Ware, Hertfordshire, UK: Wordsworth Editions, 1998.

David, Catherine, Frederic Lenoir and Jean-Philippe de Tonnac, eds. *Conversations about the End of Time*. Translated by Ian Maclean and Roger Pearson. New York: Fromm International, 2001.

Davis, Todd F. "Apocalyptic Grumbling: Post-Modern Humanism in the Work of Kurt Vonnegut." In *At Millennium's End: New Essays on the Work of Kurt Vonnegut*, edited by Kevin Alexander Boon, 149–66. Albany: State University of New York Press, 2001.

——. "Kurt Vonnegut." In *Postmodernism: The Key Figures*, edited by Hans Bertens and Joseph Natoli, 315–20. Oxford: Blackwell, 2002.

——. *Kurt Vonnegut's Crusade, or How a Postmodern Harlequin Preached a New Kind of Humanism*. Albany: State University of New York Press, 2006.

The Day After. Dir. Nicholas Meyer. American Broadcasting Company, 1983.

The Day After Tomorrow. Dir. Roland Emmerich. Twentieth Century Fox, 2004.

Dark City. Dir. Alex Proyas. New Line Cinema, 1998.

DeCurtis, Anthony. "An Outsider in This Society: An Interview with Don DeLillo," in Lentricchia, *Introducing Don DeLillo*, 43–66.

Dellamora, Richard, ed. *Postmodern Apocalypse: Theory and Cultural Practice at the End*. Philadelphia: University of Pennsylvania Press, 1995.

DeLillo, Don. "American Blood." *Rolling Stone*, Dec. 8, 1983: 21–30+.

——. *Americana*. [1971] London: Penguin, 1990.

——. *The Body Artist*. London: Picador, 2001.

——. *Cosmopolis*. London: Picador, 2003.

——. *End Zone*. [1972] New York: Penguin Books, 1986.

——. *Falling Man*. New York: Scribner, 2007.

————. *Great Jones Street*. [1973] London: Picador, 1998.

————. *Libra*. New York: Penguin, 1988.

————. *Mao II*. [1991] New York: Penguin, 1992.

————. *Running Dog*. [1978] London: Picador, 1992.

————. *Underworld*. [1997] London: Picador, 1999.

————. *White Noise*. [1985] London: Picador, 2002.

Denby, David. "When Worlds Collide: 'The Matrix Revolutions'." *The New Yorker*, Nov. 10, 2003: 128.

Derrida, Jacques. "Economies de la crise." *La Quinzaine littéraire* (Oct. 1984): 6–7.

Dewey, Joseph. *Beyond Grief and Nothing: A Reading of Don DeLillo*. Columbia, SC: University of South Carolina Press, 2006.

————. *In a Dark Time: The Apocalyptic Temper in the American Novel of Nuclear Age*. West Lafayette, IN: Purdue University, 1990.

————. *Underwords: Perspectives on Don DeLillo's Underworld*. Edited by Joseph Dewey, Steven G. Kellman, and Irving Malin. London: Associated University, 2002.

Dickens, Charles. *A Tale of Two Cities*. [1859] London: Penguin, 1994.

Di Filippo, Paul. "Literary Influences on *The Matrix*." In Haber, *Exploring the Matrix: Visions of the Cyber Present*, 74–97.

Dionne, E. J., Jr. "Interview with E. J. Dionne, Jr." *Frontline: The Jesus Factor*, PBS April 29, 2004. http://www.pbs.org/wgbh/pages/frontline/shows/jesus/interviews/dionne.html (accessed Feb. 22, 2005).

The Directors–Terry Gilliam. American Film Institute AFI, 2000.

Donnie Darko. Dir. Richard Kelly. Pandora Cinema/Newmarket Films, 2001.

Douthat, Ross. "Crises of Faith" *The Atlantic*, July/August 2007: 38–42.

Dowling, David. *Fictions of Nuclear Disaster*. London: Macmillian, 1987.

Dr. Strangelove, or How I Learned to Stop Worrying and Love the Bomb. Dir. Stanley Kubrick. Columbia Pictures, 1964.

Edelstein, David. "Bullet Time Again: The Wachowskis Reload." *New York Times*, May 11, 2003. *http://web.lexis-nexis.com/* (accessed July 12, 2003).

Eilers, Michelle L. "On the Origins of Modern Fantasy." *Extrapolation* 41, no. 4 (2000): 317–37.

Eisner, Will. *Comics and Sequential Art*. Taramac, FL: Poorhouse, 2001.

Eldredge, Niles and Ian Tattersall. *The Myths of Human Evolution*. New York: Columbia University Press, 1982.

Eliade, Mircea. *Myth and Reality*. London: George Allen and Unwin, 1964.

————. *The Myth of the Eternal Return*. Translated by Willard R. Trask. London: Routledge and Kegan Paul, 1955.

Ellegård, Alvar. *Darwin and the General Reader: The Reception of Darwin's Theory of Evolution in the British Periodical Press, 1859–1872*. Stockholm: Göteborg, 1958.

Ellmann, Maud. *The Hunger Artists: Starving, Writing and Imprisonment*. London: Virago, 1993.

Ellison, Harlan. "I Have No Mouth, and I Must Scream." In *The Mirror of Infinity*. Edited by Robert Silverberg. San Francisco: Canfield, 1970. 269–84.

Evenson, Brian. *Understanding Robert Coover*. Columbia, SC: University of South Carolina Press, 2003.

Felluga, Dino. "*The Matrix*: Paradigm of Postmodernism or Intellectual Poseur? Part I." In Yeffeth, *Taking the Red Pill: Science, Philosophy and Religion in* The Matrix, 85–101.

The Fisher King. Dir. Terry Gilliam. TriStar/Columbia Pictures, 1991.

Fitzpatrick, Kathleen. "The Unmaking of History: Baseball, Cold War, and *Underworld*." In Dewey, *Underwords*, 144–60.

Flannery-Dailey, Frances and Rachel Wagner. "Bruce Willis as the Messiah: Human Effort, Salvation and Apocalypticism in *Twelve Monkeys*." *Journal of Religion and Film*. 4, no. 1 (April 2000). http://www.unomaha.edu/jrf/Messiah.htm (accessed Aug. 2, 2006).

———. "Wake Up! Gnosticism and Buddhism in *The Matrix*." *Journal of Religion and Film*. 5, no.2 (October 2001). http://www.unomaha.edu/~wwwjrf/gnostic.htm (accessed July 15, 2003).

Fontana, Paul. "Finding God in *The Matrix*." In Yeffeth, 187–219.

Ford, James. "Buddhism, Mythology, and *The Matrix*." In Yeffeth, *Taking the Red Pill: Science, Philosophy and Religion in* The Matrix, 150–73.

Freese, Peter. *From Apocalypse to Entropy and Beyond: The Second Law of Thermodynamics in Post-War American Fiction*. Essen: Verlag Die Blaue Eule, 1997.

———. "Natural Selection with a Vengeance: Kurt Vonnegut's *Galápagos*." *Amerikastudien* 36, no. 3 (1991): 337–60.

———. "Vonnegut's Invented Religions as Sense-Making Systems." In Reed, *The Vonnegut Chronicles: Interviews and Essays*, 145–64.

Friedlander, Saul, Gerald Holton, Leo Marx, and Eugene Skolnikoff, eds. *Visions of Apocalypse: End or Rebirth*. New York: Holmes and Meier, 1985.

Friedman, Amy. "DeLillo in London—January 15, 1998." Public appearance at The Congress Centre. Oct. 7, 2003. http://perival.com/delillo/delillo_19980115.html

Frye, Northrop. *Anatomy of Criticism*. London: Penguin, 1990.

Fuller, Robert C. *Naming the Antichrist: The History of an American Obsession*. New York: Oxford University Press, 1995.

Gado, Frank, ed. *First Person: Conversations on Writers and Writing with Glenway Wescott, John Dos Passos, Robert Penn Warren, John Updike, John Barth, Robert Coover*. Schenectady, NY: Union College, 1973.

Gaiman, Neil. Overture. In *Swamp Thing: Love and Death*, by Alan Moore, 6–10. Art by Stephen Bissette, John Totleben, Shawn McManus. New York: Vertigo, 1990.

Gannon, Charles. "Neither Fire nor Ice: Postmodern Revisions of America's Post-Cold War Apocalyptic Nightmare." *The Comparatist* 23 (May 1999): 152–59.

George, Peter [Peter Bryant]. *Two Hours to Doom*. London: T.V. Boardman, 1958.

Gibbs, Nancy. "Apocalypse Now." *Time*, July 1, 2002: 40–48.

Gibson, William M., ed. *Mark Twain's Mysterious Stranger Manuscripts*. Mark Twain [Samuel Clemens] Berkeley: University of California, 1969.

Gleason, Paul. "Don DeLillo, T. S. Eliot, and the Redemption of America's Atomic Waste Land." In Dewey, *Underwords*, 130–43.

Global Warming International Center website. http://www.globalwarming.net/index.php?option=com_frontpageandItemid=1

Goldman, Albert. "The Trial of Lenny Bruce." *The New Republic*, Sept. 12, 1964: 13–14.

Goldman, Marlene. *Rewriting Apocalypse in Canadian Fiction*. Canada: McGill-Queen's University Press, 2005.

Goldsmith, Steven. *Unbuilding Jerusalem: Apocalyptic and Romantic Representation*. Ithaca, NY: Cornell University Press, 1993.

Goldstein, William. "Don DeLillo." *Publishers Weekly*, Aug. 19, 1988: 55–6.

Gonzalez, Ann. "Robert Coover's *The UBA*: Baseball as Metafiction." *The International Fiction Review* 11, no. 2 (1984): 106–09.

Goonan, Kathleen Ann. "More Than You'll Ever Know: Down the Rabbit Hole of the Matrix." In Haber, *Exploring the Matrix: Visions of the Cyber Present*, 98–111.

Gordon, Andrew. "*The Matrix*: Paradigm of Postmodernism or Intellectual Poseur? Part II." In Yeffeth, *Taking the Red Pill: Science, Philosophy and Religion in* The Matrix, 102–23.

Gordon, Devin. "The Matrix Makers." *Newsweek*, 6 Jan. 2003. *MSNBC News*. 2005. http://www.msnbc.com/news/850165.asp (accessed on July 10, 2003).

Gordon, Lois. *Robert Coover: The Universal Fictionmaking Process*, Carbondale, IL: Southern Illinois University Press, 1983.

Gould, Stephen Jay. *Ever Since Darwin: Reflections in Natural History*. London: Burnett Books in association with Andre Deutsch, 1978.

———. *The Panda's Thumb: More Reflections in Natural History*. New York: W.W. Norton, 1982.

Graham, Philip. "A Memo to the Wachowski Brothers from a Disappointed Fan." *New York Times*, June 1, 2003. http://web.lexis-nexis.com/ (accessed on Aug. 13, 2003).

Grau, Christopher. "Brain-in-a-vat Skepticism." *What Is the Matrix: "Mainframe"* Nov. 20, 2002. http://whatisthematrix.warnerbros.com/ (accessed on June 11, 2003).

Griswold, Charles L., Jr. "Happiness and Cypher's Choice: Is Ignorance Bliss?" In Irwin, *The Matrix and Philosophy*, 126–37.

Groth, Gary and Robert Fiore, eds. *The New Comics: Interviews from the Pages of* The Comics Journal. New York: Berkley, 1988.

Gunn, James. "The Reality Paradox in *The Matrix*." In Yeffeth, *Taking the Red Pill: Science, Philosophy and Religion in* The Matrix, 72–83.

Haber, Karen, ed. *Exploring the Matrix: Visions of the Cyber Present*. US: Byron Preiss Visual, 2003.

Haldeman, Joe. "The Matrix as Sci-Fi." In Haber, *Exploring the Matrix: Visions of the Cyber Present*, 168–79.

Hansen, Arlen J. "The Dice of God: Einstein, Heisenberg, and Robert Coover." Tenth Anniversary Issue: I, *NOVEL: A Forum on Fiction* 10, no. 1. (Autumn 1976): 49–58.

Hanson, Robin. "Was Cypher Right? Part I: Why We Stay in our Matrix." In Yeffeth, *Taking the Red Pill: Science, Philosophy and Religion in* The Matrix, 31–42.

Hersey, John. *Hiroshima*. Harmondsworth, UK: Penguin, 1966.

Hertzel, Leo J. "An Interview with Robert Coover." *Critique: Studies in Modern Fiction* 11, no. 3 (1969): 25–34.

———. "What's Wrong with Christians?" *Critique: Studies in Modern Fiction* 11, no. 3 (1969): 11–22.

Heylighen, Francis. "Punctuated Equilibrium." *Principia Cybernetica Web*. July 22, 1999. http://pespmc1.vub.ac.be/PUNCTUEQ.html (accessed on Jan. 5, 2005).

Hoban, Russell. *Riddley Walker*. [1980] London: Picador, 1982.

Honderich, Ted, ed. "Social Darwinism," *The Oxford Companion to Philosophy*. Oxford: Oxford University Press, 1995.

Houellebecq, Michel. *Atomised*. Trans. Frank Wynne. [1998] London: Heinemann, 2000.

Howard, Gerald. "The American Strangeness: An Interview with Don DeLillo." *Hungry Mind Review* 43 (1997): 13–16.

Hunter, Stephen. "'Matrix' Vortex; Trilogy's Center Wastes a Lot of Motion, but It'll Drag You In Anyway." *The Washington Post*, May 15, 2003. http://web.lexis-nexis.com/ (accessed on Aug. 13, 2003).

Ibuse, Masuji. *Black Rain*. London: Bantam, 1985.

Irwin, William, ed. *The Matrix and Philosophy*. Chicago, IL: Open Court, 2002.

La Jetée. Dir. Chris Marker. Argos Films, 1962.

Joy, Bill. "Why the Future Doesn't Need Us." In Yeffeth, *Taking the Red Pill: Science, Philosophy and Religion in* The Matrix, 235–75.

Kadragic, Alma. "Robert Coover–An Interview." *Shantih: A quarterly of international Writings* 2, no. 2 (Summer, 1972): 57–61.

Kapell, Matthew and William G. Doty. *Jacking in to the Matrix Franchise: Cultural Reception and Interpretation*. New York: Continuum, 2004.

Kavanagh, Barry. "The Alan Moore Interview" Oct. 17, 2000. *Blather.net* 2003. http://www.blather.net/articles/amoore/watchmen3.html (accessed on Jan. 1, 2004).

Kennedy, Louis. "Piece of Mind Forget about Beginnings, Middles, and Ends. The New Storytelling Is about Making Your Way in a Fragmented, Imaginary World." *The Boston Globe*, June 1, 2003. http://web.lexis-nexis.com/ (accessed on March 13, 2005).

Kennedy, Thomas E. *Robert Coover: A Study of the Short Fiction*. New York: Twayne Publishers, 1992.

Kermode, Frank. "Apocalypse and the Modern." In *Visions of Apocalypse: End or Rebirth*, edited by Saul Friedlander, et al., 84–106. New York: Holmes and Meier Publishers, 1985.

———. *The Sense of an Ending*. Oxford: Oxford University, 1967.

Ketterer, David. *New Worlds for Old: The Apocalyptic Imagination, Science Fiction, and American Literature*. Bloomington, IN: Indiana University, 1974.

Khoury, George, ed. *The Extraordinary Works of Alan Moore*. Raleigh, NC: TwoMorrows Publishing, 2003.

Kievitt, Frank David. "Walter M. Miller's *A Canticle for Leibowitz* as a Third Testament." In *The Transcendent Adventure: Studies of Religion in Science Fiction/Fantasy*, edited by Robert Reilly, 169–75. Westport, CT: Greenwood, 1985.

King, C. Richard and David J. Leonard. "Is Neo White? Reading Race, Watching the Trilogy." In Kapell, *Jacking in to the Matrix Franchise: Cultural Reception and Interpretation*, 32–47.

King, Stephen. *The Stand*. London: New English Library, 1978.

Klawans, Stuart. "A Dialogue with Terry Gilliam." In Sterritt, *Terry Gilliam—Interviews*, 141–69.

Klinkowitz, Jerome. *The Vonnegut Effect*. Columbia, SC: University of South Carolina Press, 2004.

Knight, Peter. "Everything Is Connected: *Underworld's* Secret History of Paranoia." In Ruppersburg, *Critical Essays on Don DeLillo*, 282–301.

Kraemer, Christine Hoff. "Alan Moore's *Promethea*: Comics as Neo-Pagan Primer and Missionary Tool." Paper given at Northeast Modern Language Association Convention, Baltimore, MD. Mar. 1–3, 2007.

Kreuziger, Frederick A. *The Religion of Science Fiction*. Bowling Green, OH: Bowling Green State University Popular Press, 1986.

Kurzweil, Ray. *The Age of Spiritual Machines: How We Will Live, Work and Think in the New Age of Intelligent Machines*. London: Orion Business, 1999.

———. "The Human Machine Merger: Are We Heading for *The Matrix*?" In Yeffeth, *Taking the Red Pill: Science, Philosophy and Religion in* The Matrix, 220–34.

Khayyam, Omar. *The Rubaiyat*. Translated by Edward Fitzgerald. Garden City, NY: Garden City Books, 1952.

LaGravenese, Richard. *The Fisher King: The Book of the Film*. Introduction by Terry Gilliam. New York: Applause Books, 1991.

Lahaye, Tim and Jerry B. Jenkins. *Left Behind*. Wheaton, IL: Tyndale House, 1995.

Lamm, Spencer, ed. *The Art of the Matrix*. London: Titan, 2000.

Lashmet, David. "'The future is history': *12 Monkeys* and the Origin of AIDS." *Mosaic: A Journal for the Interdisciplinary Study of Literature* 33, no. 4 (Dec. 2000): 55–72. *Literature Online*.

Laurence, William L. *Dawn Over Zero*. London: Museum Press, 1947.

Lawler, James. "We Are (the) One! Kant Explains How to Manipulate the Matrix." In Irwin, *The Matrix and Philosophy*, 138–52.

Lawrence, D. H. *Apocalypse*. Introduction by Richard Aldington. London: Martin Secker, 1932.

Lawrence, John Shelton. "Fascist Redemption or Democratic Hope?" In Kapell, *Jacking in to the Matrix Franchise: Cultural Reception and Interpretation*, 80–96.

LeClair, Thomas. *In the Loop: Don DeLillo and the Systems Novel*. Urbana, IL: University of Illinois, 1987.

LeClair, Tom and Larry McCaffery, eds. *Anything Can Happen: Interviews with Contemporary American Novelists.* Urbana, IL: University of Illinois, 1983.

Lentricchia, Frank, ed. *Introducing Don DeLillo.* Durham, NC: Duke University Press, 1991.

(The Official) Left Behind Series site. http://www.leftbehind.com/

Lewicki, Zbigniew. *The Bang and the Whimper: Apocalypse and Entropy in American Literature.* Westport, CN: Greenwood, 1984.

Lewis, R.W. B. *Trials of the Word.* New Haven: Yale University, 1965.

Lish Manuscripts, 1972–1991. Lilly Library Manuscript Collections. Indiana University Library.

Lloyd, Peter B. "Glitches in *The Matrix.* . . . And How to Fix Them." In Yeffeth, *Taking the Red Pill: Science, Philosophy and Religion in* The Matrix, 124–49.

"The Making of *The Matrix.*" *The Matrix.* DVD. Dir. Larry and Andy Wachowski. Warner Bros., 1999.

Malin, Irving and Joseph Dewey. "'What Beauty, What Power': Speculations on the Third Edgar." In Dewey, *Underwords,* 19–27.

Maltby, Paul. *Dissident Postmodernists: Barthelme, Coover, Pynchon.* Philadelphia: University of Pennsylvania Press, 1991.

Marine, Gene. "Lenny, You *Meshugginah,* You Can't Play the Hero!" *Ramparts* 10 (June 1972): 58–60.

Martin, Joel W. and Conrad E. Ostwalt, Jr., eds. *Screening the Sacred: Religion, Myth, and Ideology in Popular American Film.* Boulder, CO: Westview, 1995.

The Matrix. Dir. Larry and Andy Wachowski. Warner Bros., 1999.

The Matrix: Reloaded. Dir. Larry and Andy Wachowski. Warner Bros., 2003.

The Matrix: Revolutions. Dir. Larry and Andy Wachowski. Warner Bros., 2003.

Matthews, Jack. *The Battle of Brazil.* New York: Crown Publishers, 1987.

May, John R. *Toward a New Earth: Apocalypse in the American Novel.* Notre Dame, IN: University of Notre Dame, 1972.

McAlister, Melani. "Prophecy, Politics, and the Popular: The Left Behind Series and Christian Fundamentalism's New World Order." *The South Atlantic Quarterly* 102, no. 4 (2003): 773–98.

McAllister, Matthew P. "Ownership Concentration in the U.S. Comic Book Industry." In *Comics and Ideology,* edited by Matthew P. McAllister, Edward H. Sewell, Jr., and Ian Gordon, 15–38. New York: Peter Lang, 2001.

McCabe, Bob. *Dark Knights and Holy Fools.* London: Orion, 1999.

McCaffery, Larry. *The Metafictional Muse: The Works of Robert Coover, Donald Barthelme, and William H. Gass.* Pittsburgh: University of Pittsburgh Press, 1982.

———. "Introduction." In *Postmodern Fiction: A Bio-Biographical Guide,* edited by Larry McCaffery, xi–xxviii. New York: Greenwood Press, 1986.

McCaffery, Larry and Robert Coover. "Robert Coover on His Own and Other Fictions." *Genre* 14, no. 1 (Spring 1981): 45–65.

McCarthy, Cormac. *Blood Meridian or the Evening Redness in the West.* [1985] London: Picador, 1990.

McCloud, Scott. *Understanding Comics: The Invisible Art.* New York: Harper Perennial, 1993.

Mellard, James M. *The Exploded Form: The Modernist Novel in America*. Urbana, IL: University of Illinois, 1980.

Memento. Dir. Christopher Nolan. Newmarket Films, 2000.

Mendlesohn, Farah. "Toward a Taxonomy of Fantasy." *Journal of the Fantastic in the Arts* 13, no. 2 (2003): 169–83.

Merrill, Robert. *Critical Essays on Kurt Vonnegut*. Boston: G.K. Hall, 1990.

Merrin, William. "'Did You Ever Eat Tasty Wheat?' Baudrillard and *The Matrix*." *Scope: An On-line Journal of Film Studies*, Feb. 8, 2003 http://www.nottingham.ac.uk/film/journal/articles/did-you-ever-eat.htm (accessed on July 10, 2003).

Miller, Frank. *Batman: The Dark Knight Returns*. London: Titan, 1996. Originally published in single issue format, 1985, 1986.

Miller, Jonathan. "The Sick White Negro." *Partisan Review* 30, no. 1 (Spring 1963): 149–55.

Miller, Walter M. *A Canticle for Leibowitz*. [1959] London: Orbit Books, 2002.

Milligan, Richard. "Environmental Rhetoric in and around *The Day After Tomorrow*." Paper given at 2005 Joint Conference of the National Popular Culture and American Culture Associations, San Diego. March 24, 2005.

Milne, Bruce. *The End of the World: The Doctrine of Last Things*. Eastborne: Kingsway Publications, 1983.

The Mindscape of Alan Moore. Dir. Dez Vylenz. Shadowsnake Films, 2003.

Moore, Alan. *Promethea*. Illustrated by J. H. Williams III and Mick Gray. La Jolla, CA: America's Best Comics, 2000. Originally published in single issue format #1–6, 1999, 2000.

———. *Promethea 2*. Illustrated by J. H. Williams III and Mick Gray. La Jolla, CA: America's Best Comics, 2001. Originally published in single issue format #7–12, 2000, 2001.

———. *Promethea 3*. Illustrated by J. H. Williams III and Mick Gray. La Jolla, CA: America's Best Comics, 2002. Originally published in single issue format #13–#18, 2001, 2002.

———. *Promethea 4*. Illustrated by J.H. Williams III and Mick Gray. La Jolla, CA: America's Best Comics, 2003. Originally published in single issue format #19–25, 2002, 2003.

———. *Promethea 5*. Illustrated by J. H. Williams III, Mick Gray, Jeromy Cox, Jose Villarrubia. La Jolla, CA: America's Best Comics, 2005. Originally published in single issue format #26–32, 2003, 2004, 2005.

———. *Saga of the Swamp Thing (Book 1)*. Illustrated by Steve Bissette and John Totleben. New York: Vertigo, DC COMICS, 1987. Originally published in single issue format #21–27, 1983, 1984.

———. *Swamp Thing: Love and Death (Book 2)*. Illustrated by Shawn McManus, Steve Bissette, et al. New York: Vertigo, DC COMICS, 1990. Originally published in single issue format as *Saga of the Swamp Thing* #28–34 and *Swamp Thing Annual* #2, 1984, 1985.

———. *Swamp Thing: The Curse (Book 3)*. Illustrated by Stephen Bissette, John Totleben, et al. New York: Vertigo, DC COMICS, 2000. Originally published in single issue format #35–42, 1985.

———. *Swamp Thing: A Murder of Crows (Book 4)*. Illustrated by Stan Woch, Ron Randall, et al. New York: Vertigo, DC COMICS, 2001. Originally published in single issue format as *Saga of the Swamp Thing* #43–45 and *Swamp Thing* #46–50, 1985, 1986.

———. *V for Vendetta*. Illustrated by David Moore. London: Titan Books, 1990.

———. *Watchmen*. Illustrated by Dave Gibbons. New York: DC COMICS, 1987. Originally published in single issue format #1–12, 1986, 1987.

Morgan, David. "The Saga of *Brazil*: Terry Gilliam Discusses the Making and Near Un-making of his Dystopian Fantasy." *Wide Angle/Closeup* http://members.aol.com/morgands1/closeup/text/brazil.htm (accessed on April 28, 2006).

———. "'They're Getting a Gilliam Film'—On Location with *The Fisher King*." *Wide Angle/Closeup*, http://members.aol.com/morgands1/closeup/text/lafisher.htm.

Murdoch, Iris. "Against Dryness: A Polemical Sketch." In Bradbury, *The Novel Today: Contemporary Writers on Modern Fiction*, 15–26.

Musil, Robert. "There Must Be More to Love than Death: A Conversation with Kurt Vonnegut." In Allen, *Conversations with Kurt Vonnegut*, 230–39.

Mustazza, Leonard. "A Darwinian Eden: Science and Myth in Kurt Vonnegut's *Galápagos*." *Journal of the Fantastic in the Arts* 3, no. 2.10 (1991): 55–65.

Nelson, John Wiley. "The Apocalyptic Vision in American Popular Culture." In Zamora, *The Apocalyptic Vision in America*, 154–82.

Nuwer, Hank. "A Skull Session with Kurt Vonnegut." In Allen, *Conversations with Kurt Vonnegut*, 240–64.

O'Leary, Stephen D. *Arguing the Apocalypse: A Theory of Millennial Rhetoric*. Oxford: Oxford University Press, 1994.

The Omega Man. Dir. Boris Sagal. Warner Bros., 1971.

Osen, Diane. "A Conversation with Don DeLillo." *Publisher's Weekly*, March 7, 2002. http://www.publishersweekly.com/NBF/docs/wwl_curri_DeLillo.htm

Ospovat, Dov. *The Development of Darwin's Theory*. Cambridge: Cambridge University Press, 1981.

Osteen, Mark. "Against the End: Asceticism and Apocalypse in Don DeLillo's *End Zone*." *Papers on Language and Literature: A Journal for scholars and Critics of Language* 26, no. 1 (Winter 1990): 143–63.

———. *American Magic and Dread: Don DeLillo's Dialogue with Culture*. Philadelphia: University of Pennsylvania Press, 2000.

Ostwalt, Conrad. "*Armageddon* at the Millennial Dawn." *The Journal of Religion and Film* 4, no.1 (April 2000) http://www.unomaha.edu/~wwwjrf/armagedd.htm (accessed on July 3, 2003).

O'Toole, Fintan. "And Quiet Writes the Don." *The Irish Times*, Jan. 10, 1998. http://web.lexis-nexis.com/ (accessed on Aug. 27, 2004).

Outbreak. Dir. Wolfgang Peterson. Warner Bros., 1995.

Paley, William. *Natural Theology: Or Evidences of the Existence and Attributes of the Deity, Collected from the Appearances of Nature*. London: Longman, 1846.

Pappu, Sridhar. "We Need Another Hero." Oct. 18, 2000. *salon.com* http://archive .salon.com/people/feature/2000/10/18/moore/index2.html (accessed on Nov. 19, 2002).

Passaro, Vince. "Dangerous Don DeLillo." *New York Times*, May 19, 1991. http://www .nytimes.com/books/97/03/16/lifetimes/del-v-dangerous.html (accessed on Mar. 7, 2002).

Peoples, David and Janet. *Twelve Monkeys*. Script by David and Janet Peoples. http://www.dailyscript.com/scripts/twelve_monkeys.html (accessed on May 30, 2006).

Pettersson, Bo. *The World According to Kurt Vonnegut*. Åbo, Finland: Åbo Akademi University, 1994.

"Pinewood Dialogues Online: Terry Gilliam." Interviewed by David Schwartz at Riklis Theatre, American Museum of the Moving Image, Jan 6 and 7, 1996. *Pinewood Dialogues Online* http://pinewood.movingimage.us/interfaces/ammi/ pinewood/person.cgi?people_id=25 (accessed on April 28, 2006).

Poe, Edgar Allan. "The Masque of the Red Death." [1842] *The 70 Best Tales of Edgar Allan Poe*. London: Chancellor, 1992.

Porush, David. "Hacking the Brainstem: Postmodern Metaphysics and Stephenson's *Snow Crash*." In *Virtual Realities and Their Discontents*, edited by Robert Markley, 107–41. Baltimore: Johns Hopkins University Press, 1996.

Probst, Christopher. "Welcome to the Machine." *American Cinematographer* 80, no. 4 (April 1999) http://www.theasc.com/magazine/apr99/matrix/index.htm (accessed on July 3, 2003).

Puschmann-Nalenz, Barbara. *Science Fiction and Postmodern Fiction*. New York: Peter Lang, 1992.

Pynchon, Thomas. *Gravity's Rainbow*. [1973] London: Vintage, 2000.

Quinby, Lee. *Anti-Apocalypse*. Minneapolis: University of Minnesota Press, 1994.

Rapture Ready website. http://www.raptureready.com/

Reed, Peter J. "A Conversation with Kurt Vonnegut, 1982." In Reed, *The Vonnegut Chronicles: Interviews and Essays*, 3–14.

———. "God Bless You, Mr. Darwin, for Kurt Vonnegut's Latest." In *Critical Essays on Kurt Vonnegut*, edited by Robert Merrill, 62–63. Boston: G.K. Hall, 1990.

Reed, Peter J. and Marc Leeds, eds. *The Vonnegut Chronicles: Interviews and Essays*. Westport, CN: Greenwood, 1996.

Robbe-Grillet, Alain. *For a New Novel: Essays on Fiction*. Translated by Richard Howard. New York: Grove Press, 1965.

Roberts, Adam. *Science Fiction*. London: Routledge, 2000.

Robinson, Douglas. *American Apocalypses: The Image of the End of the World in American Literature*. Baltimore: The Johns Hopkins University Press, 1985.

Robinson, Tasha. "In My World: Alan Moore Interview." The A.V. Club Oct. 24, 2001. http://www.avclub.com/content/node/24222 (accessed on Nov. 19, 2002).

Rogers, Richard A. "*1984* to *Brazil*: From the Pessimism of Reality to the Hope of Dreams." *Text and Performance Quarterly* 10 (1990): 34–46. (Electronic version).

Rosen, Elizabeth K. "The American West through an Apocalyptic Lens: Cormac Mc-Carthy's *Blood Meridian*." *U.S. Studies Online* 3 (Spring 2003) http://www.baas.ac.uk/resources/usstudiesonline/issue.asp?us=3

———. "Lenny Bruce and His Nuclear Shadow Marvin Lundy: Don DeLillo's Apocalyptists Extraordinaire." *Journal of American Studies* 40, no. 1 (April 2006): 97–112.

Roshwald, Mordecai. *Level 7*. [1959] London: Allison and Bushby, 1981.

Rothstein, Edward. "A Hacker's Haunting Vision of a Reality within Illusion." *New York Times*, Apr. 17, 1999. http://web.lexis-nexis.com/ (accessed on July 12, 2003).

———. "Philosophers Draw on a Film Drawing on Philosophers." *New York Times*, May 24, 2003. http://web.lexis-nexis.com/ (accessed on July 12, 2003).

Ruben, Matthew. "*12 Monkeys*, Postmodernism, and the Urban: Toward a New Method." In *Keyframes: Popular Cinema and Cultural Studies*, edited by Matthew Tinkcom and Amy Villarejo, 312–32. London: Routledge, 2001.

Ruppersburg, Hugh and Tim Engles, eds. *Critical Essays on Don DeLillo*. New York: G.K. Hall, 2000.

Ruse, Michael. *The Darwinian Revolution*. Chicago: University of Chicago, 1979.

Sabin, Roger. *Adult Comics: An Introduction*. London: Routledge, 1993.

———. *Comics, Comix and Graphic Novels: A History of Comic Art*. London: Phaidon, 1996.

Salyer, Gregory. "Myth, Magic and Dread: Reading Culture Religiously." *Literature and Theology: An International Journal of Theory, Criticism and Culture* 9, no. 3 (Sept. 1995): 261–77.

Sawyer, Robert. "Artificial Intelligence, Science Fiction and *The Matrix*." In Yeffeth, *Taking the Red Pill: Science, Philosophy and Religion in* The Matrix, 56–71.

Schneemelcher, Wilhem, ed. *New Testament Apocrypha*. Translated by A. J. B. Higgins. London: SCM Press, 1973.

Schwenger, Peter. *Letter Bomb: Nuclear Holocaust and the Exploding Word*. Baltimore: The Johns Hopkins University Press, 1992.

Shapiro, Jerome F. *Atomic Bomb Cinema*. New York: Routledge, 2002.

Shelley, Mary. *Frankenstein*. [1818] London: J.M. Dent, 1959.

———. *The Last Man*. [1826] London: Hogarth, 1985.

Slotkin, Richard. *Gunfighter Nation: The Myth of the Frontier in Twentieth-Century America*. New York: Atheneum, 1992.

smoky man and Gary Spencer Millidge. *Alan Moore: Portrait of an Extraordinary Gentleman*. Leigh-on-Sea, UK: Abiogenesis, 2003.

Spiegel, James S. "Cinematic Illustrations in Christian Theology." *Journal of Religion and Film* 6, no. 2 (Oct. 2002) http://www.unomaha.edu/~wwwjrf/cinematic.htm (accessed on July 4, 2003).

Staples, Brent. "A French Philosopher Talks Back to Hollywood and 'The Matrix.'" *New York Times*, May 24, 2002. http://web.lexis-nexis.com/ (accessed on July 12, 2003).

Stein, Stephen J., ed. *The Encyclopedia of Apocalypticism: Vol. III: Apocalypticism in the Modern Period and the Contemporary Age*. New York: Continuum, 1998.

Steinberg, Theodore L. "Bernard Malamud and Russell Hoban: Manipulating the Apocalypse." In *Phoenix from the Ashes: The Literature of the Remade World*, edited by Carl B. Yoke, 163–71. New York: Greenwood, 1987.

Sterritt, David and Lucille Rhodes, eds. *Terry Gilliam–Interviews*. Jackson, MS: University Press of Mississippi, 2004.

Stevens, Wallace. "Adagia." In *Opus Posthumous*. Edited by Samuel French Moss. New York: Alfred A Knopf, 1957.

Stone, Brad. "Alan Moore Interview." Oct. 22, 2001. *CBR News* http://www.comic bookresources.com/news/newsitem.cgi?id=554 (accessed on Oct. 22, 2003).

Stuller, Jennifer K. "Singing the Body Imaginative: The Elemental Flesh in Alan Moore's *Promethea*." Paper presented at the Comic Arts Conference, San Diego Comic Con International, July 21, 2006. http://www.ink-stainedamazon.com/conf _cci06.html (accessed on May 28, 2007).

The Sum of All Fears. Dir. Phil Alden Robinson. Paramount Pictures, 2002.

Swatos, William H., Jr., and Kevin J. Christiano. "Secularization Theory: The Course of a Concept." In *The Secularization Debate*, edited by William H. Swatos, Jr., and Daniel V. A. Olson, 1–20. Lanham, MD: Rowman and Littlefield, 2000.

Taylor, Justin, ed. *The Apocalypse Reader*. New York: Thunder's Mouth Press, 2007.

The Terminator. Dir. James Cameron. Orion Pictures Corporation, 1984.

Terminator 2: Judgment Day. Dir. James Cameron. TriStar Pictures, 1991.

Terminator 3: Rise of the Machines. Dir. Jonathan Mostow. Warner Bros., 2003.

Testament. Dir. Lynne Littman. Paramount Pictures, 1983.

The Thirteenth Floor. Dir. Josef Rusnak. Columbia Pictures, 1999.

Thompson, Hunter S. *Fear and Loathing: On the Campaign Trail '72*. London: Flamingo, 1994.

Thompson, Leonard L. *The Book of Revelation: Apocalypse and Empire*. New York: Oxford University Press, 1990.

Trachtenberg, Stanley. Introduction. In *Critical Essays on American Postmodernism*, edited by Stanley Trachtenberg, 1–30. New York: G.K. Hall, 1995.

Turan, Kenneth. "The 'Matrix' in the Middle; 'Reloaded' Packs a Visceral Visual Wallop, but This in-between Sequel Lacks Emotional Power and Doesn't Live Up to Its Predecessor." *Los Angeles Times*, May 14, 2003. http://web.lexis-nexis.com/ (accessed on Aug. 13, 2003).

12 Monkeys. Dir. Terry Gilliam. Universal Pictures, 1995.

28 Days Later. Dir. Danny Boyle. 20th Century Fox, 2002.

Tynan, Kenneth. Foreword. *How to Talk Dirty and Influence People*, by Lenny Bruce. New Introduction by Eric Bogosian. New York: Fireside, 1992.

UNAIDS. http://www.unaids.org/en/AboutUNAIDS/default.asp

Until There's a Cure (Until) national website. http://www.until.org/statistics.shtml.

Ulin, David L. "Merging Myth and History." *Los Angeles Times*, Oct. 8, 1997. http://web.lexis-nexis.com/ (accessed on Mar. 21, 2002).

Vanilla Sky. Dir. Cameron Crowe. Paramount Pictures, 2001.

Vella, Michael W. "When Prophecy Fails: *The Brunists* and the Origins of Robert Coover's Dissonance." *Delta* 28 (June 1989): 35–51.

Voigts-Virchow, Eckart. 'The Lord of the Files'—Carnivalizing Dystopia (*Nineteen Eighty-Four*) in Terry Gilliam's *Brazil*." In *Text und Ton im Film*, edited by Paul Goetsch/Dietrich Scheunemann, 265–85. Tübingen: Gunter Narr Verlag Tübingen, 1997.

Vonnegut, Kurt. *Bluebeard*. [1987] London: Grafton, 1988.

———. *Breakfast of Champions*. [1973] London: Panther, 1974.

———. *Cat's Cradle*. [1963] Harmondsworth, UK: Penguin,1965.

———. *Deadeye Dick*. [1982] London: Panther, 1984.

———. *Fates Worse than Death*. [1991] London: Vintage, 1992.

———. *Galápagos*. [1985] London: Paladin, 1990.

———. *God Bless You, Mr. Rosewater*. [1965] London: Vintage, 1992.

———. *Hocus Pocus*. [1990] New York: G. P. Putnams' Sons, 1990.

———. *Jailbird*. [1979] London: Granada, 1981.

———. *Vonnegut MSS*. Lilly Library Manuscript Collection. University of Indiana.

———. *Mother Night*. [1961] New York: Bard, 1971.

———. *Palm Sunday*. [1981] London: Granada, 1992.

———. *Player Piano*. [1952] London: Grafton, 1987.

———. *The Sirens of Titan*. [1959] London: Victor Gollancz, 2001.

———. *Slapstick, or Lonesome No More!* [1976] London: Paladin, 1989.

———. *Slaughterhouse-Five or The Children's Crusade*. [1969] London: Vintage, 2003.

———. *Timequake*. [1997] London: Vintage, 1998.

———. *Wampeters, Foma and Granfalloons*. [1974] London: Panther, 1979.

———. *Welcome to the Monkey House*. [1968] New York: Dell, 1970.

Wachowski Brothers transcript. Nov. 6, 1999. *Matrix Events*. Warner Home Video. 1999, http://www.warnervideo.com/matrixevents/wachowski.html (accessed on April 15, 2005).

Wagar, W. Warren. *Terminal Visions: The Literature of Last Things*. Bloomington, IN: Indiana University Press, 1982.

Wallace, Molly. "'Venerated Emblems': DeLillo's *Underworld* and the History Commodity." *Critique* 42, no. 4 (Summer 2001): 367–83.

Wardle, Paul. "Terry Gilliam." In Sterritt, *Terry Gilliam—Interviews*, 65–106.

WarGames. Dir. John Badham. MGM/UA Entertainment Company, 1983.

Watson, Ian. "The Matrix as Simulacrum." In Haber, *Exploring the Matrix: Visions of the Cyber Present*, 148–67.

Weaver, John D. "San Francisco: Hungry I." *Holiday* 29, no. 4 (April 1961): 125–30+.

Wein, Len. Introduction. *Swamp Thing: Dark Genesis*, by Len Wein and Berni Wrightson. New York: Vertigo, 1991.

Wein, Len. *Swamp Thing: Dark Genesis*. Illustrated by Berni Wrightson. New York: Vertigo, DC COMICS, 1991. Originally published in single issue format as *House of Secrets* 92 and *Swamp Thing* 1–10, 1971, 1972, 1973, 1974.

Weinraub, Bernard. "In *Matrix*, the Wachowski Brothers Unleash a Comic Book of Ideas." *New York Times*, April 5, 1999. http://web.lexis-nexis.com/ (accessed on July 10, 2003).

Wells, Herbert George. *The World Set Free*. London: Macmillan, 1914.

Wells, Paul. "On Being an Impish God." In Sterritt, *Terry Gilliam—Interviews*, 125–34.

West, Nathanael. *The Day of the Locust*. [1939] Collected in *Nathanael West: Complete Works*. London: Picador, 1993.

Willman, Skip. "Traversing the Fantasies of the JFK Assassination: Conspiracy and Contingency in Don DeLillo's *Libra*." *Contemporary Literature* 39, no. 3 (Fall 1998): 404–33.

Wolfe, Gary. "Evaporating Genre: Strategies of Dissolution in the Postmodern Fantastic." In *Edging into the Future: Science Fiction and Contemporary Cultural Transformation*, edited by Veronica Hollinger and Joan Gordon, 11–29. Philadelphia: University of Pennsylvania Press, 2002.

Wolfman, Marv and George Pérez. *Crisis on Infinite Earths*. New York: DC COMICS, 2000. Originally published in single issue format #1–12, 1985.

Woods, James. "Books: Atoms of Paranoia: Underworld by Don DeLillo." *The Guardian* (London), Jan. 8, 1998. http://web.lexis-nexis.com/ (accessed on April 15, 2005).

Wyatt, Edward. "After a Long Wait, Literary Novelists Address 9/11." *The New York Times*, 7 March 2005. http://web.lexis-nexis.com/ (accessed on April 26, 2005).

Yeffeth, Glenn, ed. *Taking the Red Pill: Science, Philosophy and Religion in* The Matrix. Chicester: Summersdale, 2003.

Yoke, Carl B. "Phoenix from the Ashes Rising: An Introduction." In *Phoenix from the Ashes: The Literature of the Remade World*, edited by Carl B. Yoke, 1–11. New York: Greenwood, 1987.

Zamora, Lois Parkinson, ed. *The Apocalyptic Vision in America: Interdisciplinary Essays on Myth and Culture*. Bowling Green, OH: Bowling Green University Popular Press,1982.

———. *Writing the Apocalypse: Historical Vision in Contemporary U.S. and Latin American Fiction*. Cambridge: Cambridge University, 1989.

Ziegler, Heide and Christopher Bigsby, eds. *The Radical Imagination and the Liberal Tradition: Interviews with English and American Novelists*. London: Junction Books, 1982.

Zins, Daniel L. "Exploding the Canon: Nuclear Criticism in the English Department." *Papers on Language and Literature* 26, no. 1 (Winter 1990): 13–40.

———. "Rescuing Science from Technocracy: *Cat's Cradle* and the Play of Apocalypse." *Science Fiction Studies* 39, no. 13.2 (July 1986): 170–82.

INDEX

apocalyptic literature: plot and, xxi–xxii; popularity of, xvi, xvii–xviii; postmodern elements, 175–76; secularization of, xvi–xvii. *See also* social criticism
apokalypsis, xiii, 34, 101, 176
atomic bomb. *See* nuclear bomb

Barth, John, 126
Batman, 15
Baudrillard, Jean, 97–98, 100, 116
Bellows, Saul, xi
Berger, James, xviii, xxi
Bergoffen, Debra, xxvi, 66
biblical allusions: Babylon, 108, 110; crucifixion, 8, 89, 135; Exodus, 108–9; flood, 125, 135–36; Genesis, 108, 133, 135; Grail legend, 82, 84; immaculate conception, 125; Lucifer, 134–35; Nebuchadnezzar, 110; resurrection, xxix, 125, 127, 135; shepherding, 110–11
Bissette, Stephen, xxvii, 4
Black Rain (Ibuse), 143–44
The Body Artist (DeLillo), 145, 146
Bradbury, Ray, 98
Brazil (1985): bureaucracy as Antichrist, 79; bureaucracy as deity figure, 78–79; director as character in film, 91; fantasy, 77–76, 79–80, 81; good/evil paradigm, 80; insanity as trope, 76, 77, 80, 82, 84, 85; multiple deity figures, 81; New Jerusalem and, xxviii, 75, 77, 79, 80, 81; Sam as deity figure, 81; Sam as part of bureaucracy, 80; suspicion of technology, 75; "visionary as metaphor," 91
Broeck, Josef, xiv
Buber, Martin, xii, 66
Bulletin of Atomic Scientists, 20
Bush, George W., xvii

Cameron, James, 98
Campbell, Ramsey, 8
A Canticle for Leibowitz (Miller), 144
Carter, Jimmy, xvii
Cat's Cradle (Vonnegut), 46–47
Chapman, Dino and Jake, 1
Clarkson, Helen, 144
Cole, James: insanity of, 85, 86, 90; as prophet, 87–88, 89, 90; time travel and, 85, 86, 88, 89. *See also Twelve Monkeys* (1995)
comics: apocalyptic myth in, 1, 6, 9, 13; characteristics of, 3–4; closure and, 3–4; collaboration in creating, xxvii; DC characters' histories, 14–15; multiverse and, 14
computer graphic imaging (CGI), 116
Coover, Robert: apocalyptic writing of, xxv, xxix, 125–26, 138; biblical influence/myth, 124–25; on game-playing, 130; metafiction and, 123–24; *A Theological Position*, 125. *See also The Origin of the Brunists* (Coover); *The Universal Baseball Association* (Coover)
Cosmopolis (DeLillo): apocalypticism in, 143, 146; capitalism, 166–67; communal *vs.* personal apocalypse in, 149; connectiveness, 166; Eric as apocalyptist, 167–68, 168–69; immanent end, 145; judgment, 166; punishment, 165–66, 168–69
Cowart, David, 58, 169
The Crack of Doom (Cromie), 144
Crisis on Infinite Earths, 15, 16
Cromie, Robert, 144

Dark City (1998), 98
Darwin, Charles, xix, 47, 54; *The Voyage of the Beagle*, 52
Darwinism, 48, 49, 50, 51, 57, 58, 63
Davis, Todd F., 50, 65

ABOUT THE AUTHOR

Elizabeth K. Rosen is a visiting assistant professor at Lafayette College. She has published in the fields of visual, cultural, and literary studies, and previously wrote professionally for television.